MANAGING PEOPLE AND ACTIVITIES

Susan Curtis

Lecturer in Business Studies
Manchester Metropolitan University, Crewe + Alsager Faculty

Barry Curtis

Head of Department, Social Sciences, South Cheshire College, Crewe
Chief Examiner, NEAB 'A' Level Business Studies

PITMAN
PUBLISHING

London · Hong Kong · Johannesburg · Melbourne · Singapore · Washington DC

This book is for Laura and George

PITMAN PUBLISHING
128 Long Acre, London WC2E 9AN
Tel: +44 (0)171 447 2000
Fax: +44(0)171 240 5771

A Division of Pearson Professional Limited

First published in Great Britain in 1997

© Susan Curtis and Barry Curtis 1997

ISBN 0273 62066 5

British Library Cataloguing in Publication Data
A CIP catalogue record for this book can be obtained from the British Library

10 9 8 7 6 5 4 3 2 1

Typeset by Tek-Art, Croydon, Surrey
Printed and bound in Great Britain by Clays Ltd, St Ives plc

The Publishers' policy is to use paper manufactured from sustainable forests.

Contents

◆ Foreword

I have no hesitation in recommending Managing People and Activities by Susan Curtis and Barry Curtis to students and lecturers of HND and HNC courses in Business and Finance. The text follows the BTEC syllabus and includes useful and interesting activities and case studies which aid learning and consolidate teaching. The book is very topical and up to date, giving the student plenty of insight into what is happening in businesses today. Each topic is covered in sufficient depth to enable the student to complete assessments in the subject. Theories are explained well and there is much demonstration of how the theory operates in practice.

Rhuwina Griffiths
Chief Examiner Business and Management
BTEC

◆ Preface

Business is a fascinating area to study. It is always changing and moving in new directions. Business pervades every aspect of our lives and this book is written as a guide to understanding some of the issues which face businesses and the people who manage them.

The book has been written for students studying the BTEC core module 'Managing People and Activities', and follows the BTEC specifications. Wherever possible theory has been supported by case studies which show people at work and illustrate how managers behave in the business world.

We hope that the book is read with interest and enjoyment.

Susan and Barry Curtis

◆ Acknowledgements

The authors would like to thank the following people and organisations for their help:

Kara Regan, Ian Little, John Dodd, Ken Minor, Mick Jennings, Win Rogers, Maggie Saxon, Judy Bowker, David Levy, Larry Lorensen, Julie Brewer, Sue Wainwright, Stephen Harris, Ken Barrett, Stuart Walton, Bob Ritchie, Carol Potter, John Williams, Daryl Pritchard, Tracy Slack, Julie Palmer, Derek Tate, Dario Gradi, Lisa Statham, Peter Morris, Steve Brunsden, Alan Pinkney, Lorna Astles, Peter Cuthbert, Ruth Ashford, Neil Williams-Slaven, Sue Coles, Greg Jackson, Arthur Stringer, Caroline Tyrer, Mervyn Evans, Margalit Stott, Sue Woodall, Philip Eades, Liz Brooke, Alan Craig, Nathalie Ormrod-Brunisholz, Najah Shani, Graham Finney.

Stanley Head Outdoor Education Centre, Staffordshire; Avalon Adventure, Newton Abbot; Leadership Resources, Kenilworth; New Victoria Theatre, Newcastle; Iowa–Illinois Gas and Electric Company; Bisto Foods, Middlewich; Stoke on Trent Council; Oasis Travel, British Steel, Crewe Alexandra Football Club, Asda Stores, Kuwait Oil Tanker Company, Crewe & Nantwich Borough Council, CHK Engineering Ltd, NRS Service Centre, British Railways Board, Royal Mail, Stretton Leisure, Leighton Hospital, Genus UK Ltd, Stakis Hotels, The Wedgwood Group.

Management styles

From reading this chapter you will learn about
management styles, including:

1   the major categories of management styles;
2   the effectiveness and appropriateness of each style
     within different situations;
3   contingency theories of leadership;
4   changes in working patterns;
     ◆ flexibility
     ◆ multi-skilling
     ◆ teamworking
     ◆ empowerment.

 ## Introduction

Managing people

Traditional management theories stressed the manager as being in charge, the manager's job was to plan and organise the work while the workers carried out instructions as laid down for them. Methods of payment such as piece rates reinforced this, emphasising that the workers should do their work very precisely and they would be rewarded for doing just that and nothing else. People often felt alienated from their work, they could not identify with the task or the organisation, the work was tedious and the worker could not see how his or her small part in the production process contributed to the final product.

Although this culture is still the case in many organisations, there is a trend towards changing the organisational culture through managing people differently. The main thrust is to employ the whole person, using people's ideas and creativity, and giving people responsibility for organising their own work and for making changes which will improve the quality of the product.

Improving quality, increasing profits and market share are the main objectives of managers today. The most effective way to achieve these objectives is by making the productive process more efficient by improving productivity. The people most likely to know how productivity can be improved are the workers themselves.

The movement is towards a change in management style, managers are now coaches and leaders rather than autocrats and dictators. Workers are being empowered by being given greater responsibility. They are being encouraged to work together as a team and they are receiving training to help them work in teams and to become multi-skilled.

 # Management styles

Categories of styles of management are concerned with manager behaviour. The most common way to categorise manager behaviour is to look at where the focus of power lies:

◆ *Autocratic managers* keep the power to themselves so that only they can make decisions.
◆ *Democratic managers* share the decision-making power with subordinates.
◆ *Laissez faire* translates from French as 'let it alone'. These leaders often allow subordinates to make day-to-day decisions about their own jobs.

Autocratic

This style is sometimes known as *authoritative*. These leaders take full authority and responsibility for their group. They structure the work situation for their employees and tell them what to do and how to do it. This style can be carried out in a positive or negative way. The positive stance encourages subordinates to work by offering rewards such as praise while the negative stance forces subordinates to work by issuing threats and punishment.

Advantages of the autocratic style

◆ The positive or benevolent autocratic manager is often very motivating to work for. Everyone in the group can feel confident and secure because they understand what they should do and they receive praise and recognition for good work from their manager.
◆ The autocratic style is satisfying for the leader as he or she can feel in control of the situation.
◆ This style allows for rapid decision making. A group of individuals, particularly with diverse opinions, will take longer to reach a decision, which may be detrimental to the organisation in situations where a quick reaction is important.
◆ People new to the organisation or people not very competent at their jobs will benefit from the certainty provided by this type of leader.

Disadvantages of the autocratic style

◆ Employees often dislike the negative autocrat as the style can create fear and frustration.

◆ There is greater dependence on the manager because he or she provides the structure within which to work. The work is done by subordinates to please the leader whether his or her style is negative or positive. Without the leader, the workers have no reason for doing the work.

◆ The autocratic style may stifle innovation and creativity from group members.

Democratic

This style is sometimes known as *participative*. Authority is decentralised and decisions arise from consultation and participation between the leader and sub-ordinates within the group. There is a team atmosphere, rather than a separation between manager *and* subordinates.

Advantages of the democratic style

◆ The democratic manager feels supported by the group. He or she is not making decisions alone, as is the autocrat.

◆ Group members are encouraged to express their ideas and make suggestions which provide a greater diversity of solutions to problems.

◆ Group members feel greater commitment and motivation towards the tasks in hand because they have participated in the decision-making process. Group members can claim ownership of a decision in which they participated.

◆ Group members feel that there is respect for their own experience, knowledge and skills.

◆ Group members often have greater knowledge of events in the organisation and do not feel that they are 'always the last to know'.

Disadvantages of the democratic style

◆ The leader may not always agree with decisions made by the group. One of the problems of delegation is that others will always do things slightly differently to yourself. The leader may often feel uncomfortable with the decisions taken.

◆ Group members need to be competent in their work in order to be able to contribute to decision making.

◆ Decision making is slower when more people are involved. When there is a wide range of opinion on a subject, it may be impossible for everyone to agree.

◆ Although the manager may be democratic, the subordinates may not be. Some subordinates may have a strong need for power and attempt to seize the opportunity to take more than their fair share and may even take over from the official leaders.

Laissez faire

This style is also known as *free rein*. The *laissez faire* leadership style is a perfectly legitimate management style because the leader will carry out the functions of planning, organising, co-ordinating and monitoring of activities. There is a tendency to confuse this style with that of 'abdication' – the person who refuses to carry out his or her role as leader and avoids power and responsibility.

The manager of an adult centre which provides evening classes should have a *laissez faire* style. He or she does not need to visit classes in order to instruct the tutors on what to do. His or her role as manager is to decide upon what courses to run, to advertise them, co-ordinate timetabling and rooms, organise an enrolment evening, bank the money and perform many other tasks which the tutors would not see as their job. The manager is a distant figure whose role is so crucial that there would not be an adult centre without them, yet many tutors and students think of this sort of manager as superfluous.

Advantages of laissez faire

◆ Group members have autonomy over the day-to-day aspects of their job.

◆ *Laissez faire* style offers opportunities for personal growth to group members.

◆ This style often produces more successful results than the other styles when the group members are highly motivated and have expertise in their field.

Disadvantages of laissez faire

◆ A lack of direction from the leader could cause people to work at cross purposes or pursue irrelevances.

◆ Group members often do not realise the amount of work involved in leading the group and may feel a lack of respect for the manager. Informal leaders may emerge, creating disharmony.

QUIZ

1.1

Rate yourself on leadership style

		Agree	Disagree
1	I believe that the less people know about the business, the less trouble they get into.	☐	☐
2	I give very precise instructions about how things should be done.	☐	☐
3	My subordinates know that I am available to help them and they sometimes telephone me at home.	☐	☐
4	I have a reputation as a problem solver, so when things get difficult, they are brought to me.	☐	☐
5	My employees come to me regularly for advice and instruction.	☐	☐
6	I know what's going on in my department at all times.	☐	☐
7	It is important for a manager to be in control at all times.	☐	☐
8	Subordinates only wish to be involved with decision making so that they can find out what is going on before everyone else.	☐	☐

	Agree	Disagree

9 It is much faster and more efficient if the manager takes all the decisions. ☐ ☐

10 Many subordinates have insufficient experience at work to be involved with decision making. ☐ ☐

11 My subordinates cannot deal with anything out of the ordinary unless I watch them. ☐ ☐

12 People like to be told what to do, otherwise they are anxious and uncertain. ☐ ☐

If you answered 'Agree' to more than two of these questions, you may not be managing effectively. Your management style is too autocratic and you have great difficulty in delegating work to your subordinates. This shows a lack of trust in those who work for you and a tendency to want to control everything and everyone. You need to consider 'letting go' of more of the responsibility, it will probably not turn out as disastrously as you fear, and will free your time for more important tasks such as planning for the future.

CASE STUDY 1.1

Dario Gradi, Manager, Crewe Alexandra Football Club

Dario Gradi has been Manager of Crewe Alexandra Football Club for the past twelve years. He qualified as a P.E. teacher and then specialised in teaching soccer. He was coach at Chelsea Football Club, Assistant Manager at Derby County and Manager at both Wimbledon and Crystal Palace Football Clubs. In order to survive financially, Crewe Alexandra Football Club nurtures young players they know will have to be sold. The club has become a football player manufacturing company by training many youth teams and having a Centre of Excellence at the club.

Dario Gradi manages the playing side of the football club which includes all the players, the Youth Coach, the scouts and the Centre of Excellence.

'The aim of the team is to try and win at football matches. It's quite important for the town to have a football team. A town without one loses something, it's the national game. The town has adopted me and I've been able to put a lot of effort into the club. There are three reasons why I've stayed here so long. First, the board here is unusual, there's never been a power struggle, it's very democratic and the board are genuine fans of the club. The big advantage I've got is that Crewe Alex. have never known good times.

Second, I get reasonably well paid now, which I wasn't when I first came. Third, is that we've got some good young players in the pipeline and it would be a shame for somebody else to enjoy them. When we started the Youth Policy I realised it was a good catchment area.

Fig 1.1 Dario Gradi, Manager, Crewe Alexandra Football Club

As well as a Youth Team of YTS trainees, there are seven other youth teams covering every age from under sixteen to under ten. There are Sunday matches for the youth teams, and they train at Crewe Alex's ground every evening, except for Fridays. Boys have to live within an hour's travelling distance of Crewe in order to qualify for membership of a Youth Team.'

Management style

'I don't have a style. It's the sort of thing you're not trained for. You drop into it and do whatever takes your fancy. I try to be what I am. I'm not trying to adopt any style. I try to be fair, and I think that's what I wish to be known as with whatever disciplinary decisions have to be taken. I like to be in charge but I don't like to flout my authority, that's poor management. I think respect is something you have to earn, it's not your right.

I've always liked them to call me by my christian name, some people call me gaffer. I hate the word "boss". It's easy now most of the players have been kids with us, they find it easy to call me Dario. I like discipline to be self-discipline. I like to think we teach them the right habits and discipline for themselves. My players aren't subjected to the same pressures, adulation and attention as superstars. David Platt came from here and he handles himself very well. We hope we've had a part to play in that. We won't develop a badly behaved player here. We'll have either cured him or released him before he gets to that level. Those players whose attitude we've been worried about, we let them drift off to other clubs. Sometimes you're fighting against the home background and it's difficult to put that right.

I don't think very much of my job is motivating the players. I think that's an over-emphasised aspect of football. I think the motivation comes from the work they do during the week. We practise to improve the players and we practise to improve the team. There's a purpose to the work we do: as a team and as individuals we're trying to better ourselves. I'm trying to produce players and a good team, so there's an objective. When they play I can merely say we're trying to put into practice the things we do in training.

Players train for two hours each day, four days a week and also play two matches each week.

You can't really train for more than two hours a day, apart from the physical effort there's the weather and the facilities. The younger ones train more and the ones that aren't in the first team train even more than that. Once they're in the first team, if they train too much, they get weary. We watch videos of our own game and the bulk of comments come from me. You have to be careful with the suggestions from them. If you ask for their opinion, they might not have thought anything about the situation, but once you've asked them they'll start to think and they'll tell you the first thing that comes into their head. When you dismiss that as utter rubbish, that will then become an issue with them and they actually then believe it even more vehemently and they hadn't even considered it five minutes earlier. That's a big danger of the democratic way of ruling. That's quite different to you telling them what's wrong and them standing up for themselves and adopting a different approach. I do encourage them to speak up for themselves and go to great pains to emphasise that they can say what they like. There's no punishment for any verbal abuse or criticism coming my way. I want men, not mice, working for me and they've got to feel free to express themselves.

CASE
STUDY
cont

The coaching staff watch the videos of our games with me during the week and what they say will have more effect on me than what the players say. The players are too close to the problem and they haven't got as much experience as us.

I think most people think that managers have to be tough, it's an image they have of them. I think managers have to be strong minded and be prepared to be unpopular. If you want to be popular, don't go into management. I think that's a mistake a lot of managers make, they want to be popular with their players.

They'd want me examined if I tried to be democratic. They don't want it. Most people want to be disciplined, they want to be organised and they want to be led. If there was a sign of weakness, players would be trying to wrestle for power. If the board start talking to the players as to what's wrong, that can be a problem. The board have always been strong here. I've never felt any cracks here. Some managers hide behind the board and say, "The board won't let me give you any more money". I'm the one who pays them and I'm the one who sacks them, I don't pretend otherwise.'

Planning

'As far as planning goes, I've just been preparing the wage bill for next season; deciding which players I'll be keeping and offers I'll make to them. I've just sold a player for £350 000. We plan a week ahead on some things, we have to be able to change it all because of the weather or somebody is injured. It's not very often I do things off the cuff and neither am I meticulous. I'm very much aware of the quality of the 11 and 12 year old boys we've got, so you can say that I plan that far ahead. I've got some good players and some valuable players. Our finances are never okay, we lose money every year unless we sell players. We were promoted last year to the second division; it's the best run that Crewe have ever had in their history.'

Organising

'The Assistant Manager organises the scouting, that's his speciality. The Youth Coach organises the coaching of the youth teams. I have a considerable input on that. The Youth Development Officer is part-time and he is responsible for recruitment into the lower age groups.'

Monitoring

'That's mostly video. We don't have team meetings. I'll always talk about the game to the team and individual performances. I'm watching individuals and continually assessing them, both in training and during games.'

DISCUSSION QUESTIONS 1.1

1 What is the management style of the Board of Directors and what difference does this make to the work of the manager?

2 What is Dario Gradi's leadership style? Does this differ between the players and the coaching staff?

3 Why does Dario Gradi say that he doesn't have a management style?

4 Why does Dario Gradi say that his players don't want democratic leadership?

5 To what extent does the financial position of the club affect the work of the manager?

The effectiveness and appropriateness of each style within different situations

Whether managers are autocratic, democratic or *laissez faire* depends upon the situation they find themselves in. The factors which may be taken into account when managers decide upon whether or not to share the power to make decisions with their subordinates include:

◆ the time available

◆ the subordinate

◆ the nature of the task

◆ the organisational culture

◆ organisational structure

◆ the level of delegation

◆ the amount of power the manager holds

◆ the manager's preferred style.

The time available

It may be appropriate to be autocratic when a deadline is approaching. In this case it would be more effective for the manager to instruct the subordinates as to what to do and how to do it, rather than letting them have a say. Time may be very short and group decision making is much more time consuming than when one person makes a decision alone. Managers can be more democratic when there is plenty of time to spare. The *laissez faire* manager will leave the subordinates to make their own decisions on day-to-day operations and will expect them to achieve the deadline on their own initiative.

The subordinate

When the work experience of subordinates is very limited, they will need instructing as to how to do the job and an autocratic management style is appropriate. The autocratic style is also effective when subordinates' motivation and commitment to the job is very low as they will not be as interested in taking part in the decision-making process as they would have been if they had seen the task as worthwhile.

When subordinates have ideas and suggestions to contribute, a more democratic style is appropriate. For subordinates who are well trained, well educated, very competent in the job or very committed to the task, a democratic or *laissez faire* management style is often the most appropriate.

The location of the subordinates in relation to the manager is also a factor in the choice of management style. People who are distant from their manager, such as drivers and salespeople, cannot consult him or her frequently on how to proceed with the job, and therefore a democratic or *laissez faire* style may be the most effective. Some managers work away from the office a great deal, or are located in different buildings or on different storeys of the same building from their subordinates; they will also find it difficult to adopt an autocratic style as their subordinates will frequently need to make their own decisions about the work.

The task

Complex tasks with which individuals are unfamiliar need explanation or training sessions to remove uncertainty and allow the individuals to acquire the knowledge to carry them out. It may be seen as unfair for a manager to adopt a *laissez faire* style in this type of situation and leave their subordinates to 'sink or swim'. The subordinates will feel insecure and if they are left alone to cope with a difficult task, they should be reassured occasionally that they are doing the job correctly.

Trainers often adopt a democratic approach and during a training session on, for example, dealing with a difficult customer. They will involve the trainees and ask their opinions on what should have been said and done in a given situation. This helps the trainees to learn how to give better customer service by gaining their commitment to the procedure for dealing with customers.

A democratic style is also effective in situations where the subordinates are familiar with the task and can give suggestions as to how the quality of the product or service can be improved. It is appropriate for the manager to share decision-making power about how the task should be carried out when subordinates are competent at their jobs.

Often quite straightforward tasks are so simple that there is little or nothing in the way of decisions to be made about how they should be carried out. In this case, an autocratic management style would be appropriate.

Organisational culture

This is the way things are normally done within the organisation, and it will often influence the choice of management style. Organisational culture reflects assumptions about the way work is performed and what behaviour is acceptable and unacceptable. Unacceptable behaviour might include dressing informally or gossiping with customers. Assumptions about the way the work is performed could involve the organisation's policy towards customers. One firm of accountants might value long-term relationships with their customers, and consider it important to keep in touch and entertain them socially; while another firm of accountants might take the view that customers come and go easily and employ a sales team to attempt continually to get new business. These sorts of assumptions are often taken for granted and firms do not realise that their competitors are operating with a totally different culture until a merger or takeover takes place. Differences in culture then become a serious problem for the merged companies as they find they are incompatible in the ways they work.

According to Edgar Schein, there are three levels of culture: artifacts and creations, values, and basic assumptions.

◆ *Level 1: Artifacts* This is the physical and social environment. It includes space and layout, technological output, written and spoken language and the behaviour of group members. The physical and social environment of a hospital ward is very different to that of the shopfloor of an engineering company. Not only are the layouts and standards of hygiene different, but the language used also differs. The hospital ward deals very closely with its customers and their confidential and personal details; the behaviour of the staff is therefore more discrete than it would need to be in the engineering company, where shopfloor workers may never meet their customers.

◆ *Level 2: Values* An organisation's members often come to share beliefs as to how people and situations should be handled. These beliefs as to the correct way to behave are their values. Many organisations strive for zero defects in their production, but cannot achieve it. British Telecommunications ensures that the Phone Book contains no errors by checking all new entries three times. British Telecommunications' belief in zero defects causes them extra work but no-one in the organisation would consider allowing the Phone Book to be delivered to the customer containing mistakes.

◆ *Level 3: Basic Underlying Assumptions* When a solution to a problem is repeatedly successful, it becomes taken for granted that this successful procedure is then the way to deal with the problem. Many of these procedures develop over time and form the assumptions about how things should be done, guiding organisational members' behaviour. They also determine how group members perceive, think and feel about things.

As organisational culture determines people's assumptions, beliefs and behaviour, it will naturally have an effect on management style. In certain organisations managers will be expected to behave autocratically, as that is the way things are done in that organisation. Charles Handy classified cultures into four different types. Each culture illustrates the preference for a particular management style.

Types of organisational culture

Power culture

The leader is the source of power. The leader controls everything that happens in the organisation. Information is fed to the leader from all departments or functions of the organisation as workers wish to gain favour with the leader and influence the leader's decision in their favour. The only person who knows everything that is happening in the organisation is the leader. A leader may allow free access, which means that he or she is constantly bombarded by employees wanting to ask or tell things. Another leader may restrict contact to a senior team. Everyone else uses the grapevine as an information source to try and find out what is going on.

In-fighting, especially at the top, can be fierce. Decisions made on all kinds of things, from pay rises to who leads the new product launch, are the result of power struggles rather than reasons, such as seniority or fairness. Those holding power value their own success most. They often have personal charisma and charm. They have many sources of information and connections with useful people. They often work on intuition and take risks.

The successful leader in a power culture will be well respected and considered to be unique and inspiring. Yet other cultures might see him or her as untrustworthy and as a 'wheeler dealer' type. Their leadership style will almost always be autocratic.

Role culture

The role culture is a bureaucracy. Rules, procedures and job titles are all of great importance. All the functions work according to the overall plan, so senior management merely have to co-ordinate departments to make sure they are meeting the plan. Individuals are selected to do certain tasks. These tasks should be completed exactly to a specification, no more or less. Anyone doing more than the specified amount of work is considered a threat. Colleagues and superiors would be suspicious of their motives for doing extra work.

Power is determined by rules and procedures and the allocation of work. A role culture can only operate properly in a stable environment. There has to be an unchanging external environment or the firm must have a monopoly position in the product market. Banks and the civil service are examples of role cultures, though these are now beginning to change. Role cultures cannot cope with a changing environment – some organisations go through constant crises and product innovations, entering new markets with new customers – these would not suit the role culture.

Creative and innovative people would be frustrated by working in a role culture. Role cultures are the most common type of organisational culture. When firms grow, they may have an area that remains task or power culture dominated, but the rest of the organisation will usually change to being a role culture. Managing large numbers of employees does require job titles and specifications, defined areas of responsibility and procedures to follow. The management style in a role culture will normally be autocratic.

Task culture

The task culture often consists of people who like to solve problems in teams or groups. Each person has their own area of expertise and he or she shares this with the team for the benefit of the project on which they are working. People are respected for their technical expertise. Individuals' attitudes are often more positive towards their own group than to the organisation as a whole. People's status in the organisation and their job title is of little importance compared to their knowledge, working relationships and their respect for the competence of the other team members.

Controlling the workforce is difficult in task cultures. Control is achieved by senior management allocating projects, people and resources. The actual control of projects is left to project or team leaders. Team members' attitudes can become negative in task cultures if there is a lack of growth in the organisation or in their project area. Resources may be cut or diverted to other areas where there is growth. Morale and job satisfaction will fail and the team will lose interest in their project.

Task cultures are suitable for organisations going through constant change as they are good at planning and problem solving. As work in most organisations is routine, task cultures are not usually appropriate. Management style is democratic or *laissez faire*.

Person culture

The person-orientated culture serves the individuals in the organisation. Procedures and roles are there to meet the needs of individuals in the organisation and they are subject to change, according to the wishes of the individuals. Very small professional businesses may have this type of culture. It is the most unusual organisational culture. Specialists in larger organisations, such as hospital consultant and computer analysts, may have this type of culture between themselves. They may feel more loyalty to one another than they do to the larger organisation. They often support each other and form an elite friendship group in the organisation. Although they are difficult for senior management to control, the culture may easily change if members leave. The most appropriate management style is laissez faire.

Organisational structure

Structure is the pattern of relationships among positions in the organisation and among members of the organisation. The structure indicates what work is to be carried out, who is responsible for what, who should be in charge of different activities and how people should communicate with one another. The purpose of structure is the division of work among people in the organisation, and the co-ordination of their activities so they achieve the objectives of the organisation.

Organisations will have varying levels of command, with small organisations having perhaps a general manager and deputy, with a salesman and administrator. This may give three or four levels of authority, and these levels are known as the *scalar chain*. Larger organisations will have longer scalar chains, although the trend in organisations towards cutting out layers of management has reduced the average size of scalar chains. The longer the scalar chain, the more likely it is that the style of management is autocratic as commands tend to be passed down through the layers of people with little discussion.

Another factor in organisational structure which affects management style is the *span of control*. This refers to the number of subordinates who report directly to a given manager or supervisor. When only one or two people report to a manager, the manager can adopt an autocratic or democratic style, depending upon other factors in the situation. When the manager has 30 or 40 individuals reporting to him or her, a more *laissez faire* style has to be adopted as the manager would not have sufficient time to see them all.

The level of delegation

A manager who is an effective delegator will find subordinates are more motivated in their jobs. In addition having more tasks delegated to individuals enables them to receive some basic training for being managers themselves in the future. They then have a stronger case when applying for promotion than other individuals whose manager did not delegate so much responsibility. The delegator, in the meantime, has more time to think about planning and objectives.

Some managers continue to find it difficult to delegate even though they are aware that it is a shortcoming. Perhaps the only solution to this is to increase the manager's workload so that he is forced to pass work on. The following are some of the reasons why managers may find it difficult to delegate:

◆ they feel insecure when they give power away

◆ they are perfectionists with insufficient confidence in others

◆ they worry that they will become out of touch with things about which they are accustomed to knowing

◆ they feel that the subordinate may refuse to accept the work

◆ they wish to keep the enjoyable parts of the job for themselves

◆ they fear that the cost of a mistake may be high

◆ they worry that trust may be abused or misused.

The main delegation problem is the trust/control dilemma. If a manager always retains control a subordinate will sense a lack of trust, and so if the manager wishes to increase trust he or she must release some control. Managers with an autocratic style will find it difficult to let go of control of a situation. Even managers with a democratic style still enjoy plenty of control because they share the decision-making process and do not give away control completely. It is only the *laissez faire* manager who truly has the confidence to delegate to his or her subordinates.

Sometimes, of course, delegation does result in errors or difficulties. The following are some reasons for failure of delegation:

◆ the task is not possible – the manager may not have given it enough thought to realise that it is not a feasible task

◆ the task is not clearly defined, with the result that the subordinate makes a mistake

◆ the subordinate does not have sufficient training to do the task

◆ the subordinate does not have the authority to carry out the task.

The type of power the manager holds

Leadership is about motivating individuals to pursue goals; power is being able to get someone to do something they would not otherwise have done. Power can be achieved in different ways. Some people have no other power than their job title which gives them the right to direct others while others have a lot of personal power because they are popular or because they have a natural air of authority and can easily influence others. The choice of management style is concerned with the sharing of power to make decisions. The source of the manager's power may well influence his or her willingness or ability to share that power and hence dictate their management style.

Sources of power

1 *Legitimate power* is based on the manager's status and the fact that his or her job title gives them the right to direct the work of others. When a person has no other source of power and is unpopular with their subordinates, they are likely to be reluctant to share their power and will adopt an autocratic management style.

2 *Reward power* is the extent to which a person controls rewards that are valued by another. If a manager has almost total control of the pay his or her subordinates receive, can make recommendations about promotions, and has considerable discretion to give job assignments, he or she has a high level of reward power. Some subordinates may be motivated by a desire for recognition and acceptance, and praise from their manager is an additional form of reward power. It may be appropriate in some circumstances to adopt a democratic leadership style in the allocation of rewards, but this can encourage organisational politicking which can often be destructive. A *laissez faire* style may be impossible when allocating rewards, with the exception of the allocation of tasks.

3 *Coercive power* is based on the ability of one person to punish another for 'incorrect' behaviour by withholding praise or making threats. Some managers may berate subordinates in front of others, belittling their efforts and generally making their lives miserable. Certain forms of coercion may be subtle, news that the organisation may be restructured and some job losses are expected, employing people on temporary contracts, the possibility of staff being transferred to a dead-end department, all affect the security of employees and make them feel that their jobs are threatened. Coercive power will normally be used by autocratic managers.

4 *Referent power* is power through identification and usually surfaces as imitation. People will use the manager with referent power as a role model, copying their behaviour and dress. Referent power is similar to the concept of charisma in that it often involves trust, acceptance, willingness to follow and an emotional liking for the role model. This type of power is present naturally and does not have to go along with a particular status in the organisation. The manager with referent power will be able to adopt autocratic or democratic styles, according to the situation, but will find it difficult to be *laissez faire* as subordinates feel it natural to refer to them for guidance and advice.

5 *Expert power* is based on the belief that someone has a specific, although limited, area of knowledge which others in the group may not have. This power can easily be used to reinforce an autocratic management style as knowledge and information can be withheld until the moment of the decision, when the expert can step in and give incontrovertible reasons as to why a certain decision should be made.

The extent and mix of these powers will depend on the individual leader and the situation. The use of one power may reduce the effectiveness of another – if a person is disciplined for lateness by a manager this may reduce the referent power of that manager. From the viewpoint of the organisation, reward power is most useful because it can be exercised directly down the hierarchy. However, this does not mean that it is the best source of power to motivate individuals. Research indicates that the most important powers for organisational effectiveness are expert and referent power.

The manager's preferred style

The role of the manager involves overseeing the task and the people and it is possible that some managers may put more emphasis on one than the other. A manager may be very good at getting the job done well and on time, but in the process may upset staff and have a high rate of staff turnover and absenteeism. It will be expensive for the organisation to employ this manager, as despite the good work produced, the long-term effects will be low morale and the continual cost of recruiting new people and sorting out the grumbles of the existing staff.

Alternatively, a manager may enjoy people's company and not worry very much about getting the job done. The staff may have full attendance and enjoy going to work for the companionship or fun, but they will not be getting the task done to the best of their ability.

Managers need to achieve the fine balance between getting the task done and making sure that the staff are happy. Democratic managers are likely to take people into consideration, whereas *laissez faire* managers may tend to assume that their subordinates are self-motivated. Autocratic managers are not necessarily more concerned about the task than the people, benevolent autocrats do not share the power to make decisions with their subordinates but they are concerned and pleasant when dealing with staff.

The Ohio State and Michigan Studies

The Ohio State and Michigan Studies were two different research studies which looked at the behaviour of leaders and whether they emphasised the task or the people in a situation.

Ohio State

These investigations began by attempting to identify the differences in the behaviour of leaders. Two factors emerged as the major differences:

1 people orientated (called 'consideration structure') This includes behaviour between supervisor and subordinates which indicates trust, respect and warmth, and

2 task orientated (called 'initiating structure') including behaviour in which the supervisor organises group activities without consulting the group as to their opinions and how it should be done.

The researchers found that leaders who scored high on 'consideration structure' had subordinates who were satisfied with them, who had fewer absences and lower grievance rates than leaders who scored low on 'consideration structure'. According to these studies, it is possible to score high or low on both people and task orientation.

Michigan studies

Researchers looked at what type of behaviour made leaders effective. They called the differences they found in leader behaviours 'production centred' and 'employee centred'.

◆ Production centred leaders:
  - set rigid standards
  - organised tasks in detail
  - dictated exactly how the work was to be done
  - 'supervised subordinates' work closely.

◆ Employee centred leaders:
  - encouraged the workers to participate in setting goals and other decisions about the work
  - inspired trust and respect in the workers.

The leaders who were most effective in terms of high production were:

1 Employee centred rather than production centred. The focus for communication between supervisor and worker was 'How are you getting on?' rather than 'How is the work coming alone?'

2 Less likely to supervise the work closely.

3 More likely to be doing different work to that of their subordinates (although this was not found to be true in all the studies carried out).

According to the Michigan research, the more effective leaders:

(a) have relationships with their subordinates which are supportive and make them feel important and worthwhile;

(b) use group rather than individual methods of decision making and supervision;

(c) tend to set high performance goals.

It is probably more appropriate to be autocratic or task-centred in times of danger, emergency or approaching deadlines. The people-centred style is suitable for circumstances like the solution of a complex problem such as the design of a staff training programme to preventing shoplifting in a retail store.

The most important factors determining appropriateness and effectiveness of managerial style are the subordinate and the task. Experienced, well motivated individuals will not need telling exactly what to do and how to do it and will not benefit from autocratic management. Also, some tasks can be done in a variety of ways and may be achieved more effectively if a democratic or laissez faire style of management is adopted. Other tasks require no decisions as to how best they can be done and therefore a democratic approach would not be appropriate.

The trend in organisations is towards delayering with flatter organisational structures and fewer layers of management. Responsibility is being pushed downwards so that individuals at the lowest levels in the organisation have more decision making power in carrying out their jobs on a day-to-day basis. This means that organisations generally are adopting a more democratic or laissez faire approach in their management of human resources. The changes in working patterns towards multi-skilling, flexible hours of working, teamwork and empowerment all have implications for the leadership style managers adopt. The trend towards teamwork also gives greater responsibility for decision making to groups of workers. Teams can make many decisions between themselves as to who should do the work and how targets can be best achieved.

Giving individuals responsibility for decisions on day-to-day matters frees managers to plan and spend their time on more strategic issues such as where the organisation should be going next.

CASE STUDY 1.2

People talking about their boss

Steve, Marketing Executive

'We are a public relations and marketing company. I handle new accounts and enquiries to the business. I also handle my existing client base and all aspects of their marketing. If I get a new contact I will go out and meet them, introduce our company and all our products and services, the existing client base and the profit we've made for them. I also go on site to visit existing clients at least once a month. Its basically an update; I monitor how their work is going and give them feedback, try to keep the business

Fig 1.2 Steve, Marketing Executive

on-going which is very important. I spend at least two hours per day at the office, sometimes it's a whole morning or afternoon.

My boss's field is public relations. His client base varies from motor cars, to laser eye treatment to confectionery. The buck stops with him, he owns the business. Myself and a colleague, Tony, have a lot of input into the system side – the computers, and the marketing of our company and how we project ourselves.

We have eight staff, this has reduced from 24 as people do not like working for the company and leave. The boss has the attitude of "Its my business, I'll run it how I want and I don't see why I have to change". The secretary has been there the longest, 18 months, and she only stays because it's ten minutes from her house to work.

The boss sits back and lets business come to him. It's a contradiction in terms, he should be going out and finding new business. After one week of working for my boss, I came to realise that he had a very off-hand, gruff attitude. He tends to leave myself and Tony to run the business. If anything goes wrong with the computers, systems, anything electrical, Tony will handle that. I deal with all new business enquiries. I turn away business or accept business, depending on how busy we are at the time. The boss tends to leave us alone and he concentrates solely on his public relations work. It gives us a lot more responsibility, which is a good thing, it proves that there is trust there. I try to see both sides of the coin. I think he's got to the stage where he realises that he has got good people in his team, and myself and Tony are capable of looking after the business when he's not here. He feels completely confident with the situation, to leave us to it. We've pointed this out and said to him "Yes, you've given us more responsibility, but you're not rewarding us for it or giving us any recognition for it". He tend to take us too much for granted. I've pointed it out to him twice before. He tends to be very dismissive of it and says it's what we want anyway. It's nice to be recognised and have appreciation shown.

There is a positive side, I'm looking for alternative employment and this gives me a great experience to be able to say that I handle the business. I'm very pleased in some ways, because its one of the best opportunities I've had for a long time. I think the business has so much potential, but the boss is content to take as much money as he can from the business and just relax. That's not helping myself or my colleagues. Tony and myself could set up in business, but it requires a lot of capital. I aim to be in my own business in the next five years. I have the marketing and the advertising knowledge and Tony has the systems knowledge, so we have talked about it many a time.

The annoying aspect is that we do so well on our own, the office runs so calmly. Everything fits into place, there is no adverse pressure on any people in the office. When the boss comes into the office he brings pressure with him which we all feel. Everyone just shuts up and gets on with their work, it's a very intense atmosphere and there's no freedom. As soon as he comes in he says "I want to know what's going on, stop what you're doing and tell me now what has gone on for the last week". I can't tell him exactly at the drop of a hat, I would like to make a regular time for sitting down and going over the week's activities, but he's out on business. We sit down and discuss it between ourselves, but he isn't there. He comes in on a Monday or Tuesday and wants to know what has gone on during the previous week.

CASE STUDY cont

I do enjoy the responsibility and so does Tony. The boss has given us a £2500 rise each and the other people in the office have all had £500 minimum, so I think that shows he does appreciate us. Its partly due to a state of panic because he realises that he's got a good team and we have made it known that we're not going to hang around and it's his way of saying "I'm trying to change, give me time".

When a third colleague, Nigel, joined the company he had no keyboard skills, nor had he ever done any telemarketing work or anything to do with marketing. He was taken on because of his enthusiasm. His training was limited to the boss giving him half a day on a computer. This was on the Friday. On the Monday, the boss, myself and Nigel went over to the plastics division of a large company which is an important new client of ours. While we were there we met the American boss who works in the UK, and he outlined a marketing plan for their company, to create more awareness of their company and its services and prices. This was Nigel's account and it was a very large account to give to someone of his inexperience. The boss asked me to go along and we sat there in front of the whole board of directors, and the managing director asked us to introduce ourselves and tell them about ourselves. The boss and I had plenty of experience to mention, but when it came to Nigel all he could say was that he'd been a buyer and that he had no experience in marketing. The American said incredulously, "You're going to be looking after our account?" Nigel was sitting there feeling inches tall, I felt for him, I wished the ground would swallow him up for his own sake. Not only was he faced with all the directors of this large and important company, but all the field sales representatives were there as well. So then I had to come in and say that I would be working alongside him and that I would be handling it during his training. The boss looked at me and gave me a wink and sighed with relief. But the point is now that they always come to me and I don't know anything about the account, I've already got my client base. This large company has three different databases which Nigel has to use to do their marketing. Nigel has got them like spaghetti junction, he trundles along as best he can. Tony has to sit down with Nigel whenever the boss is out and try and sort things out. It is crass the way it has been left to Nigel to try and make sense of it; just imagine giving someone a car who can't drive. He has to type with one finger and has never used a keyboard in his life, he's expected to handle complex data, it's one of the boss's major pitfalls, he has no forward planning for things like this. It's a matter of "I've given you half a day on it, what more do you want?" It's cost time and money and should have been sorted out in the first place.

The boss totally relies on us to do things. We'll do it because we like to think of our own standards of work practice, so we have no problems there. The major drawback was with Nigel and the problems coming in thick and fast with the computer system, and the boss would come into the office expecting everything to be hunkydory. When things weren't, he'd just say "No, it can't be the system, a bad workman always blames his tools".'

DISCUSSION QUESTIONS 1.2

1 Why is Steve's boss's management style the most appropriate for the situation he is in?

2 What factors within the situation enable the boss to adopt a *laissez faire* management style?

3   Why has the *laissez faire* approach failed with Nigel? How could the situation have been handled differently?

4   What benefits does the *laissez faire* approach have for the experienced staff?

5   Has the boss behaved in a way which indicated that he underestimated the skills and experience which Steve possesses? If so, discuss further.

CASE STUDY 1.3

People talking about their boss

Sue, PC Support Officer

Sue's job involves helping colleagues in a department with their computing needs and includes writing systems, supporting people and solving individuals' problems with their computers. Although Sue is attached to a department to provide computer support, she is actually a member of a 12-strong PC Support Team and her boss, David, is the team leader of that group.

'David is the best boss I've ever worked for. You can say what you feel to him, get annoyed with him, and the next day it's all forgotten. He's responsible for the management of the team and he represents the site for all IT issues. We each have an hour's slot with him every month to air any issues that we have. He's interested in anything that may affect your work and in the way that you're interacting with your customers. ('Customers' here refers to other employees in the pharmaceutical company – the members of the department to which Sue is attached). *You feel motivated after you've seen him. You don't feel just a link in the chain, he makes you feel as though you are worth something. He gives you feedback which he's had from customers which is always nice to hear because you don't often hear it from them. He's very interested in what you've done and loves to get involved and offers any suggestions where he can. He encourages us to take the lead with the customers as well, he encourages us to be fair but firm. He doesn't expect us to be able to meet all their requirements. He's completely encouraging in that way and supportive. If you've said that you can't deliver something to a customer, then that's good enough for him. There are no hard and fast rules at all. If he feels that you're a hard worker, he's very fair. I've never had a monthly slot with any of my other managers in this company.*

If David knows that a particular person in the team is open and honest, then he'll support them all the way. He is less supportive of those who are not as committed, but will not stand in the way of anyone's career development. If David thinks we're under pressure, he'll do everything he can to relieve that for us. If that means staying behind and helping us, he will do. It does get to the point though where he will step in and say, "No more". He's sent me home on some occasions at the stroke of four – when I've been working late a lot and things are getting very stressed.

Although I don't see the other members of the PC team, because they're a good 15-minute walk across the site from me we do have a monthly meeting. David chairs the meeting and it deals with current issues, things we need to know. We have to take it in turns to take the minutes and he's open to suggestions on the agenda beforehand. We use it for information sharing. If we've come across a particular problem that it would be useful for the others to know and understand, then David encourages us to share the information that we've all got. If somebody tries to dominate the meeting, he'll intervene, he treats us all the same.

Occasionally on a Friday lunchtime, he'll ring us all up and buy us all a beer. He treats us all well at Management Reward time. We don't get an annual increment, we get rewards according to performance. It may be performance related pay or other reward the company has on offer. The company is very creative with the rewards.

David leads the IT support issues on site and coordinates the team actions required to meet targets. The majority of day-to-day issues are dealt with locally with no involvement from him, but help and advice is always there if we require it. He's very receptive of new ideas, he encourages us all to think about how we could do things differently and he often does more investigating on the idea.'

DISCUSSION QUESTIONS 1.3

1 What is David's management style?

2 Why is David successful in motivating his staff?

3 What similarities and differences are there between David's management style and the management style of Steve's boss in the previous case study?

CASE
STUDY
1.4

People talking about their boss

Carol, Auditor

Carol works for Stoke City Council. She is one of a team of auditors who audit the accounts of local authority departments. Carol's team is responsible for a diverse range of council departments from recreation and leisure to engineering. Carol goes out and tests computing, financial and accounting systems.

'I see Sue, my manager, at the start of an audit and, although I see her most days, I sometimes go out to do an audit and go home straight from the location. I ring in once or twice a day to let Sue know what's happening and if there's any problem I'll ring her just to get her opinions and advice. Sue is very approachable but there's a slight distance – she isn't on the same friendly level that you would all go out to lunch together. I would say the rest of the team would all go to her with any queries they have, she's well respected by the team because of her expertise and her management style. The team happens to be all women, its the only one in the office, the others are all a mixture. You could go to Sue with confidential matters if you wanted to.

Sue takes full responsibility and authority for the work. You know what Sue wants. She's very clear in a calm way. She tells you what she wants to come out of the audit and how long you will have to tackle the job. Probably because she knows that I've had several years' experience, I don't need to be spoon-fed. I know she monitors the situation. She is happy

CASE STUDY cont

for myself and other team members to go back and report to her any problems we find and will guide and assist us.

I've just done a systems review of a leisure centre, to highlight strengths and weaknesses in the system – payments, income and expenditure, stocks and wages. You have to have quite a range of skills to cover all the areas. We need to know the income and expenditure and how it has been recorded so that we can ascertain whether it can be manipulated fraudulently. At a leisure centre they have small items which generate income such as hairdryers, lockers, telephones. If there aren't adequate controls over the auditing of such things and paying in then there is a potential for fraud. We have to go round the whole leisure centre and check bar stocks, catering stocks, security arrangements and equipment.

My job is to highlight potential problems and to recommend management solutions. I have to do a series of testing after documenting the system. Compliance testing is to ensure that the system is as they told me and all is working well. If I feel that there is an area of weakness, we do substantive testing – examining a greater volume of transactions in a smaller area. I determine whether there has been any problems and I draw up a consultative document. To find out something like whether there has been fraud with the sweet machine, my suspicions might be aroused by frequent emptying and yet no banking of monies from that machine for several months. There might be a system of manual documentation as well as computerised and I might be able to cross-reference entries and it may be that the manual records are incomplete, they may have paid more money into the bank than they claimed to have emptied out of the machine. I can recommend a new system for documenting this more effectively.

My recommendations to the leisure centre management in my discussion document (a draft report) were not read by Sue. She felt happy that I had achieved what she wanted, she had been kept informed by me throughout the process, I felt trusted and it gave a great boost to my motivation. We went through the discussion document with the leisure centre manager. It was extremely thick because there were so many problems at the centre, it took us several hours. He had the document prior to the meeting, so he'd had chance to read it, and he was aware of a lot of issues as they had been raised with him prior to the meeting. Sue allowed me to lead the meeting and at every stage, if I needed support or he needed clarification, Sue was there in a supportive role. The manager was very receptive as he's new to the department and therefore the report wasn't criticising him.

Decisions are made democratically, we talk it through and come to a joint decision. We're incredibly like-minded in the way we work. That's very very nice. I find that very reassuring. She's very supportive of the whole group. She does encourage you to express your ideas and make suggestions. She's under a great deal of pressure with work and she's out of the office a lot, but she still makes time for us, even in her own lunch hour. We can see there's a great commitment from her which we find motivating. There's a good team spirit, partly because of Sue's leadership. Team members do things for her personally, we would work extra hours and would take on more pressure purely because of her. There's a greater commitment from us because she supports us.

Sue will, to a certain extent, tell us what to do and when to do it. Her level of telling would be amended according to the person's experience. You would never feel that you weren't sure what was required and I've noticed that if she's needed work to be carried out by the

CASE STUDY cont

team fairly quickly, she always thanks you for doing it. She keeps a close watch on what's going on, but in a diplomatic and subtle way.

When I first started, she introduced me to people, but now she doesn't need to. She did take me to the venue the first time and took me round and introduced me to various areas within the division. She also made sure that I had some introductory training to the computer system. I wasn't left on a limb and that gave me the foundation to carry on.

One day, we were coming back in the car from an audit and I noticed during our conversation that Sue's opinions on the case were identical to mine. I was elated at having a boss who thought in the same way, it was like listening to myself talking, it was weird.'

DISCUSSION QUESTIONS 1.4

1 How does Carol's boss alter her management style to suit different situations?

2 Why does Carol seem to be so happy with Sue's management style?

CASE STUDY 1.5

People talking about their boss

Sue, Audit Manager

Carol's boss talks back

Sue Woodall is Audit Manager at City of Stoke-on-Trent, City Treasurer's Department. The Treasurer's Department has four Assistant Treasurers who are in charge of Accountancy, Revenue and Benefits, Audit Services and Financial Services. The Treasurer's Department has an independent appraisal function and acts as an internal police force within the Council. The Department's officials have the power to inspect any documents within the Council. Within the Audit Department, there are three teams. Sue Woodall's team of four auditors are responsible for services provided by: leisure and recreation, planning and architecture, engineers, legal property and administrative services, payroll, museums and cultural services and insurance provision for the City Council. The insurance provision is not an audit function, but has been added on as an extra responsibility.

Sue's boss is Assistant Treasurer for Audit Services. He agrees the work for the division and each of his managers allocates the work to their team. All managers deputise for the Assistant Treasurer as well as covering for one another when they are on holiday and out of the office. The four managers have team briefings each Monday morning, they try to ensure that they are not all out of the office at the same time. The managers are in the process of rotating jobs. Sue has been in her present job for one year and was previously manager of a different area.

'*I know what the other managers are doing in a general way. The rotation has meant that we've had to advise one another and that has given us experience of other City Council functions. The idea is to make sure that there is cover for everyone. It was very demoralising at first, we were specialists and then we were given jobs we didn't know. You think you know about the job until you get in there and get your hands dirty. You do get complacent, it would be negative to say that it hasn't been beneficial. The rest of the division have been doing job rotation, so it has helped us to lead by example, if its good enough for them we can do it.*

Fig 1.3 Sue Woodall (right) with her team: Geetha, Sharon, Sue and Carol

I did management as part of my CIPFA qualification, but I don't think of myself as a leader. I look to gain the support of the people involved. If everything is explained in a positive way, the reasons why things have got to be done, rather than instructing them, people become more committed. The work that we do is really an on-going process of discussion, we won't do an audit at the same venue again for two or three years. We've got very mixed and varied work and it's attractive work to be involved with. We spend around 50 per cent of our time working at sites out of the office. If there's a problem team members won't carry on on their own, they'll come back and discuss it, but they're professionals and you don't expect to have to go and keep an eye on them. They're representing the division wherever they go and carrying with them the image of our office. You've got to leave them to get on and be aware of their capabilities.

The old image of auditors was very austere, sitting with a pile of books and ticking things off. The nature of the work is now assisting managers. Not only do we do a financial audit, but we can help in a management consultant function, checking if venues are getting value for money from their suppliers and helping them to implement quality systems such as BS5750. We work alongside people rather than against them.

For new starters there is a basic induction package administered by the Personnel Section. They then need to be acquainted with Council procedures and documentation, to be aware of procedures across the whole spectrum of our services. Not only have they got to know the people in our office, but the layout of the Council, the idea of committees, councillors and the politics behind it. I would go with a new starter to a venue and introduce them, show them around, introduce them to key personnel. I make sure they are comfortable and settled before I leave them, then I feel easier in my mind. I do protect my team – whatever they do reflects on me and the impressions I give out affect them. There is a team spirit, we have to provide cover for lunchtimes as we are expected to continue to provide the service throughout lunchtimes. I don't sit with them, it's an open plan office, but I like to feel that I'm approachable. We often discuss issues as a team, or with whichever team members are in the office. Newcomers can listen in and get to know how we think. We don't go out socially. The team isn't static as people are rotated through various groups as part of our Fair Recruitment and Selection Programme. We can't recruit into a team and guarantee that team members will always be together.

I don't think it makes any difference that the team are all women. Characters matter more than whether team members are male or female. As long as they get on with one another, that's the main thing.

Carol and I are likeminded because we've both worked for such a long time in auditing. She has only been with us with two months, but she had already got a good knowledge of council work from her previous job. There wasn't a great need for a long induction period. she's very able to mix and get on with people she doesn't know. I've been out with her to venues for audit and I can now leave her to introduce herself. I wouldn't leave her entirely to herself to get on with things, but she's got the knowledge and experience already and knows what the work involves. Everyone in the team is willing to help her out. She'll always come back with any queries when she feels that she's got a problem.

Carol is positive in the way she tries to find solutions to problems. The nature of the work we do causes people to expect criticisms, but if we can turn that around it's more forward thinking and people are more likely to go along with you.'

DISCUSSION QUESTIONS 1.5

1 Have Sue and Carol got a different attitude towards their work?

2 How does Sue distance herself from her team?

3 Are there differences in Carol and Sue's account of Sue's management style?

4 In each of the three case studies of Steve, Sue and Carol, all their bosses appear to adopt a laissez faire management style. What similarities and differences are there in the accounts of the behaviour of the three managers and their management styles?

5 Which manager would you prefer to work for and why?

Contingency theories

Hersey and Blanchard's situational leadership theory

This theory was devised by American consultants Paul Hersey and Ken Blanchard in 1982. Management style should be chosen according to the work experience of the subordinates (or followers). For example, new and inexperienced workers in an organisation will need plenty of guidance and support, whereas 'old hands' who have been working in the organisation for several years can be left to get on with their work.

The choice of management style is determined by the situation the leader finds themselves in. According to Hersey and Blanchard, there is one factor which determines the situation – the 'maturity' of the followers. By 'maturity', Hersey and Blanchard mean:

◆ the amount of experience the follower has had doing their particular job; and

◆ how well motivated the follower is.

These two definitions of maturity, though, do not necessarily go together. People who are new in a job may be willing to accept responsibility and are keen to achieve success in doing it. In the same way, people who have been doing their jobs for many years are not necessarily well motivated.

Hersey and Blanchard believed that both aspects of maturity (task experience and motivation) should be taken into account when deciding upon a management style.

Four different management styles were identified by Hersey and Blanchard. These can be listed as levels, depending upon the job experience of the subordinate.

1 *Telling (No experience).* Specific instructions are given as to how to do the job, not only when the employee first joins the organisation but also while they are still learning their job. Communication is largely one-way – from boss to subordinate – and there is little behaviour which could be classed as a personal relationship.

2 *Selling (Some experience).* The manager continues to provide instructions as to how to do the job when needed. As the employee becomes familiar with the work, there will be more relationship behaviour. Communication becomes two-way and more open between the boss and subordinates. The boss will explain why the job is carried out in a certain way, which gives the subordinate a clearer understanding of the job and their role in the organisation.

3 *Participating (Experienced).* The subordinate is now so experienced at the job that there is little task support needed and interactions with the leader consist of such matters as discussion on the wider role of the job and organisational politics.

4 *Delegating (Expert).* There is very little communication with the manager about the job itself. The subordinates are experienced enough at the job to complete it alone and they do not feel the need of emotional support from the boss in order to do the job.

The theory helps to give guidance to managers facing the dilemma of whether to adopt an authoritarian or participative style with their workers. The motivation of the subordinates also has to be taken into account because unwilling subordinates may need more direction or attention from their leader than willing followers. Highly motivated people may be able to start at the 'participating' level rather than at the 'telling' level.

However, Hersey and Blanchard's theory does not consider different types of jobs, or that some organisations have such flat organisational structures that it might be impossible for the leader to give all subordinates directions.

Fig 1.4 Hersey and Blanchard's theory

Some organisations have an overlap period of time when the person leaving shows the new starter how to do the job. Someone on the same level may act as mentor to the new person and the leader does not need to give any instructions. The theory is useful, however, for pointing out that the varying amount of experience people have in doing a job will require different management styles. It also introduces the idea of using different management styles with each individual subordinate.

Fiedler's contingency theory

A person may be very successful being democratic, having meetings and getting the whole team to contribute and feel committed to the work. In a different job and a different situation, there may only be one way to do the work, and it would be more appropriate to adopt an autocratic managerial style. The democratic manager may not do their job as successfully in all situations and may need to change his or her style to fit the circumstances.

Frederick Fiedler categorised different situations in which leaders might find themselves as:

◆ favourable to the leader

◆ unfavourable to the leader

◆ moderately favourable to the leader (a mixture of the two).

Fiedler recommended that managers should adopt an autocratic management style if the situation is either strongly favourable or unfavourable to them and a democratic style if the situation is moderately favourable.

There are three factors which determine whether a situation is favourable or unfavourable for a leader. They are:

1 *Leader–member relations.* How well the manager gets along with subordinates or group members, and the degree to which they feel supported by their members.

2 *Task structure.* Whether the task is clearly laid down and structured. It may be flexible and there could be many ways of completing the job. Or it could be clear-cut and programmed as to goals, procedures and measurable progress.

3 *Position power.* How much power the leader has over such things as hiring and firing of the subordinates. The leader may be involved in recruitment and selection, the allocation of pay rises and promotions. The manager may also be responsible for giving verbal and written warnings for such things as lateness or absence. Some leaders have no power over any of these matters.

What is meant by a 'favourable situation':

◆ the leader is liked and trusted by the group (leader–member relationships)

◆ the task is clearly laid down and well defined (task structure)

◆ the power of the leader is high and he or she can reward and punish subordinates (position power).

What is meant by an 'unfavourable situation':

◆ the leader is disliked by the group

◆ the task is ambiguous and there are several possible ways in which it can be carried out

◆ the leader has no power to reward and punish subordinates.

What is meant by a moderately favourable situation:

A moderately favourable situation is a mixture of favourable and unfavourable together. A popular leader may have no power to hire and fire and an unstructured task, so can therefore be democratic and ask the opinions of the group as to how the task should be carried out. This may be suitable when people are working in teams and on one-off projects such as designing computer systems. When the group members are experts in their own field or the problem they are working on is a creative one, then plenty of different suggestions and perspectives on the problem will be helpful to the leader.

Fiedler's approach is useful because it reminds us that there are occasions when it pays to be distant and task-centred rather than democratic. The main strength of the theory is that it points out that leaders need to be autocratic in certain situations.

The theory's advice on when to adopt a democratic style is more problematic. Mixing together the three variables of task structure, position power and leader popularity does not always provide a situation in which a leader can be democratic and share power with subordinates.

It is difficult to be democratic with a highly structured task as there is very little to discuss. If swissrolls have to be taken quickly from a conveyor belt and loaded into boxes, the ways it could be done are very limited. A democratic approach may be to let workers reorganise their work in terms of job rotation so that people only have to do a certain task for an hour and then they change over to something else – but this is not always possible.

Also, it is difficult for an unpopular leader to be democratic as the members may not feel co-operative enough to put forward ideas and helpful suggestions to their manager. There may be a lack of trust in the manager or respect for the manager's expertise in the job. It is possible though, for the leader to be *laissez faire* and leave the members to do the task as they see fit. This would not be appropriate in all situations.

Events cropping up in addition to the daily routine can be dealt with in a democratic way. Workers can contribute to the solution of problems such as how to tighten security against burglars or shoplifters. They can provide suggestions on changes such as new layouts to the office or factory, what new staff should be told in an induction programme and how they should be trained.

Managers who are used to being autocratic and taking all the decisions them-selves may forget that it is possible to involve staff occasionally. When changes are made in an autocratic way, staff can feel frustrated and that they are 'always the last to know'. This especially causes bitterness when the decisions are told to a few people, so that most staff find out what has been decided through the grapevine or rumours.

Managers who normally have an autocratic leadership style as a result of their situation can alter it in certain circumstances so that staff feel involved with and committed to changes.

 # Changes in working patterns

Flexibility

There are around 25 million people working in Great Britain today, 6 million work part-time and the remainder work full-time or are on government training schemes. Fewer than 19 million people work full-time and of those over 15 million have permanent employment contracts, 1.5 million are employed on temporary contracts and over 2 million are self-employed. The government gathers statistics regularly to find out about changes in the labour market and the movements in the figures indicate trends towards fewer people being employed permanently or full-time, and more people working part-time and temporary. It would seem that men's full-time jobs are being lost and replaced to some extent with women's part-time jobs, although the total number of people in employment falls each year.

The continual move away from permanent full-time contracts towards atypical contracts – part-time, temporary and sub-contracting, indicates that employers are seeking greater flexibility in various forms from their workforces. In the UK there is no definition of a contract of employment; this gives employers a free rein to employ workers on any basis.

There are three types of flexibility being used increasingly by employers:

1   *Functional flexibility or 'multi-skilling'.* Employees can perform several jobs. Individuals are trained to do more than one job so that they can interchange jobs in a teamwork situation, or be redeployed into other areas of the company where there is a manpower shortage. Functional flexibility means that fewer employees are required, as individuals have almost always got something to do, absent colleagues can be covered for and teams can train one another in addition to new recruits.

2   *Numerical flexibility.* Employing people on atypical contracts. This enables the organisation to increase or decrease employee numbers quickly in response to changes in demand. Seasonal trends and peak periods of the day or week can be more easily coped with by employing extra part-time or temporary staff for the busy periods only.

3   *Financial flexibility.* Changes in the organisation's payment systems. Firms are keen to pay 'the going rate' for the job rather than across the board increases in order to keep in line with the external labour market, that is in comparison

with wage levels in other firms in the locality or in the same industry. There is also a trend towards individualised payments such as performance related pay. Financial flexibility allows firms to bring in new payment systems as they wish rather than negotiating with the union on similar pay increases for all.

Core and periphery

In order to achieve increased flexibility, firms are increasingly segregating their workforces into a 'core' group and one or more 'peripheral' groups. The core group tends to consist of employees with full-time permanent status and is central to the longer term future of the organisation. Employees in this group are likely to be well trained and flexible. They are more likely to enjoy good career and promotion prospects and have a higher degree of job security than those in the peripheral groups.

Research undertaken by the Institute of Manpower Studies in 1984 showed that there were two sub-groups within the periphery. The first group consists of full-time employees with skills readily available in the labour market, such as clerical, secretarial and low skilled manual workers. The second peripheral group provides greater numerical flexibility and includes part-timers, casuals, fixed term contract staff, temporaries, sub-contractors and public subsidy trainees, with less job security than the first peripheral group.

Companies using core and peripheral working arrangements are often referred to as 'the flexible firm'. Flexible firms find many advantages of using atypical contracts:

1 costs are lower as:
   (a) workers are employed only when needed;
   (b) savings are made on employment benefits such as sick pay and pensions;
   (c) recruitment costs are saved for the core as new core workers can be picked from the periphery;

2 core workers coming from the periphery have demonstrated their competence before the firm commits themselves to giving permanent contracts;

3 firms do not have to face uncomfortable redundancy situations if a downturn in trade occurs;

4 part-time and temporary workers are more productive than full-time workers. Part-time workers are often more enthusiastic about their work due to shorter hours and temporary workers are motivated by the fear of losing their jobs. Sub-contractors are self-employed and wish to satisfy the customer, which is the flexible firm;

5 firms have greater control over peripheral employees, who are often not represented by unions. Companies who have had power struggles with the trade unions in the past may feel that it is important to assert their right to manage the business. This can be done more easily with a larger proportion of the workforce on atypical contracts.

The change from firms having full-time permanent employees to becoming a flexible firm has been facilitated by several factors (many of which arose because of the recession in the 1980s):

◆ reductions in the size of the workforce, which has led firms to examine how best to make use of the remaining employees' time

◆ high unemployment, which has meant that employees and trade unions have been more prepared to consider different ways of working to retain jobs

◆ the creation of a pool of unemployed people prepared to take on more marginal work, such as part-time or temporary employment

◆ a change in company philosophy – concentrating on the 'core' activities and letting others provide 'peripheral' services in order to achieve more flexible ways of meeting changes in demand without the commitment to employing permanent staff

◆ increased competition from abroad which has led companies to look at the working patterns of their foreign competitors

◆ a need to be more flexible in response to the market, for example, Sunday opening, smaller and more frequent deliveries exactly when the customer requires them, gaining efficiency by contracting out certain services rather than producing them within the firm.

Flexible hours

Permanent and full-time staff have experienced greater flexibility in their hours of work over recent years.

Flexible working hours

This is the longest-running of the flexible hour systems; it became widespread by the 1970s and is most usually referred to as 'flexi-time'. Two and a half million people are working flexible hours. Most of them are office workers.

The firm's working day has to be longer than the working hours for individuals in order to implement flexi-time. People then flex their hours according to the needs of the business and their individual preference.

There is a band of time, say, from 8 am–6 pm when employees could work their contracted seven or eight hours. The employees can choose what time to go into work, and as long as they work a 'core time' of approximately 10 am–4 pm, their employer is happy for them to work their contracted hours when they wish. Employers control this by having a 'settlement period' within which time off must be taken so that build-ups of days off do not get over-large.

Compressed working week

Some organisations close early on Fridays, or do not work at all on Fridays, and therefore longer hours are worked on the other working days.

Compressed annual hours

Some employees are contracted to work a certain number of hours per year. Compressed annual hours involve working many hours in a short period of time. This is suitable for people working away from home such as oil rig workers. They can work intensively for a period of time and then take a long break.

Job sharing

Two people agree to share a single job. The employer has two contracts of employment, one with each person. The distribution of work is for the workers themselves to decide. Employees find the arrangement beneficial as the job is usually of a more interesting nature than many part-time jobs. Most job shares disappear when one person leaves and the other takes it over as a full-time job.

Homeworking

It is feasible for people to work at home with a computer terminal connecting them to their office. This has introduced the concept of 'the virtual organisation', which means that an organisation as a body of people all working together in one building has ceased to exist. It was once thought that future generations would all be working from home. This has not happened due to problems of isolation and loss of personal contacts. Women who work at home tend to do jobs related to the textile industry such as sewing.

Telecottages

Teleworking, telecommuting or remote working all refer to the practice of working at a distance for an employer, either at home or at a telecottage, according to the Association for Teleworkers and Telecottages and Telecentres. The Association reports that there are around 600 000 estimated self-employed teleworkers in the UK. Teleworkers work in a whole variety of fields, for example, accountancy, bookkeeping, translating and data inputs, as well as on a wide variety of contracts for large organisations at a distance.

A telecottage is a local centre that provides low-cost access to information techno- logy and communications. Users may be small businesses, community groups, or individuals who work from home and need additional support. A typical tele- cottage may be located in primary schools, colleges of FE, high schools, doctors' surgeries, libraries and converted village buildings. A telecottage would usually consist of a training room containing computers, printers and scanners, a working area also containing computers, printers, scanners, photocopier and fax machine.

Teleworkers work from telecottages and at home, if they have the equipment. The work usually comes from contracts which have been obtained from organisations who contract out certain jobs which could be completed in a remote location and sent back via modem or fax. This should eventually allow the worker to become competent in working with IT equipment and ultimately work at home being self- employed, or employed by an organisation.

An example of an organisation shipping work from the office to the home is British Telecommunications. Ten British Communications Directory Enquiry operators took part in a year-long work-at-home experiment and reported several benefits. The experiment began in June 1992, when ten directory assistants had sophisticated communications equipment installed in their homes in Inverness, including a video telephone. The experiment was successful. The benefits included the willingness of operators to do overtime, less time lost due to illness and also the environmental consideration of not travelling to work by cars.

The Telecottage Association built on the ACRE (Action with Communities in Rural England) Telecottage and Teleworking project. It was established by a group of practitioners with a wealth of experience in teleworking, and the establishment and management of the UK's first telecottages.

The Association states that it's aims are:

'To improve the opportunities and choice in employment, training and services for people living in rural areas and the development of local economies through the use of information technology and telecommunications, including shared facilities in local centres.'

Members of the Association obtain a quarterly newsletter, telecottage equipment starter pack (which is a package of Apple equipment and software available for rent to new telecottages to help them get started, including computers, scanners and laser printers), publications, training, and advice and referral service, conferences and personal fact files. More than 40 per cent of the UK's major companies are running pilot teleworking schemes. There are now over 70 telecottages in the UK, mainly in rural locations; this is the fastest growing network of telecottages in the world.

'Telecottages' written by Ruth Ashford, Lecturer in Business Studies, Manchester Metropolitan University. (Copyright reserved)

Multi-skilling

Multi-skilling is training or enabling workers to be competent at performing several different jobs. Multi-skilled individuals can perform many tasks skillfully, which enables them to cover for absent colleagues, work alone or as part of a small team to complete the production of a whole product, or train others in the skills they possess.

The design of jobs affects the variety of tasks which have to be carried out to complete the job. Changes in job design have the potential for both degrading and improving jobs. Change can lead to the 'de-skilling' of previously skilled jobs so that fewer tasks are performed by one person. Change can also enhance and supplement an individual's skills.

Traditionally, workers made their own decisions about how their work was carried out and were often craftsmen producing masterpieces of quality, tailored individually for each customer. The twentieth century has seen the advent of mass production and a change of the design of jobs so that many have become the repetition of one task. Although this has provided faster production and cheaper goods, it has often resulted in individuals feeling distanced from the production of the whole product and alienated from the organisation. They feel that their contribution to the production process is so small that they do not matter to the organisation. This can result in absenteeism and high staff turnover. This idea of separating out tasks in order to increase production is attributed to F.W. Taylor and Henry Ford and is sometimes referred to as Taylorism or Fordism.

F.W. Taylor's scientific management

Frederick Winslow Taylor was born in America in 1856 and was trained as an engineer. While he was working at the Bethlehem Steel Works, he observed how tasks, such as shovelling coke, were carried out. He experimented with different shovel sizes and measured daily outputs. Taylor designed a method of working using an exact shovel size which would be best for the job and which allowed for rest breaks. When Taylor's method of doing the work was used, output increased by nearly 400 per cent and wages increased by over 60 per cent. Costs were reduced considerably over a three year period as the number of workers needed fell by over 260.

Taylor believed that every worker in an organisation should only perform a single function. The principle of studying work and designing a 'best way' of doing the work was called 'scientific management'. Taylor's ideas were so successful at increasing production and caused such a lot of interest throughout America that they were tried out by other industries, although not always with happy results. In 1912, there were labour troubles at Watertown Arsenal, Massachusetts, caused by an attempt to apply his principles. As a result of the strike, he was asked to report upon his methods to the Special Committee of the House of Representatives.

Taylor believed that decisions about how the work should be done should be taken by management so that some order and precision could be given to the organisation of the factory or office – but separating the 'doing' part of the job from the 'thinking' part made jobs less interesting for the workers. When workers have no say in how the work is done and have a repetitive task to perform, they feel a lack of involvement, both with the job and the organisation as a whole.

Frederick Taylor is often blamed for the modern work organisation problems of assembly line boredom and alienation. Taylor did recommend organising work into small and separate tasks, but his plan was not to make things difficult for workers. Since the sixteenth century, workers had been ill-treated, exploited and underpaid by the employers and Taylor had the intention of putting this right. Taylor was implementing his ideas in 1911 with the intention of increasing production and workers' wages. F.W. Taylor's Scientific Management aimed to improve the workers' situation and make work organisation more efficient.

Taylor was the father of work study, the timing of tasks to calculate more efficient ways of working. 'Taylorism' could be said to be the implementation of these 'efficient' working methods – jobs designed by managers or work study specialists to provide maximum output. Taylorism actually seems to result in jobs made up of repetitive tasks and treatment of the workforce as if they were only capable of physical effort and not of contributing their ideas or thoughts to the work process.

Henry Ford

Henry Ford originated the idea of the moving production line for the mass production of cars. The early part of the twentieth century, when cars were first introduced, they were a symbol of status and wealth. Ford intended to change the fact that cars were only for the rich. The Model T was to be for the masses – a car almost everyone could afford. To make a cheaper car, Ford introduced various efficiency measures. He mechanised wherever possible and broke down tasks into their smallest parts. One worker would perform the same task over and over again, producing just one very small component of the whole operation.

The work was not enjoyable and by 1913, employees of the Ford Motor Company were leaving the company at such a rate that Ford had to hire ten times more workers than he needed just to keep the production line moving. Ford decided to double wages in order to get the best people and motivate them to work hard.

Henry Ford wanted to use the most up-to-date ideas about production, particularly those of F.W. Taylor. Charles Sorensen, one of Ford's top production people, started an assembly line by pulling a Model T chassis slowly by windlass across 250 feet of factory floor, timing the process. Behind him walked six workers, picking up parts from carefully spaced piles on the floor and fitting them to the chassis. By installing an automatic conveyor belt, a whole car was eventually assembled in 93 minutes. Many firms have since followed the lead of the Ford Motor Company and have used their production line methods to cut costs and increase efficiency.

Ford is credited with the invention of the production line. 'Fordism' is the philosophy of mass production, jobs designed so that they are made up of repetitive tasks which are only a tiny part of the production process. Fordism often results in the design of tedious jobs and workers who feel alienated from the organisation as they do not see the whole product produced and assume that their part in its construction is unimportant and unvalued.

Job design

Job design is concerned with the characteristics of jobs and how these affect people's behaviour. Job factors can be divided into two broad classes: quantitative and qualitative factors. Quantitative refers to the amount of work involved in the job, white qualitative refers to the perceived quality of that work. Many people at work would like their job redesigned to allow them to take on more responsibility. Their managers are willing for them to do this, just so long as they take on the responsibility as an extra to their existing job and do not drop any of the less interesting tasks they have to do as part of their job. There are three types of job redesign, all of which are forms of multi-skilling:

1 job rotation – moving workers from one job to another;

2 job enlargement – increasing the number of different tasks in one job;

3 job enrichment – giving workers more responsibility for, and control over, their work.

Job rotation

Employees' motivation can be improved by their movement from one job to another. Job rotation can be organised by managers or the workers involved. In the packing department of a sweet factory, workers could change between:

◆ taking packets of sweets from the conveyor belt and packing them into cartons

◆ labelling and wrapping the cartons

◆ lifting and stacking the cartons.

This change could occur weekly, daily, half-hourly or whatever the workers or management consider is most desirable. Job rotation provides variety and helps people avoid the strain of repeating the same physical movements all day, every day.

This form of job redesign can often be done at no extra cost to the organisation as no new machinery or equipment is needed. It increases the flexibility of the workforce as employees can perform one another's jobs. This is useful during periods of sickness and at holiday time.

Job rotation can have disadvantages in that:

◆ mistakes are difficult to trace, or workers feel blamed for the errors of another person

◆ more training is needed for all the workforce if tasks are complex, and this is costly for the organisation

◆ bad feeling may arise at changeover time if workers inherit untidy areas, half-finished tasks or work shoddily done

◆ the amount of variety within one job is still limited.

Job enlargement

The worker's job is expanded to include tasks previously performed by other workers. Before enlargement, workers perform a narrowly defined, specialised task; afterwards, they have more tasks to perform as part of their job. Unfortunately, job enlargement often fails to motivate individuals or to provide a more interesting job. If the entire production sequence consists of simple, easy-to-master tasks, merely doing more of them does not meaningfully change the worker's job. A few more similar tasks often do not provide sufficient challenge and stimulation.

Job enrichment

If motivators are incorporated into a job, the job will be enriched and more motivating for employees to perform. The motivators to incorporate in order to achieve a more motivating job are those highlighted by Herzberg's research:

◆ opportunity for achievement
◆ opportunity for recognition
◆ work itself
◆ responsibility
◆ opportunity for promotion.

The worker's involvement in the organisation and the job is increased by incorporating one or more of these motivators. Employees can complete a whole job, or a much larger part of the job than they did previously. The job is often enriched to include tasks which were performed by the manager or supervisor. The job therefore involves increased decision making.

Enrichment of many factory jobs may lead to abandoning the conveyor belt and production line, which are efficient methods of production. Costs may rise as a result of job changes. Firms may lose business as a result of changing job design.

Reorganisation of firm's structures, through re-engineering or continuous improvement schemes, may alter office as well as factory jobs. Managerial and other workers' responsibilities may be increased as a result of such measures as reducing the number of layers of management in an organisation. People may feel demotivated if they consider that they have been given a lot of extra work for no extra rewards. But if people feel they are achieving more and receiving recognition for their work, they will be motivated and have positive attitudes towards work.

Multi-skilling and job characteristics

Job design researchers Richard Hackman and Greg Oldham developed the job characteristics model in 1980 in order to guide job enrichment efforts. The model identified five core job characteristics:

1 *Skill variety* The extent to which the job entails a number of activities that require different skills.
2 *Task identity* The degree to which the job allows the completion of a major identifiable piece of work, rather than just a fragment.
3 *Task significance* The extent to which the worker sees the job output as having an important impact on others.
4 *Autonomy* The amount of discretion allowed in determining schedules and work methods for achieving the required output.
5 *Feedback* The degree to which the job provides for clear, timely information about performance results.

The more these core characteristics are reflected in jobs, the more motivating the jobs are likely to be. Multi-skilling normally involves all of these characteristics. Multi-skilled workers may feel that the work is meaningful, know that they are responsible for the outcomes, and find out about results. According to the model these feelings lead to outcomes which include higher work motivation, greater satisfaction of growth needs, higher general job satisfaction, and increased work effectiveness. The increased work effectiveness usually stems from higher work quality, although greater quantity may sometimes result.

In order to implement multi-skilling, organisations must be prepared to train the workforce and individuals must be prepared to undergo training and to perform several different jobs once they have received the training. Some individuals are happy to continue with the same job all the time, whilst others wish for the variety which multi-skilling offers.

CASE STUDY 1.6

Oasis Travel

Oasis Travel has two branches; one in Alsager, Cheshire, and the other in Tunstall, Stoke-on-Trent. The Alsager branch has been open for eight years and is staffed by three people: Daryl Pritchard, Manager; Tracy Slack, Assistant Manageress and Sales Consultant; and Julie Palmer, Office Clerk. Oasis Travel caters for a mixture of business and pleasure holidays. They do little advertising and manage to be very successful, with most business coming from personal recommendations from existing customers. On average they deal with around 150 customers per week.

Fig 1.5 Daryl Pritchard, Manager, Oasis Travel Agency

Daryl

'I've been working for Oasis since I left school, I started in the Tunstall branch and became manager here when it opened. The travel industry is very low paid, but I wouldn't change it for any other job, it's something different every day. There aren't many perks to the job, nowadays we don't get many cheap holidays. I'm left to run this branch without interference, we have one meeting a year with the Tunstall branch and that's all.

We don't have targets set for us, the targets we work to are our own sales figures from previous years, we try to keep the figures at least the same as last year, or hopefully better. In travel agents where they have multiple branches, they are much more pressured, they get commission on each sale, they are constantly under pressure from their head offices to sell more and meet strict targets. Our owner is easy going and as long as we keep doing our job, he's happy that the branch is well run. Overheads go up every year, so the only way we can see how we're doing is to match last year's figures. In the past few years we've done it, this year has been tricky for the whole of the travel trade. People are not booking holidays, agencies are reducing staff. The good summer of 1995 was bad for all travel agents because people stayed in Britain for their holidays. Even during the recession people had found money for holidays, but I don't know what is happening at the moment, we'll be glad when this year is over. I never expected the travel trade to be in this mess.

I go on holidays to gain experience, it's essential to know about locations in order to do this job. I don't get much discount, often the general public get bigger discounts than I do. The experience of seeing different holiday venues helps me to advise people. In a couple of weeks I'm going to Florida and California. I'm quite well travelled, it's my thirteenth trip to the States and still counting. I've been to Australia and the Far East. In some agencies the staff have never been on holiday and they're not much help to people needing advice.

My job mainly involves dealing with the public, sorting problems out and smoothing out staff problems. I'm the one who organises the staff, I share the work out. I push the business and try to get our name across as much as I can. The three of us work together as a team, we're pretty well organised and we all know what has to be done and whoever is free can cope with it. We all get on well and no-one argues. The job involves calming down the public quite a lot, both before and after their holidays. We're here for two things; to do bookings and to help to sort out problems if they occur. There are times when bad things happen as well as good.

I'm my own boss, I can make decisions on all sorts of things from advertising to agreeing on discounts, everything it takes to run the office. We have commissions with different tour operators and I have to organise those. It depends on what business we're doing and what different rates we can get.

Head Office decide on times of opening and staffing. The times are 9 am–5.30 pm, six days a week. I don't believe in working six days a week, but I have to, to keep the business going. If I have a day off I get double the work the next day, so many people come in who will only talk to me. I don't get much social time apart from week nights and Sundays. That's made up for by the extra holidays, I take about five or six weeks a year. In quieter times I do have a day off but the quieter times vary and it isn't a particular time of year any more.

Customer service is important. You've got to be friendly and go out of your way for clients. We're not the sort of agents who just book whatever people ask for. We do the searching for the holiday they want and go out of our way to find that holiday. By giving more of a personal service we ensure that customers will come back. The way I train staff is the way I would work. It does the trick, we get customers constantly coming back. Our staff are well known in the village, we're known on a first name basis.'

Tracy

Tracy has worked at Oasis in Alsager for seven years. She started straight from school and attended college on a day release basis to gain her COTAC (ABTA certificate for travel agents). Tracy's job involves selling holidays, administration, dealing with customer inquiries and problems both on the telephone and in person, organising tickets for customers, telephoning clients when they return from holidays to ask whether the holiday experience was successful.

'In the mornings we come in and we open the post, sort out the paperwork, there are confirmations to print out. I file through my notes to see what's the most important job to do. If a client hasn't come back to us we give them a ring. We have coffee and then all through the day we're answering enquiries. If a client comes to pay their balance, we print the receipts off. We have bad debt letters on Monday, asking for the balance or payment due. If the client has had a change of times or repricing of the holiday we have to send that out as well. There are odd jobs like making cards for the window, stamping newly delivered brochures and putting them on the shelves.

Fig 1.6 Tracy Slack, Assistant Manageress and Sales Consultant, Oasis Travel Agency

Daryl is going on holiday in a couple of weeks and I run the office while he's away. Someone will come to help out from the Tunstall office, but it's me who knows how the office works and how our computer system and the accounts work. So I'm in charge yet again. The public tend to know us and they will come to Julie and myself rather than the person from the Tunstall branch. I enjoy the responsibility of covering for Daryl to a point, but sometimes it has its downside. Often when clients have a complaint, they lash out at whoever is in charge. During Daryl's last holiday a client arrived at the airport and there was no reservation for her, she was in a panic. Only Julie and myself were in the office, I was worried but I managed to sort it out, it was the airline's fault.

I'm quite happy, most of the time it's nice dealing with the public. I looked into being a flight attendant, but I've got a friend who has done the job and she was mostly at home, because she was just "on call" and couldn't go anywhere. I wouldn't mind being a sales representative within the industry, working up and down the country and going to different travel agents.

It's nice to have a day off during the week. Being an independent agent we're not pressured to sell things, and when you get on well with your boss, it makes for a pleasant atmosphere. It's satisfying to deal with the public when they tell you all about the holiday they want and it's available for them to book. They come back to you afterwards as if you're a friend. The perks of the job are the educationals which are trips abroad run by tour operators and the concessions on holidays. The salary and the holidays are not good. We get very little holiday entitlement – 18 days a year. Once you've had a two-week holiday, there's not much time left. There aren't many educationals now, the last time I went anywhere was three years ago for three days in Cyprus. All the agents and tour operators are cutting down. It's nice to know the resorts yourself when you're advising clients instead of getting the brochure out and telling them what it says. Although nowadays the brochures do give more information and it's a lot better for us and for the client to see what's on offer. I like the agency meetings we have in Tunstall once a year. We can discuss how we're getting on and how we can improve our sales, and we're not nagged at, it's good.

The downside of the job is dealing with some of the public; some are easy going, some fussy. People can be miserable, the majority of the time they're not fully happy with the holiday they've booked. Sometimes people come in for late offers and there's a bargain they can take advantage of and they're on top of the world, it's nice when you feel as though you've done them a favour. When companies go into liquidation it causes us problems, checking all the *paperwork. Sometimes clients have disputes with tour operators and we fight for the client.*

Working Saturdays impinges on your social life. It would be nice to have a long weekend off. Sundays go by quickly and then it's Monday and back to work again. Saturday is the busiest day as most people can only come in at the weekend, we're shattered by the end of it and so Sunday is a late wake-up day.'

Julie

'I've worked here for about six months. The job involves all sorts of things, from dealing with the public to making coffee, sorting the post, answering the phones. I enjoy it. I do everything Daryl and Tracy do. I enjoy doing the bookings the most, you feel that you've achieved something at the end of the day. You do get all different people in here, some can be really nice and others are unpleasant with you. I go to college one day a week and I'm doing GNVQ level 2 course in Travel and Tourism and the ABTA course, they run alongside each other. We learn more about the geography side of things, about different countries and regional tourist boards in Britain.

Fig 1.7 Julie Palmer, Office Clerk, Oasis Travel Agency

I did a week's work experience before I came here, so I knew something, but it was at the quiet time so there wasn't really a lot to do. Then I started working Saturdays here before I became full-time, that made me sure that this is what I wanted to do. I might be a flight attendant later. There isn't anything about the job I don't like, except having to work every Saturday. That's the problem, but we do get a day off in the week.'

DISCUSSION QUESTIONS 1.6

1 Is it essential for Daryl, Julie and Tracy to work together as a multi-skilled team?

2 Are there any tasks which Julie would find difficult to carry out if she were left to run the office alone?

3 How do cutbacks by tour operators impact on the skills of travel agents?

4 The staff at Oasis Travel Agents are a very cohesive team, what factors have contributed to Daryl's success in building such a team?

5 How is customer service improved by the team's method of working?

6 What disadvantages are there to a career as a strong travel agent?

Teamworking

Teams are capable of increasing productivity, raising morale, and nurturing innovation. These benefits only result if the right type of team is chosen for the task to be accomplished. Teams consume time, energy and money. They must be carefully formed and to be effective team members need training, good communication links, and details of the job they must carry out. A major pitfall for companies using teams is their tendency to create teams when they are not really needed. Some people are better left to work alone and some tasks can be better accomplished by individuals. Before a team is formed, management should analyse the work to be done, decide whether a team approach is preferable, and then select the best type of team.

Team types

The benefits of the team approach and the reduction of the workforce in many organisations have produced different types of team:

1 *Problem-solving teams* These comprise of knowledge workers who gather to solve specific problems and then disband.

2 *Product-development teams* These normally consist of workers who produce the product. Ideally they should also include, or at least consult with, people from marketing and sales who understand consumer needs.

3 *Management teams* Consists mainly of managers from various functions, like sales and production. They coordinate work amongst the other teams. Managers often have most difficulty in operating as a team, even when they have a teamwork philosophy within the organisation.

4 *Work teams* Work teams produce the product or service. When empowered, they become self-managed teams.

5 *Quality circles* A group of people from the same work area who meet regularly to solve work problems and improve work processes.

6 *Virtual teams* Geographically dispersed teams who interact via computer.

The teams most popular today consist of two types: work teams, which include self-managed teams, and problem-solving teams.

Work teams

Work teams are relatively permanent in nature. Small numbers of people with complementary skills perform the day-to-day work of the organisation. If the work team is empowered with the authority to make decisions about how the daily work is done, it is a self-managed team or autonomous work group. Self-managed teams can take actions such as deciding on the order of the tasks they do and often have their own budgets. Teams at Rover Group have the authority to call in suppliers if a component consistently fails. The team leader can discuss the problem with the supplier without calling in a manager. The team is responsible for their own quality checks and have all the information they need to make decisions.

Self-managed teams are most effective when they combine employees with a range of skills and functions. Members are trained to be multi-skilled so that they can perform each other's jobs as needed. Empowering these teams with the decision making authority necessary to perform their role in the organisation often means allowing them to select fellow team members, spend money, solve problems, conduct meetings in work time, decide how they wish to achieve any targets set for them, evaluate their own results and plan future projects.

Problem-solving teams

These are temporary combinations of workers who gather to solve a specific problem and then disband. The problem-solving teams differ from quality circles in important ways. Where quality circles are permanent committees designed to handle whatever workplace problems may arise, problem solving teams have specific tasks to deal with. Multi-functional teams may look at the processes which the organisation's products go through in order to cut out unnecessary processes. This is a sort of business process re-engineering and can be done much more cheaply by internal problem-solving teams than by management consultants.

The use of autonomous working teams allows managers more free time for planning and strategic issues rather than having to spend time resolving day-to-day problems. The team members appreciate the trust management place in them and often enjoy the increased responsibility and independence the team ideal gives them. Teams can take years to develop into fully effective and cohesive working units, but if individuals are committed to teamwork and the task, then an effective team can emerge fairly quickly.

Empowerment

Empowerment is power sharing, the delegation of power or authority to subordinates in the organisation. It means giving power to others in the organisation so they can act more freely to accomplish their jobs. Top managers believe giving up centralised control will promote speed, flexibility and decisiveness and help them cope with an environment of intense global competition and new technology.

Reasons for empowerment

Empowerment can make an organisation more flexible and effective in two ways. The first is that empowerment increases the total amount of power in the organisation. Many managers think that they must give up power in order for someone else to have more. But delegating power from the top can create a larger total amount of power, so that everyone has more. The manager who gives away power often receives a payment for it in terms of increased commitment and creativity from his or her subordinates. When employees have power, they may find ways to use their abilities for positive results for the organisation. Managers' fear of power loss is a big barrier to empowering employees, but if they took the attitude that they would actually gain power, delegation would be easier for them.

Empowerment can also increase employee motivation. Individuals like to feel that they are effective and can produce results themselves. Increasing employee power heightens motivation for getting the job done because people improve their own effectiveness, choosing how to do the task and using their creativity. Most people enter an organisation with a desire to do a good job, and empowerment enables them to release the motivation already there. Their reward is a sense of personal achievement and competence.

Elements of empowerment

Empowering employees involves giving them four motivators which enable them to accomplish their jobs more effectively.

1 More information about company performance. In companies where employees are fully empowered, no information is secret.

2 Employees have knowledge and skills to contribute to company goals. Companies can use training to give employees the knowledge and skills they need both to do their own jobs and also to contribute to wider company performance, such as training in quality awareness.

3 Employees have the power to make decisions. Many organisations give workers the power to influence work processes and quality through quality circles and autonomous work teams. The Body Shop has made the ultimate step in empowering its workers, by giving them the business. In some of The Body Shop stores, workers are buying the shop with the use of the profits they have made in their store, they have formed a management team and manage the shop with guidance from Body Shop International.

4 Employees' rewards are based on company performance. Two of the ways in which organisations can reward employees financially based on company performance are through profit sharing and employee share ownership. Usually, profits are given to employees on a half yearly basis, but ownership of shares is normally bought through a scheme which entails the employee saving for the shares from their wages for five years and then the shares are purchased at the original price, giving the employee an instant profit if they choose to sell them

The empowerment process

The empowerment process often consists of three stages.

1 The first stage is the diagnosis of conditions within the organisation that cause powerlessness for subordinates. Factors such as too many rules, little task variety, being stuck in a remote location, rewards for routine output rather than innovation, and lack of opportunities for participating in decisions, all reduce power.

2 The second stage is to develop new ways of working which will increase power at lower levels. Employees are given access to knowledge and skills, information, power to make decisions, and rewards based on company

performance. This stage usually starts with a clear goal or vision, publicly stated by top management and involves a complete change in the way the organisation is structured and the jobs individuals do.

3   Stage three involves feedback to employees that reinforces their success and feelings of effectiveness. Employees learn how they are getting on. Many companies place emphasis on pay for performance, so employees' success is rewarded through pay. Other companies give more opportunities for promotion, or positive feedback to reinforce employees' feelings of effectiveness, so that they become comfortable and improve at their jobs under empowerment. The organisation that has empowered employees will be different, with major changes in structure, information sharing, and decision making responsibility.

Individual and interpersonal behaviour

From reading this chapter you will learn about individual and interpersonal behaviour, including:

1 motivation;
2 personality;
3 perception;
4 why female managers find it difficult to get into senior management positions;
5 attitudes to work;
6 internal and external factors affecting behaviour.

The main function of managers in organisations is to motivate their employees to pursue enthusiastically organisational objectives. Motivation is the basis of managing people and achieving objectives.

 Motivation

Motivation is the cause of an action. Individuals are motivated to eat because they are hungry, motivated to look both ways before they cross the road to keep themselves safe and motivated to take college courses for their own self-esteem.

A manager may be able to motivate his or her employees by encouraging or praising them; by giving them responsibility to carry out the work as they wish, or by offering them rewards such as increased wages or the possibility of future rewards such as promotion.

Some people may be highly motivated and far exceed what was expected of them after praise from their manager, others will not alter their work rate as a result of the praise. Certain people may actually reduce their work rate as they are convinced that the manager has an ulterior motive in giving the praise, and is attempting to get more work out of them for no extra pay. They may be determined that their manager is not going to take advantage of them and therefore the praise is seen in a negative light. There are a variety of ways of motivating people as well as a variety of different reactions to motivators.

Theories of motivation

Theories of motivation originate from:

1 ideas people have had in the past as to what motivates individuals to work; and

2 research done on motivators at work, such as payment systems and how they affect people's willingness to work.

The theories can help managers to understand how individuals are motivated at work and how to improve individual motivation.

Hierarchy of needs theory

Abraham Maslow formulated his theory of motivation in 1935. In his article, 'A Theory of Human Motivation' he put forward the theory that individuals are only motivated by needs which are unmet. His idea was that we have a basic need for such things as food and sleep, and once we have had a good night's sleep or a large meal, we will not be motivated to eat more food or doze off. Once needs are met we move on to meeting needs on a higher level. Maslow categorised different needs into five levels, individuals will only move from one level to another when their needs are around 75 per cent met at that level. The five levels consist of:

Higher order needs	self-actualisation needs (being everything one is capable of being)
	ego or self-esteem needs (the need for praise and recognition, to feel good about oneself)
	social needs (the need for companionship and friendship)
Lower order needs	safety and security (the need to feel safe from attack and to be able to feel secure enough to make plans for the future)
	basic or physiological needs (circumstances which enable individuals to function effectively, e.g. sleep, food, air to breathe, freedom from illness, correct temperature).

The higher and lower order needs differ in that it is possible to meet the lower order needs fully. The higher order needs tend to be insatiable in that the more we get of them, the more we want. If we are praised and told what a good job we are doing, we want to hear more; the ego or self-esteem need can never be satisfied fully.

There may be conflict between needs for employers wishing to help their workers meet needs at work. In order to meet social and self-esteem needs the manager may introduce teamwork which should encourage all team members to feel valued. Occasionally though, teamwork can mean that some individuals are demoted from being supervisor or assistant manager and are now just another team member and this adversely affects their ego needs. People who had status within the organisation before teamwork or flatter structures were introduced may never come to terms with the situation, as newer more competent people may contribute a great deal to the group and be more useful than the person who previously held a position of higher status. The person who has lost status would have been deferred to in the past and now they may feel ignored and mistreated under the teamwork system. Also, conflict can arise when people are working in groups and disagreements occur. Some disagreements may take the form of open arguments and fights, whilst others take place behind the scenes with gossip about a disliked team member or complaining to the manager about the team member. Social needs are not being met for all group members when the group goes through a period of conflict.

Another need which is difficult for employers to meet is self-actualisation. This means that the individual is doing a job that they really enjoy and feel that they are being challenged so that they are performing to the best of their abilities. Talented people are sometimes in exactly the right job for them and they are happy at work. Other individuals have sufficient freedom in their job to choose which tasks they wish to work on and can negotiate with their managers about what they would like to do and what they would like to leave out. Other people are given set tasks as part of their job and if they feel that these are not interesting enough for them they can volunteer to do more responsible tasks, but they also have to complete all the less interesting ones too. Sometimes employers have very mundane jobs which they need to employ someone to perform and they can do very little to make the jobs more interesting. This means that some of the people working on these jobs are frustrated and bored with the work; others are happy because they get along well with the other people at work, or they may have time-consuming hobbies and interests outside work and the job is a means to support their leisure interests and therefore they are fairly content in their work.

◆ ACTIVITY 2.1

Match the following facilities/motivators to a category of need: basic, security, social, ego or self-actualisation.

1 Work organised in groups so that employees can chat to one another while carrying out their work.

2 Award for the best production team of the month.

3 Canteen facilities.

4 Pension.

5 Health and Safety Officers.

6 Praise for good work.

7 Re-organising the work so that individual employees can choose which tasks they carry out.

Criticisms of the Hierarchy of Needs

Research carried out to substantiate Maslow's theory that individuals must satisfy one need before moving on to the next has not found the theory to be completely true. People can be doing a job that they love and therefore be meeting their needs for self-actualisation. Yet they may work on a temporary basis and not have any job security, be working alone and not meet their social or ego needs. Because their job is so fulfiling to them, they can be quite happy in their work when one or several levels of need are missing. Therefore the theory that people are only motivated by needs which are unmet is not completely correct. Certain needs can be left unmet and the individual can move onto the next level and not feel any motivation to meet the missing need.

However, Maslow's theory is useful as it provides a guide for managers as to why workers may be discontent in their jobs. Although the theory gives an indication of problem areas, in that the work does not meet the needs of the employee, it does not give advice as to how to change the situation in order to meet individual's needs other than in a very general way.

Herzberg's two-factor theory

Frederick Herzberg's research into the factors which motivate individuals to work indicated that certain circumstances would cause people to be motivated to work, whilst other circumstances would create dissatisfaction at work. Herzberg and his researchers questioned 200 accountants and engineers in Pittsburg, USA, about what they liked about work and what they disliked about work. Herzberg then categorised these answers into those factors which provide satisfaction at work and those which cause dissatisfaction. He called the two factors motivators and hygiene (or maintenance) factors.

Motivators	Hygiene factors
Achievement	Working conditions
Recognition	Pay
Responsibility	Company policies
The work itself	Relationship with supervisor
Promotion prospects	Interpersonal relationships

Motivators

Achievement. This may mean a feeling of having done something well, of having created something, helped someone, overcome a difficult challenge; a job accomplished of which the individual feels proud.

Recognition. This entails some form of acknowledgement of the good work performed from the individual's manager or employer. It may be praise, a pay rise, an announcement to colleagues, an item in a newsletter, an award, any message which the individual feels demonstrates that their boss appreciates their work.

Responsibility. This often entails a feeling of being in charge of the task and being able to take decisions as to how it will be done. Being given responsibility for a task or for managing people signifies that the manager has faith in the ability and competence of the person to whom he or she gives responsibility.

The work itself. When individuals find their work interesting and worthwhile they are motivated by the job itself. The content of the job is the most important factor in individual motivation. When factors such as responsibility and promotion prospects are weak, these become peripheral to the enjoyment of the work which is being undertaken all day, every day.

Promotion prospects. Few people do not wish to progress in their career. Being given a more prestigious job title, a higher grade or rank in the organisation is seen as a reward, a sign of faith in the individual's competence and a boost to the individual's ego as management are indicating that the individual is superior in their work performance to other possible candidates for the position. As well as the factors which enhance an individual's self-esteem, there is usually an increase in salary, which is valuable in itself. The increase in status which comes with promotion enhances the image of the individual, both within the organisation and in society.

Hygiene factors

Working conditions. Certain jobs entail unpleasant working conditions – strong smells, hot or cold temperatures, working outside in all weathers, loud and persistent noise, handling hazardous substances or dangerous machinery, unsocial hours or standing or sitting for many hours. Herzberg considered that if working conditions were poor, then individuals would be dissatisfied with their jobs. On the other hand, if working conditions are good, people would not be motivated to work any harder, they would just be happy to stay in the job.

Salary. Herzberg's research was with professional, salaried people who were not paid according to a piece rate system. His research findings were that salary does not motivate. This was due to the fact that his respondents did not earn more if they worked harder. Many jobs entail bonuses, commission, piece rates and merit rises and the individuals who are entitled to these payments are motivated to work harder to earn them. For individuals who earn a monthly salary which does not increase even if they work overtime, salary will not motivate them. These individuals will usually aim for promotion if they wish to earn a salary increase.

Company policy. A policy is a declared mode of action for the future. Organisations may have no-smoking policies or equal opportunities policies which indicate how they plan to act in present and future situations. Individuals are often strongly affected by company policies – cutbacks on spending, new training policies, contracting out of services or production which used to be undertaken in-house, taking on temporary or part-time staff, will change the daily working lives of employees. Herzberg's theory was that if individuals were adversely affected by company policy, they would be dissatisfied at work, but if company policies suited them they would not be motivated to work harder.

Supervisors. Herzberg considered that if the individual's relationship with their supervisor, team leader or manager was poor they would be dissatisfied with their work. According to his two-factor theory, if relationships with superiors are good individuals are not motivated to work harder, but in practice this relationship is extremely important in the motivation of individuals. People who manage the work of others have the most power and opportunity to motivate those individuals through their daily interactions.

Interpersonal relationships. Many people enjoy the companionship which work provides, they make friendships at work and often socialise outside working hours with colleagues. Although Herzberg's two-factor theory maintains that if relationships are happy, individuals will not be motivated to work, this is often untrue as peer pressure to perform well and a fear of letting the team down are a great motivating force. Many individuals who could get away with doing little work or putting in a shoddy performance do not do so because they would not want their colleagues to think badly of them.

Criticisms of the two-factor theory

Herzberg's two-factor theory asserts that motivators and hygiene factors are not overlapping, and a factor such as salary cannot both be motivating and demotivating in different circumstances. However, it often is the case that the same factor can motivate and demotivate individuals. If the job itself is interesting and varied, this will be motivating, whereas a tedious, repetitive job will usually be demotivating for people. Nevertheless, the theory does have some very good points:

◆ The motivators are good indicators of the factors that influence individual motivation. If a manager wishes to improve the motivation of his or her workforce, these factors will provide useful pointers

◆ Many of the hygiene or maintenance factors do not provide motivation, as Herzberg asserted. Good working conditions will not encourage people to work harder: a new office carpet is attractive and improves conditions, but individuals often consider improvements in their working environment to be justified as part of the building up of corporate image and marketing of the organisation rather than as a reward for themselves

◆ Some of the hygiene factors do have the effect of maintaining the workforce in their present positions rather than motivating them to work harder. Good salary, working conditions and relationships at work often increase loyalty to the organisation rather than motivating individuals to put in more effort in their jobs.

Acquired needs theory

David McClelland formulated a theory based on needs as motivators. People learn in early childhood that certain ways of behaving lead to good things happening to them. The child who tries hard at school may get praise from parents or teachers. This brings pleasure from feelings of achievement in having performed a task well. The child who is a bully can make other children do what she wants; as can the friendly, charming child. These children enjoy the feelings of control they have over other people and develop a need for power. The child who is sociable and interested in others has plenty of friends. They find that they are happy when they have warm friendships and can avoid conflict. According to McClelland, being rewarded for certain behaviours in childhood causes people to develop a need for these rewards.

McClelland argues that there are three basic needs, which he abbreviated to N-Ach, N-Aff and N-Power.

1 ACHIEVEMENT (N-Ach) People who have a need for achievement want to 'get the job done'. Their focus is the task.

2 AFFILIATION (N-Aff) People who have a need for affiliation want approval from other people. Their focus is other people.

3 POWER (N-Power) People who have a need for power want influence and control over others. Their focus is themselves.

The need for achievement

People with a need for achievement prefer to work on their own and like to have quick feedback on whether their efforts have been successful. They do not depend on others for approval, they set their own targets for themselves and are happy to strive for them alone. They are 'doers', the action people in the organisation, and they like to get things done. They cannot understand people who enjoy chatting all day or who hesitate in making decisions. If they are extremely task oriented, they will not be popular with others and may be unsuitable for management positions. One of the functions of a manager is to smooth conflicts: the manager with a high need for achievement often does not see the need to bother with people and can actually be the cause of conflict. This is not necessarily the case, as sometimes the task oriented manager or individual may have a job which involves dealing with people and is therefore conscientious about making sure the customers or workers are kept happy as they see this as part of their job.

The need for affiliation

People with a need for affiliation are sensitive to the needs of others. They seek approval, both from management and subordinates. They prefer to do their work by working with others, or by liaising with other people. Some people have such strong N-Aff needs that they spend a great deal of time socialising and do not manage to get much work done. Other people also have N-Aff needs, but not at the expense of doing their jobs. They are interested in the feelings of others which may well make them the best sort of leaders or managers. As they are very people-oriented, they are suited to working with people and would be unhappy working with machinery or by themselves. It is occasionally difficult to distinguish people with N-Aff needs from those with N-Power needs, as those desiring power over others are often charming and sociable in order to exercise their personal power.

The need for power

There are different ways of gaining power: through status and position in the organisation, the ability to reward people, bullying, aggressive behaviour, or the ability to punish people, having expertise which others need, or through personal influence and communication. People with a need for power have a strong desire to be liked and those who fail to gain promotion will often devote much of their time to developing friendships and extending their personal influence. Those who gain power through achieving status may have to wait longer to meet their needs than those with a need for achievement. The need for achievement is satisfied every time a task is successfully completed. N-Power people like competitive situations and having the power to make decisions. It is essential for managers to have a fairly strong N-Power as their job involves having power over others to motivate them to work.

Approaches to motivating people at work

Individuals with different needs will be motivated by different rewards. The people with high N-Ach are motivated by being given an interesting and worthwhile job to do. They can be trusted to carry out the work unsupervised and so long as they know what their objectives are and that the work is valued and appreciated, they will be well motivated. Landscape gardeners get a feeling of achievement every time they see a garden they have designed and worked on completed. Individuals with a need for achievement must have their work recognised, so that they feel accepted and of worth themselves. To the task oriented, or achievement oriented person, their work *is* them, it is an extension of themselves, and therefore any criticism of the work is a personal criticism. For them to be told that their work is excellent is interpreted by them as meaning they themselves are excellent. For their work to go unnoticed or unrewarded means that they are not valued and that they have probably made an error when carrying out the work. Recognition of an individual's work can take many forms – a public announcement, a mention in the newsletter, pay rises – all dependent upon the usual forms of recognition in the organisation. The individual with a high need for achievement will want whatever form of recognition is the norm.

Motivating people with a high need for affiliation could involve organising thee work so that the work can be carried out with others. Repetitive tasks can be done in groups and the seating arranged so that people can talk while they are doing the work. Meetings to discuss problems at work or team briefings can be arranged away from the workplace so that social interaction is encouraged. Some individuals may not have sufficient social contact and are unable to develop friendships. If their manager has reason to believe that they have a high N-Aff then the individual could be given a different job as soon as one arises, have a job designed for them which involves liaising with other people, or have certain tasks added to their existing job which require increased social contact. People with high N-Aff will enjoy dealing with customers and colleagues, but may need training for coping with awkward or unpleasant situations such as conflicts and customer complaints.

Individuals with a high N-Power wish to control others and will be motivated by the prospect of promotion or leading a team. If they cannot be given a job which involves supervising or influencing others, they will often achieve this through personal means – becoming very popular with their colleagues or politicking. Individuals with strong N-power often have good leadership potential and should be considered for positions which involve managing others. Certain individuals with strong N-Power, however, do not have good leadership potential. This may be due to a lack of interpersonal skills which means that their method of gaining power is to bully others. The use of aggressive behaviour will not necessarily stop if they achieve leadership status and therefore these individuals are probably unsuitable for positions which involve the management of others.

Not everyone has a dominant need and may have two or three needs in balance. These individuals will often be easier to manage than those with one extremely strong need.

Expectancy theory

Victor Vroom developed his expectancy model of motivation in 1964. His theory is based on the idea that needs cause behaviour. Important points which the theory makes are:

1 Motivation comes in different strengths – sometimes we want an outcome very much and other objectives may not be quite as important, even though we are still motivated to achieve them.

2 Motivation strength is determined by the perceived value of the outcome or reward. The motivation we feel to achieve a goal depends upon how valuable that goal is to us. We will be less motivated to work for objectives we feel are not so useful or valuable.

3 Motivation strength is also determined by the perceived probability that the behaviour will cause the outcome or reward to occur. If we expect to be able to achieve the objective through our actions, we will be motivated to 'go for it'.

Rachel's motivation depends upon:

1 How valuable is the reward or outcome? (promotion).

2 Will it happen? (What is the probability of the promotion occurring?)

Fig 2.1 Rachel dreams of becoming a manager

Vroom's expectancy theory of motivation as an equation:

Motivation strength	=	Probability that the outcome will occur following the action	×	Value of the result or goal

Rachel's motivation:

Highly motivated to work hard	=	She thinks it very likely that she will achieve promotion	×	Wants promotion and a managerial career very much
Not motivated to work hard	=	She thinks it highly unlikely that she will achieve promotion	×	Would quite like promotion, but is not concerned at present

People will be less motivated to try for promotion if they feel it is not really worthwhile, or if they think they will not achieve it even if they work hard and apply for it.

Vroom and approaches to motivating people at work

Vroom's theory is very useful as it reminds managers that providing good employee benefits and incentives will not necessarily motivate employees to work hard. People will only value the benefits and incentives if they see them as worthwhile. They will only work hard towards the incentives if they think they can achieve them.

Many firms provide benefits such as healthcare. Some individuals do not value this very highly, despite the fact that it is expensive for firms to provide it. Also, many organisations give bonuses to encourage individuals to achieve their targets. If the targets are very difficult to meet, people will feel that they are unachievable and will not be motivated to work for them.

Managers can check that employees value the benefits and incentives provided by the organisation by consulting them or allowing them to choose which benefits they receive. Employees' confidence that they can achieve goals also needs to be boosted, and care taken about setting goals which are possible to achieve. Appraisal interviews are useful for talking to employees about their aspirations for the future and how they can reach them. New goals can be negotiated which the employee feels are achievable and worthwhile which should then result in their feeling motivated.

CASE
STUDY

Julie Brewer, Vice President of Communications, United Way of Quad Cities, Moline, Illinois

The United Way is an umbrella organisation which raises funds for many charities. This enables businesses and individuals to donate to several charities at the same time and costs are saved on the marketing and publicity activities necessary to raise funds. Julie Brewer is Vice President of Communications which involves obtaining publicity through the media.

'I am responsible for creating all our printed materials and we make a film every year, I produce that. If a reporter or anyone connected with the media calls, they talk to me. This year, for the first time we worked with all the major television studios in our communities and I got them to do a prime time special, The United Way. It was a real big deal for me because it was the first time I had ever written a television script, researched all the stories and produced it. That's my job – anything that deals with communications comes through me.

Fig 2.2 Julie Brewer, United Way

There are 23 people working at United Way and my job involves networking with everyone to make sure that we have looked at every news angle our organisation offers and exploit it and get it out there. I create my work plan for the year by looking at what needs to be done from a communications aspect and what other departments need as far as communication goes. I write my own public relations plan for the year from this, so that sets the mood for knowing what the big projects are and I set my time schedule around that. I have more control over my work than I did in the past with other jobs.

What motivates me to do any of the three jobs I've had is the ability to sell the product. No matter what sort of organisation you work for, in public relations you have a product to promote. It may be promoting a cause, a material product, an experience, or a person. The goal of good public relations is to target your audience, the people who would give donations to United Way. The aim is to get information in front of the audience in a correct, frequent and exciting way. Writing a news release and sending it to the media is just the beginning. Dealing with mass communications, no matter how sophisticated it gets, is still very much like telling a story. I tell you something and you tell somebody else and as it goes along the story changes. When you are in public relations and work with the media it is your job to make sure the information is correct and accurate and is interpreted correctly. You have to be able to write for the audience, communicate with them, understand their limitations and know your product or subject. You have to educate them in a way which isn't patronising. That's what I find exciting, being able to get the message out there.

The part of the work I don't like is the way charity work is put under the microscope and scrutinised by the public. You have to be so careful about what you say, because your survival depends on the generosity of the community. You may like something we're doing, but your neighbour doesn't – how can I do something to please you both? We service 350 000 people in our area and you have 350 000 different opinions – so how do you stay in the good graces of all those people? There are going to be people who want you to fund Aids projects and people who don't want you to fund Aids projects. There are going to be people who want you to fund religious motivated organisations and others who would be offended if we fund a religious motivated organisation. It's just a very complicated business and you are constantly at the mercy of public opinion.

My attitude to work is that I feel it defines who we are as people. It's not just a job I get paid for, it's me. Some people's attitude is "I'm hired to work nine to five and when five o'clock comes I'm out of here". That isn't my attitude, I think you should work until it's done and it's done correctly, you walk away only when you know that you have done

CASE
STUDY
cont

everything you can to make whatever you are doing the best it can be. That way you achieve pride in your work.

My last job was in public relations on a riverboat casino. This position doesn't impinge on my social life as much as the casino because not only is it open 24 hours a day, but its most alive at night. If someone won a $60 000 jackpot at two o'clock in the morning, they would call me to go in and organise the publicity. The first time I took a day off at the casino they gave me a bleeper, the second time I took a day off they gave me a car phone. There was always that umbilical cord of communication and I felt haunted by my job – anything could happen at any minute. The casino employed 1200 people and they all had to sign a confidentiality policy agreeing not to talk to the media. I was the recognised spokesperson for the media, so they needed me to be continually available. My life was the casino and that's part of the reason why I made the decision to leave. The other part of the reason was that the Mid-West is not a very big market and if I stayed there too long I would have a hard time finding another public relations job because everyone would identify me with the casino. When I took the job at United Way I decided that my life had to stop being work all the time. The job only impinges upon you as much as you let it.'

DISCUSSION QUESTIONS 2.1

1 What factors make Julie Brewer's job interesting?

2 What do you think motivates Julie to work hard?

3 Why does Julie feel that there are disadvantages to working in a charitable organisation?

4 Why did Julie find working for a riverboat casino very difficult?

5 Why is Julie concerned about getting the details of her job precisely right?

6 Why do you think some people have the attitude that they want to leave work at exactly five o'clock and not stay until everything is done to the best of their ability?

Personality

Personality is what makes one person different from another and includes the characteristics of an individual. Personality is not a rigid way of behaving at all times, it is merely a tendency to behave in certain ways.

Differences between individuals mean that they vary in their reaction to their job, their manager and their colleagues. The quality of someone's performance at work is determined by both their personality and the situation. People differ in the way they carry out their work and how well they get along with other people. They may frequently come into conflict with others and have difficulty with relationships, this causes problems for their manager as well as themselves. The variety of personalities with which managers have to deal makes the job of management much more difficult and demanding than if they had to deal with inanimate objects such as figures or machines. Managing people is always the most challenging part of a manager's job.

Personality traits

There are several personality characteristics which can be reduced down to a few categories of personality. The most common categories are 'stable–unstable' and 'introvert–extrovert'. These four dimensions were identified by psychologist Hans Eysenck. The 'stable–unstable' category is concerned with emotional stability. Those with high stability tend to be calm and even-tempered, whilst those with low stability are anxious and moody. The trait of 'extroversion–introversion' is commonly used in everyday language. Extroverts tend to be outgoing and sociable, while introverts are more reserved and quiet.

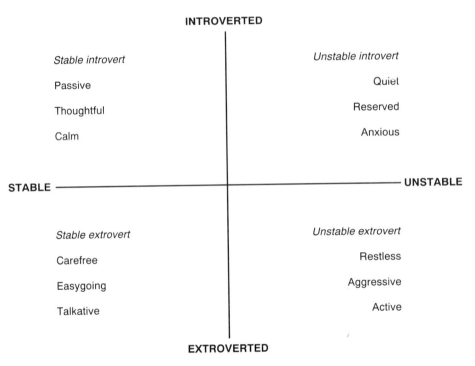

Fig 2.3 Adaptation of Eysenck's typology of personality

QUIZ *Personality test*

2.1

	Yes	No
1 Do you like going out a lot?	✓	
2 Would you call yourself tense or 'highly strung'?		✓
3 When people shout at you, do you shout back?		✓
4 If there is something you want to know about, would you rather look it up in a book than talk to someone about it?		✓
5 Are you usually carefree?		✓
6 Do you like doing things in which you have to act quickly?	✓	

Score

Give yourself 5 points per question, if you answered 'Yes' to numbers: 1, 3, 5, 6
Give yourself 5 points per question if you answered 'No' to numbers: 2, 4
Add these together, this gives you your score on the extrovert–introvert dimension

For your score on the stable–unstable dimension:

'Yes', 5 points for 1, 5
'No', 5 points for 2, 3, 6

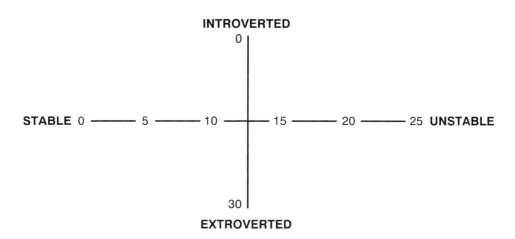

Fig 2.4 Plot your scores on the graph

Although personality tests are sometimes used for recruiting new people into jobs, there is no one particular personality which is best for a particular job. A balance of personalities in an organisation helps the organisation to function as a team, not everyone can be the star of the show or work quietly in the background.

Personality attributes

There are other personality attributes which are more relevant to managers than the extrovert–introvert category. These are:

Locus of control. Some people believe they are in control of their own lives and have an *internal locus of control.* Others think that what happens to them is a result of fate, chance, luck or the behaviour of other people. An employee who fails to get promotion might blame their boss or their colleagues, rather than their own lack of skills or poor performance record. These people think that forces beyond their control dictate what happens to them and they therefore have an *external locus of control.* Those people with an internal locus of control may be easier to manage in jobs in which they are required to work on their own initiative or come up with their own ideas. Those with an external locus of control will be reactive rather than proactive and consider that they ought to be told what to do and how to do it.

Self-efficacy. This is a person's beliefs about his or her capabilities to perform a task. People with a high self-efficacy believe that they are capable of performing well on a specific task, and people with low self-efficacy are more prone to doubt their ability to perform a specific task. Some people have more confidence than others and their belief in their ability to perform a task effectively results in their being more self-assured and more able to focus their attention on performance.

Authoritarianism. This is the extent to which a person believes that power and status differences are important in organisations. A person who is highly authoritarian may accept orders from their boss purely because of their boss's status in the organisation. Alternatively, a person who is not highly authoritarian may still carry out reasonable orders from the boss, but he or she is more likely to question things, express disagreements with the boss, and even refuse to carry out orders if they feel the orders are objectionable. A manager who is highly authoritarian may be autocratic and demanding, and subordinates who are highly authoritarian will be more likely to accept this behaviour from their leader. A manager who is less authoritarian may allow subordinates a bigger role in making decisions, and less authoritarian subordinates will respond positively to this behaviour.

Dogmatism. This refers to the rigidity of a person's beliefs and his or her openness to other viewpoints. A manager may have such strong beliefs about how certain procedures should be carried out that she is unwilling to even listen to a new idea for changing them. The manager is close-minded or highly dogmatic. Another manager in the same circumstances might be very receptive to listening to and trying new ideas. This manager is more open-minded or less dogmatic.

Machiavellianism. This concept is named after Niccolo Machiavelli, a sixteenth-century Italian author. In his book entitled *The Prince*, Machiavelli explained how to gain the power to control the behaviour of others. Individuals who score high on Machiavellianism tend to be rational and unemotional, they may be willing to lie to attain their personal goals, put little weight on loyalty and friendship, and enjoy manipulating others' behaviour. Individuals who score low on Machiavellianism are more emotional, are less willing to lie to succeed, value loyalty and friendship highly, and get little personal pleasure from manipulating others.

Self-esteem. The extent to which a person believes that he or she is worthwhile and deserving. A person with high self-esteem is more likely to seek higher status jobs, be more confident in his or her ability to achieve higher levels of performance, and derive greater intrinsic satisfaction from their accomplishments. A person with less self-esteem may be more content to remain in a lower-level job, be less confident of his or her ability, and focus more on extrinsic rewards.

Risk propensity. This is the degree to which an individual is willing to take chances and make risky decisions. A manager with a high risk propensity might experiment with new ideas and gamble on new products. She might also lead the organisation in new and different directions. The same manager might also jeopardise the continued well-being of the organisation if the risky decisions prove to be bad ones. A manager with low risk propensity might lead to a stagnant and conservative organisation, or help the organisation to weather turbulent and unpredictable times successfully by maintaining stability and calm. The potential consequences of risk propensity to an organisation are dependent on that organisation's environment.

DISCUSSION QUESTIONS 2.2

1 Consider the personality attributes of:
   (a) locus of control;
   (b) self-efficacy;
   (c) authoritarianism;
   (d) dogmatism;
   (e) Machiavellianism;
   (f) self-esteem;
   (g) risk-propensity.
      (i) How would you describe yourself on each attribute?
      (ii) Do you think you are difficult to manage?
      (iii) Choose the attributes of a person you would most like to work with or to be manager of. Are they different from your own?
2 Which attributes would make a person very difficult to manage in your view?
3 Which attributes would make a manager difficult to work for and why?

Type A and Type B personality

Type A and B theory is concerned with how people respond to stress. In 1959, two researchers, Friedman and Rosenman, observed that there seemed to be two distinctive ways that people went about working in high-pressure environments. They were particularly concerned with managers and executives in stressful occupations. One group of managers seemed to respond to their situations by acting very intensively. They were typically rushed and hasty, highly competitive, found it hard to delegate responsibility and tended to be extremely alert, even at times nervous. Friedman and Rosenman referred to this type of behaviour as Type A.

A second group of managers, however, went about their work in a very different way. They tended to be much more relaxed, and found it easier to delegate responsibility. Although they were just as concerned with getting the job done as Type A individuals were, they were less competitive, seeing setbacks as obstacles to be overcome rather than as challenges or races. If something couldn't be done on a particular working day, they accepted that it would have to be finished the day after. They didn't take their cares and stresses home with them. In all, they tended to live at much lower levels of stress than the other group did, although they were just as productive. Friedman and Rosenman described this group as Type B.

Friedman and Rosenman's research found that the Type A individuals in the group were almost twice as likely as the Type B people to develop stress-related diseases, in particular coronary heart disease, even after differences in other factors, like age and smoking, had been controlled.

Type A and B theory is not a complete theory of personality in itself: it is a partial theory, which can work together with other theories of personality in providing a picture of an individual.

Perception

Perception is the way in which people see things and interpret the behaviour of others. It is a person's viewpoint on a situation. The way in which a person understands situations depends upon his or her own values, needs, cultural backgrounds and circumstances of the moment. People may interpret the same situation differently, depending upon their experience of dealing with people and the situation itself. A difficult customer who complains to a sales assistant has a different perception of the situation than the sales assistant or other on-lookers. Because perception plays a role in a variety of workplace behaviours, managers need to have a general understanding of basic perceptual processes.

Selective perception

The process of screening out information with which we are uncomfortable or that contradicts our beliefs. For example, a manager may think highly of a particular worker. This means that the manager has a very positive attitude about the worker and thinks he is a top performer in his job. One day the manager notices a mistake on a task for which the worker is responsible. Selective perception may cause the manager to assume that someone else had completed that task on this occasion. Similarly, if the manager had formed a negative image of a particular worker, a mistake would be immediately attributed to that particular worker and would merely confirm the manager's opinion of him. If the worker did produce some excellent work, the manager would assume that he had received help from others, or would soon forget the high performance. Selective perception can be beneficial because it allows us to disregard minor bits of information which are not important or relevant. Although, if selective perception causes us to ignore important information, then it can become detrimental.

Stereotyping

The process of categorising or labelling people on the basis of a single attribute or characteristic. Common attributes from which people often stereotype are race and gender. Stereotypes along these lines are inaccurate and can be harmful. Other less obvious stereotypes are characteristics such as age, size, style of dress and regional accents. If a manager is prejudiced against older people or overweight people, he may be missing out on some valuable talent by not employing individuals with these attributes. People who are stereotyped in the minds of others may actually behave as anticipated by the prejudiced person because of the way they are treated. Research done with interviewers who were racially prejudiced showed that with black candidates, the interviewers smiled less, were curt and unsympathetic and paid less attention to the interviewees' answers than when the interviewees were white. This caused the black interviewees to perform less well than the white interviewees. Similarly a young woman who is the first female on a board of directors may feel that when she makes a presentation to the board, the other board members are paying more attention to her appearance than what she is saying. This may cause her performance to be of a lower standard than if she considered that the other board members were taking her seriously as an equal member of the board.

Attribution theory

This theory suggests that we observe behaviour and then attribute causes to it. That is, we attempt to explain why people behave as they do. The process of attribution is based on perceptions of reality and these perceptions may vary widely among individuals. We observe either our own, or other people's behaviour and evaluate that behaviour in terms of three categories: consensus, consistency or distinctiveness.

◆ *Consensus* is the extent to which other people in the same situation behave in the same way
◆ *Consistency* is the degree to which the same person behaves in the same way
◆ *Distinctiveness* is the extent to which the same person behaves in the same way in other situations.

As a result of various combinations of consensus, consistency, and distinctiveness, we form impressions or attributions as to the causes of behaviour. We may believe the behaviour is caused internally (by forces within the person) or externally (by forces in the person's environment).

For example, you observe that one of your subordinates has got the giggles and is disrupting the work of others. If you can understand the causes of his behaviour, you may be able to change it. If the employee is the only one engaging in the disruptive behaviour (low consensus), if he behaves like this several times a week (high consistency), and if you have seen him behave like this in other settings (low distinctiveness), a logical conclusion would be that internal factors are causing his behaviour.

However, you may observe a different pattern: everyone in the person's work group has got the giggles (high consensus), and although the particular individual often laughs uncontrollably at work (high consistency), you have never seen him behave this way in other settings (high distinctiveness). This pattern indicates that something in the situation is causing the behaviour, that is, that the causes of the behaviour are external.

It is important to distinguish between causes which apply to only one or two situations and those which could apply generally to several different settings. The cause of an employee suddenly failing to win an important contract when she normally performs well, will probably be due to some external factor which occurred on the day, rather than a sign that she is incompetent or is losing interest in her work.

Why female managers find it difficult to get into senior management positions

Although women are as qualified as their male counterparts, they are still not entering the ranks of senior management. While it seems easy for women to gain employment at the lower levels of management, it is still proving difficult for women to make it through to top managerial positions, and even fewer have made it to the executive suite. Women experience barriers and problems from the first day they enter an organisation. Some of these problems include the biased attitudes of both men and women. There are three main sources of problems which face women:

1 home versus workplace;
2 male attitudes to women;
3 women's attitudes to other women.

Home *vs* workplace

Some of the reasons for the shortage of women in management appear to centre around a conflict between the role of a woman as a homemaker – wife, mother and housekeeper – and as an employee external to the home environment. Women's extra domestic responsibilities have the potential to create role conflict and overload, and this can spill over to affect women's performance at work. When the demands of a female manager's job come into conflict with her domestic role demands, she may leave the organisation for a different, less stressful, employment situation. The turnover rates for female managers are higher than for male managers, that is, they leave organisations at higher rates than their male counterparts.

In addition, many women live in 'dual career marriages' in which both partners have professional commitments and have to deal with the issues associated with the management of two careers and family life. Although both men and women in dual career families deal with these responsibilities, the impact on their careers is generally much greater for a woman. Men will normally share in domestic tasks but leave the main organisation of the household to the woman.

Male attitudes to women

Many men still assume that organisations should be run by men and not by women. The sex-typing of management as a male occupation poses a major barrier to women who would otherwise qualify and excel in positions of leadership. Men may:

◆ overlook women for transfer and promotion

◆ direct them into 'female' job areas

◆ not offer them challenge and opportunity

◆ not give sufficient feedback to women on how well they are doing in the job, what they should improve upon and what direction they should take

◆ exclude them from important informal discussions.

Male prejudice and traditional attitudes in the workplace are therefore still overwhelming barriers to women gaining influence in senior management. In the traditional male culture of management, women are stereotyped as less competent than men, reinforcing beliefs that women are too soft, or not confident enough. Even women directors are likely to be treated not as a business partner or colleague, but as a woman. Men see the female director as being out of place, and because this becomes large in men's imaginations, they start to fantasise that women are taking over. If a female director speaks at a board meeting, her male colleagues are more likely to notice her dress, voice, body and manner, than what she actually says; men do not hear women because they are not listening.

Women are viewed primarily as sex objects, and secondly as servants. These stereotypes reinforce male prejudice that women lack ability and cause female managers to be seen as inadequate. Also, men continue to perceive women as the rearers of their children, so they find it understandable and appropriate that women should renounce their careers to raise families.

Women's attitudes towards women

Much of the resistance to female managers and professional advancement comes from other women. Women in most organisations have positive or negative attitudes towards other women, especially those in unusually senior positions. Women themselves are often in conflict as to how to react to a male-dominated organisation. For example, women may assist men in excluding women from responsible positions and the two types of women who do so can be classified as follows:

The Queen Bee. she has achieved a responsible position and will make sure that she is not challenged, by excluding other women who might be seen as a threat. She relishes her unique position as the only female among the male senior managers and will not risk having any other woman taking it away from her.

The Traditionalist. Their view is that serious work is a man's job. She is critical of women who are ambitious and will discourage women from taking responsibility. She may refuse to work for a woman, or if she does, will do so reluctantly.

Encouraging women into senior management positions in organisations

Supporting the career aspirations of women makes good business sense. Employers must be motivated to retain and promote women, not because it is the right thing to do, but because it is the only thing they can do to remain competitive. Already, many corporate executives recognise that to ignore the retention and advancement of women threatens their very survival. Top executives need to:

◆ have the will to act

◆ develop and communicate the cause of women's advancement throughout the organisation

◆ identify within the corporate culture the barriers to retaining and advancing women's careers

◆ implement corporate initiatives to eliminate the attitudinal, cultural and organisational biases

Through understanding and implementation, corporate leaders and male managers within the organisation must be prepared to act upon the fact that women's advancements up the corporate ladder is a business imperative. In a ferociously global economy, no organisation can afford to waste brain power simply because it wears a skirt.

Reference: Langrish *et al.*, (1984) *A development programme for women in management*, Gower.

('Why female managers find it difficult to get into management positions' written by Elizabeth Brooke, BA (Hons) Business Administration student, Department of Business and Management Studies, Crewe + Alsager Faculty, Manchester Metropolitan University)

 ## Attitudes to work

Attitudes are beliefs and feelings people have about specific ideas, situations, or other people. They shape the way people respond to events and other people. Two people may have totally different attitudes towards the prospect of making a sales presentation to new customers. One may have a positive attitude and be full of enthusiasm and excitement, the other may have a negative attitude and be terrified at the thought of doing the presentation. These attitudes determine their feelings, thoughts and behaviour. There are three parts to an attitude:

1 feelings or emotions;

2 thought or knowledge; and

3 behaviour (how the attitude affects what the person does).

Attitudes determine the way we feel about things, the way we behave and our beliefs about people and objects. Attitudes are not visible, it is the way people behave which gives clues as to the attitudes they hold. A person who works very hard obviously believes that it is a good thing to do. They may think it will get them promotion or praise, or they may have been brought up to believe that you should put maximum effort into everything you do.

Attitudes provide people with a basis for expressing their values. A manager who believes strongly in everyone working hard may consider subordinates lazy if they go home at the appointed time instead of working voluntary overtime every evening.

An understanding of attitudes is important as attitudes help people to adapt to their working environment. When people are treated well by their supervisor, they are likely to develop a positive attitude towards management and the organisation. They will be more comfortable working for that organisation if they feel appreciated and important. People's attitudes to work are interlinked with their motivation to work. If they are well motivated they will be loyal to the organisation and work hard. They will need less supervision and be less like to come into conflict with management. Attitudes are affected by factors such as the nature of the work, individual needs, the culture (the way things are done and the structure of the organisation) and how the company is organised.

Measuring attitudes

It is useful for employers to know how their workforce feel about various aspects of their work, their department and the organisation's policies. There are a number of techniques which could be used to measure attitudes, the two most common being direct observation and self-reporting techniques.

Direct observation involves observing others and assessing their attitudes on the basis of their communication style (both verbal and non-verbal) and their behaviour. This is an example of an informal approach which is unsystematic and based on an understanding of social cues. Conclusions reached by this method may be wrong: the employee who comes to work dressed rather shabbily may appear to be less conscientious than her well-dressed colleague. It may be that she is spending all her money on mortgage repayments and her colleague is still living at home with her parents and can afford to spend more money on clothes.

Self-reporting techniques are attempts by organisations to measure systematically employees' attitudes through the use of attitude questionnaires. Organisations which assess their employees' attitudes by using attitude questionnaires (self-reporting techniques) are attempting to gauge systematically and measure these assumptions. Attitude questionnaires are time-consuming and expensive to design and administer. Companies often employ external research consultants to administer the questionnaires. Attitude questionnaires are used by many companies so that the managers can be in touch with employees' views and feelings.

The Staff Opinion Survey used by Genus, a company which now specialises in cattle breeding but which was formerly part of the Milk Marketing Board, includes questions on Management Style, Communications, Job Satisfaction, Customer Perception, Genus as a Whole, 'About Yourself', and an open section for comments. Examples of questions from two of the sections of Genus' Staff Opinion Survey follows:

SECTION ONE: MANAGEMENT STYLE

TICK ONE BOX ONLY FOR EACH QUESTION

	Agree strongly	Agree	Unsure	Disagree	Disagree strongly
1 My department/unit's objectives are clear to me	☐	☐	☐	☐	☐
2 I have an up to date job description	☐	☐	☐	☐	☐
3 I believe the annual performance review system is an effective, objective way of measuring my performance in the job	☐	☐	☐	☐	☐
4 I have clear and appropriate personal objectives	☐	☐	☐	☐	☐
5 My supervisor/manager has reviewed the objectives set at the annual performance review at least once since they were set	☐	☐	☐	☐	☐
6 My supervisor/manager asks my opinion and listens to my views	☐	☐	☐	☐	☐
7 The people I work with are encouraged to co-operate to get the job done	☐	☐	☐	☐	☐
8 I have been encouraged to attend regular team meetings/briefings in the last year	☐	☐	☐	☐	☐
9 I am allowed to make most decisions and only key things need to be checked with my manager	☐	☐	☐	☐	☐
10 My manager really appreciates all the efforts I make	☐	☐	☐	☐	☐
11 Overall my manager is doing a good job	☐	☐	☐	☐	☐

Fig 2.5 Example of questions from the 'Management Style' section of the Genus' Staff Opinion Survey
With thanks to Philip Eades, Quality Department, Genus Ltd

SECTION FOUR: CUSTOMER PERCEPTION

WHILST WE WILL SHORTLY BE CONDUCTING CUSTOMER SURVEYS DIRECTLY IT WOULD BE A GREAT HELP TO LEARN YOUR OPINIONS OF WHAT YOU BELIEVE YOUR CUSTOMERS FEEL ABOUT GENUS.

PLEASE TRY TO ANSWER THESE QUESTIONS FROM THEIR POINT OF VIEW.

TICK ONE BOX ONLY FOR EACH QUESTION

		Agree strongly	Agree	Unsure/ Not applicable	Disagree	Disagree strongly
28	Customers are now much happier with the presentation of Genus invoices	☐	☐	☐	☐	☐
29	Customers are now much happier with the presentation of Genus statements	☐	☐	☐	☐	☐
30	Customers remain dissatisfied with the accuracy of Genus invoices	☐	☐	☐	☐	☐
31	Customers are satisfied with the quality of service provided by Genus	☐	☐	☐	☐	☐
32	Customers welcome Genus' move into new products and services	☐	☐	☐	☐	☐
33	Customers want Genus to be a successful company	☐	☐	☐	☐	☐
34	Overall, customers think that Genus' products and services are too expensive compared to our competitors	☐	☐	☐	☐	☐
35	Customers are interested in whether their shares increase in value	☐	☐	☐	☐	☐
36	Customers think Genus should concentrate on reducing costs and focus on its traditional products	☐	☐	☐	☐	☐
37	As competition for business gets tougher, I think my customers will stay loyal to Genus provided we deliver quality and value	☐	☐	☐	☐	☐
38	Customers feel the structure of Genus makes it a difficult company to deal with	☐	☐	☐	☐	☐

Fig 2.6 Example of questions from the 'Customer Perception' section of the Genus' Staff Opinion Survey
With thanks to Philip Eades, Quality Department, Genus Ltd

Attitudes and organisational culture

All managers, regardless of status, contribute to the maintenance of the organisation's culture. Managers play a key role in personifying the culture. Attitudes are not just individually formed but arise out of interaction with others. They become taken for granted, regarded as obvious and mere common sense and are often overlooked. They have become part of the organisational culture without employees noticing. New employees and people external to the organisation such as suppliers and customers will notice that everyone in the organisation believes that things should be done in certain ways, and that they all hold the same attitudes.

McGregor's Theory X and Theory Y

Douglas McGregor's theory of managerial attitudes emphasised that the way managers feel about human nature will affect the way they treat their employees and consequently this treatment will have an effect on the way those employees behave in future. McGregor believed that if we are treated by our manager as if we are hard working and well motivated individuals, our way of behaving and attitudes will be affected by this. We will be motivated to work hard for our manager and have positive feelings about work. Similarly, if we are threatened by our manager and treated as if we are lazy, we will begin to adopt negative attitudes towards work and behave in ways which prove the manager's attitude towards us to be true.

McGregor's theory categorised managers' attitudes into two extremes:

1 Theory X managers believe that people do not want to work.
2 Theory Y managers believe that people do enjoy work.

Theory X assumptions

1 Average human beings have an inherent dislike of work and will avoid it if they can;
2 because of this human characteristic, most people must be coerced, controlled, directed and threatened with punishment if they are to put in adequate effort towards the achievement of organisational objectives;
3 average human beings prefer to be directed, wish to avoid responsibility, have relatively little ambition, and want security above all.

Theory Y assumptions

1 The expenditure of physical effort and mental effort in work is as natural as play or rest;
2 external control and the threat of punishment are not the only means for bringing about effort toward organisational objectives. People will exercise self-direction and self-control in the service of objectives to which they are committed;

3 average human beings learn, under proper conditions, not only to accept but also to seek responsibility;

4 the capacity to exercise a relatively high degree of imagination, ingenuity, and creativity in the solution of organisational problems is widely, not narrowly, distributed in the population;

5 under the conditions of modern industrial life, the intellectual potential of the average human being is only partially utilised.

According to Douglas McGregor's theory, Theory X managers are likely to treat workers as just 'paid hands', while Theory Y managers are likely to treat workers as people capable of contributing a lot to the organisation. They will encourage workers to participate in the achievement of organisational objectives. The attitudes held by managers about human nature will often pervade the whole organisation so that there will be a Theory X or a Theory Y culture in which all communications, payment systems and the way everything is done is built upon a belief that either people are lazy and need to be threatened, or that people are conscientious and willing to work. It is quite natural for people to adopt their manager's attitudes. If they are shouted at and threatened, it will be difficult for some of this not to rub off on them when they deal with colleagues or subordinates. Some individuals can never fit into the dominant culture of their organisation and always feel uncomfortable with the way things are done and the attitudes other people hold with whom they work. These individuals would be happier working in a different organisation where the attitudes of the employees match theirs more closely than in their present organisation.

QUIZ 2.2 Are you a Theory X or Theory Y manager?

Tick *agree* or *disagree* to answer the following statements.

Statement	Agree	Disagree
1 People are capable of contributing a lot more to their jobs than they do. Their brain power and ideas are not utilised.	☐	☐
2 People are capable of contributing a lot more to their jobs than they do. They do the minimum they can get away with.	☐	☐
3 Most people enjoy having responsibility in their jobs.	☐	☐
4 Most people want to be involved with creative problem solving in their jobs.	☐	☐
5 Most people want to be told exactly what to do and not have to use their initiative.	☐	☐
6 It should be made easier for employers to sack people who are not pulling their weight.	☐	☐
7 People like to work because it gives them the chance of fulfilment and job satisfaction.	☐	☐
8 People like the status and opportunities work gives them.	☐	☐
9 If people at work were not constantly watched, they wouldn't do any work at all.	☐	☐

Statement		Agree	Disagree
10	The majority of people have only got the brain power to do menial jobs.	☐	☐
11	Most people would resign from their jobs immediately if they had enough money to live on.	☐	☐
12	Everyone hates the thought of having to go to work when they wake up in the morning.	☐	☐

Score your answers as follows:

Statement	Agree	Disagree
1	10	5
2	5	10
3	10	5
4	10	5
5	5	10
6	5	10
7	10	5
8	5	10
9	10	5
10	5	10
11	5	10
12	5	10

90 or more?

You are a *Theory Y* manager. You believe that people do want to go to work and do a good job. With your attitude to your subordinates you should be able to get the maximum contribution from them in terms of work, as you will encourage them to solve problems and contribute their ideas to getting the job done.

Less than 90?

You are a *Theory X* manager. You believe that people are lazy and need to be threatened to make them do any work. With these assumptions you will get the minimum out of your workforce.

DISCUSSION QUESTIONS 2.3

1 Assuming there are such people as Theory X and Theory Y managers, which is it easier to be, a Theory X or Theory Y manager?

2 Do you think the following statements are always correct?

> *The Theory X manager is never wrong. If the work is going badly, it must be the workers' fault because they are lazy. If the work is going well, then it is because the workers are so good.*

> *The Theory Y manager is always wrong. If the work is going badly, it must be the manager's fault because he or she has good workers who do their job well. If the work is going well, it is down to those good workers.*

3 How could you tell whether a manager held Theory X or Theory Y assumptions?

4 What sort of wording would a Theory X manager use in communications such as memos and notices to their staff?

5 Is it possible to be a manager with Theory Y assumptions in an organisation full of managers with Theory X assumptions about human nature?

Fig 2.7

Royal Mail

Arthur Stringer is the Automation Systems Manager at Royal Mail, Crewe.

'My job is to ensure that standards of automation performance and maintenance are sustained and improved in a cost effective manner. Currently we're working on enhancing the production we get from the culler/facer/canceller machine. This culls the mail, which means it separates the manual from the machinable mail. It looks for size, the mail comes in all shapes and sizes and we can machine-sort mail up to C5 size. The actual performance of the automated machinery very much depends upon the way people use it. The present scheme to improve productivity in all of Royal Mail's Automated Processing Centres is called total productive maintenance (TPM).

Some of the operators were not unduly concerned about how effectively the equipment was working. All they were interested in was tipping the mail in at one end of the culler/facer/canceller and it came out the other. They just minded the machine, they weren't too concerned how effectively the machine was working, they saw that as an engineering problem. It wasn't their job – there were some people who felt the work was boring and saw breakdowns as beneficial. The culture we're trying to instill is that if the machine is working properly, their job is easier. If it isn't jamming, they haven't got to keep clearing blockages. All the faults were passed to the supervisor who radioed the engineers for assistance.

We have a lot of minor production problems, we don't have many major breakdowns that cause mail failures. There are lots of small stoppages and jams, we're not processing identical products, mail is all different shapes and sizes, it's not an easy thing to handle. If you're canning cola or bottling milk, it's all the same. The first stage of TPM was to involve the engineers more within the processing team. We're trying to integrate the team and get the operators to drive the machines better. If you know a little about how a car works, you'll look after it better, you won't ride the clutch and you'll be careful not to damage it. So what we're trying to do with TPM is to make the people into better machine operators. As part of that they will learn how the machine works and we're using the engineers to deliver that training to them. They are telling the operators the basics of how the machine works. On this particular machine – the culler/facer/canceller – we're using five engineering technicians to train 40 operators. On site there are 11 engineers, but they're on a rotating shift so that there are around three on a shift. The operators learn to drive the machine better, having completed the training. As part of the basic training, there's a practical application phase: showing the operating team how the machine works gradually over a three month period.

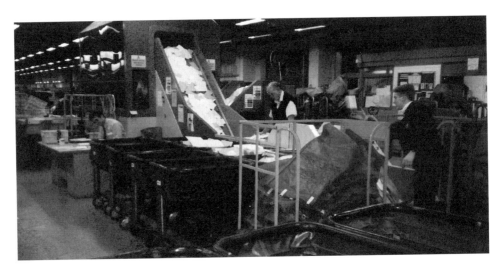

Fig 2.8 Culler/facer/canceller machine, Royal Mail

We won't be giving the operators hand tools, but they will be able to clear minor blockages, clean photo beams, and other minor cleaning tasks and replace simple belts. There are some complicated belt runs that have many twists in them and you need tools to change them. The engineers don't actually lose work as a result of the operators being able to carry out the minor maintenance work. We're giving the engineers more higher grade work to do. Maintenance is made up of three different elements: predictive, preventative and corrective. We're expecting that the engineers will be able to do more predictive maintenance when they are freed from their current tasks by the operators taking on their basic preventative and corrective maintenance work.

Royal Mail is continually looking at all the processes as to how we do things and then we're re-engineering them where necessary. It's continuous improvement of the automation system. We were not always getting to the root cause of the problems, everyone was blaming one another. We needed to pull the engineers and operators together. Ideally, accidents, breakdowns and rejects should be reduced to zero. These are the ultimate aims of TPM. We needed to get them working as a team to move towards achieving our TPM goals and to improve the performance of the equipment.

We are putting the machine operators through an eight-module foundation training course. It's 16 hours of training to tell them what TPM is all about. The modules include

CASE STUDY cont

how to operate equipment in a safe and effective manner, understanding the importance of safety procedures, measuring equipment losses leading to continuous improvement, identifying equipment losses, keeping the immediate environment clean and tidy, equipment refurbishment, the purpose of specific equipment components and the reason why maintenance is essential.

It's getting them to see that there are better ways of doing things than they've been used to in the past. They are not operating as an effective team. We're working at integrating the engineers into the operational team. We're trying to get rid of all the inefficiencies and you can't do it without working together.

The training helps them in teambuilding, we're using the engineers to train and coach the operators. Often, the operators say to the engineers "I've got a problem" and then there's no further discussion. At the end of the day what we're proving to the engineers is that the people who know most about the machines' health are the operators. They are there all shift, they notice if things are starting to go wrong, if there's a change in noise, vibration; any tell-tale sign which gives an early indication of breakdowns. Managers, engineers and some trained operators deliver this training programme to the machine operating team.

We then start to show the operators around the machine components. They get involved in doing an equipment appraisal. Which is to improve the understanding of the equipment and look at ways of improving it, the engineers and operators will go and look at a part of a machine in small groups. The engineer will explain to them what that area of the machine does, how it works. They will score each component of the machine and decide whether there are any areas which need renewal work. They are looking at the equipment in its current condition with a view to bringing it up to its original as new condition. Whether we can put it right very much depends upon cost. That's where I come into it, because there are certain areas of the machine that are not crucial to have in perfect order and it would cost a lot of money to bring them back up to their original condition.

Having done the equipment appraisal during the three month period, the whole team of operators will know the basics of the machine. Also, the engineers and operators will know one another much better. We then move on to advanced training which involves a further training course and the operators undertake minor engineering tasks such as changing belts. By the end of the advanced course, they have to demonstrate their competence to carry out these tasks. Having proved their competence, we get to a position in which we can formally hand over the work currently being done by the engineers onto the operators. The engineers are losing the work they used to do and they are naturally worried about their jobs. The work hours given to the operators are shown on a balance sheet and additional work is found for the engineers in predictive maintenance techniques. Final handover of engineering work to the operators only takes place when the engineering work hours transferred to the operators is equal to the new hours in the engineers' workload.

The operators' jobs are not very interesting at present, because of this initiative the jobs will become more interesting and a lot of them appreciate this. Hopefully from that we'll get the benefits of better performance, because if the job is more interesting they'll be more motivated. There will be commitment from them to achieve better machine performance.

The engineers also benefit in that they will be doing more interesting diagnostic-type work rather than routine repairs. I find that the operators would rather clean their own machines, it improves ownership in the same way as they would clean their car at home, the machine belongs to them for the time they are working with it. The culler/facer/canceller has got five different work stations on it, there are five people all working their own areas, all knowing how different parts of the machine work, and they can all help one another. If we achieve less breakdowns, the machines are performing better and productivity will improve. When we get losses we have to double-handle the mail, and this results in wasted time and effort. Now that the operators are better trained, there's less likelihood that mail will be delayed during the sorting process.'

TPM is not only applicable to operation and maintenance activities. The best practice is to include TPM at the design stage in partnership with the machine manufacturers. In the latest generation of automation equipment, Royal Mail operators, maintenance technicians, and managers have had a practical input into the design. Joint continual discussion workshops focus on improving accessibility, maintainability and availability. The introduction of TPM into equipment design provides a secure foundation for continuous improvements throughout the machine's life-cycle.

DISCUSSION QUESTIONS 2.4

1 What were the attitudes of the operators towards machine breakdowns at Royal Mail prior to the introduction of TPM?

2 How does the TPM training affect the attitudes of the operators?

3 What are the benefits of the operators taking on some of the engineers' tasks, to the operators themselves, to the engineers, and to Royal Mail?

Internal and external factors affecting behaviour

Factors affecting an individual's behaviour can come from:

1 *Internal sources.* Aspects of attitudes, personality, perception and motivation which come from within a person.

2 *External sources.* Factors in an individual's environment or situation.

Internal sources

A worker may be highly productive simply because he enjoys working hard or is satisfied by the feeling of having done a good job. A student may read a book for the sheer love of reading or a desire to have something explained, regardless of coursework assignments to be completed. Intrinsic motivation is concerned with the pleasure or value associated with the activity itself. Behaviour is intrinsically motivated when actions are valued for their own sake, and are carried out without any external inducement. Internal factors affecting behaviour are often more powerful than external, as people who are self-motivated can be more productive than those who need external inducements to persuade them to work.

In addition to the value an individual may get from the physical or mental activities involved in a task, he or she may also gain satisfaction from knowing that his or her efforts have led to a completed product or accomplishment. This fulfils the need for achievement. The greatest satisfaction in accomplishment is derived by people with a high need for achievement who are successful in performing a difficult task. The intrinsic rewards of task accomplishment can be improved by increasing the responsibility of workers or the importance of the tasks they perform.

Ways of increasing intrinsic motivation

Task variety. A greater assortment of tasks can be performed by the individual on a single job or, if this is impossible, he can be rotated periodically from job to job.

Task uncertainty. Very mechanistic tasks do not provide satisfaction for most individuals. A task that involves the processing of information or a limited amount of problem solving may be of greater intrinsic interest than a totally predictable task.

Social interaction inherent to the job. When social interaction is part of the job, most individuals derive greater intrinsic motivation and satisfaction from carrying out their work. Teamwork increases interest in the job and previously isolated workers may derive satisfaction from interacting with colleagues or customers.

Task identity. Many jobs are so specialised that the worker cannot see the relationship between his small task and the final finished product. In order to increase task identity, jobs can often be redesigned. Individuals can produce a larger part of the final product or a small team of workers can be formed to complete an entire assembly process.

Task significance. Individuals often feel that their efforts go unnoticed, or that their job is less important than the work of others. Intrinsic motivation can be improved by increasing the perceived significance of a person's work output. This can be done by changing the individual to a more important job or by increasing the importance of his present output. This could be done by emphasising the usefulness of the person's work or by placing the person in direct contact with the customers who will be using his product.

Responsibility for results. If an individual does not feel responsible for his work output, it is doubtful that he will place a high value on task accomplishment. Only when the person can experience success or failure on a task is he likely to value the rewards of task accomplishment. To increase intrinsic motivation, a person might be given a larger amount of discretion over how they carry out their task, and held more accountable for results.

Barriers to task accomplishment. Sometimes there are barriers which prevent well motivated individuals from doing well in their jobs. Lack of training, ability, insufficient materials or tools, and lack of encouragement and support from the supervisor may all contribute to an individual failing to complete a task competently. Restructuring a job to remove external barriers to accomplishment and providing training and supportive supervision may increase an individual's intrinsic motivation.

Knowledge of results. If an individual does not know anything about the effect of his performance at work, it will be difficult for him to derive satisfaction from accomplishing the job. It is important for supervisors or managers to inform workers exactly how they are doing. This feedback should be on a continuous basis so that the individual can quickly change his behaviour. Ideally, a feedback system should be built into the work itself.

Advantages of using internal factors to affect motivation

Increasing intrinsic motivation has several advantages as a motivational strategy. First, when individuals get satisfaction from completing a task, there may be a reduced need for extrinsic rewards to motivate behaviour. This may be important in situations where managers have a limited supply of extrinsic rewards or where individuals do not value the rewards provided. Second, the need to supervise and monitor an individual's work performance is reduced. Third, intrinsic motivation costs the organisation very little and can often be sufficiently powerful for individuals to work unpaid overtime or continue in less well-paid jobs for much longer periods of time than they would have done if they had not found the work to be so satisfying.

External sources

Motivation is external or extrinsic when an individual performs an act for a goal outside of the activity itself. Working for rewards such as pay, fringe benefits, promotion, and public acknowledgement is an everyday feature of organisational life. Rewards are tailored by organisations to retain the loyalty of existing employees and to attract new employees to the firm. Organisations are not legally obliged to provide benefits other than pay, but most provide a benefits package which reflects the image they wish to portray to the outside world.

Cafeteria-style benefits

One of the more cost-effective ways of providing benefits for employees is to allow them to choose between a range of benefits, so that they compile their own benefit package. This allows each employee to obtain the benefits most useful to themselves. An individual who does not value private medical insurance will therefore avoid choosing this option and elect to take more holiday or more pay, as they wish. Each employee has a package of a given financial limit and they can choose their benefits within this. The name 'cafeteria-style' benefits comes from the idea of choosing from a menu of possible rewards.

Linking rewards to performance

The most effective way to increase extrinsic motivation is to link rewards to performance. There are many ways of designing a contingent reward system. When the task is easily defined and measurable, it is feasible to create a piece-rate incentive system. The level of extrinsic rewards is based upon the quantity and/or quality of performance. Often, however, the task is neither clearly defined nor easily measured. In these cases, a judgement of the individual's performance is required by a supervisor or the manager who is responsible for allocating rewards. Any error in evaluation or sudden change in the criteria of performance will reduce the individual's perception that working hard leads to rewards. The perceived objectivity or fairness of the appraisal system can be as important in determining the individual's motivation as the actual link between rewards and performance.

CASE STUDY 2.3

Employee benefits at Stakis Hotels

Stakis plc is a hotel, casino and leisure group consisting of 45 hotels, 24 casinos and in excess of 25 leisure clubs situated throughout the country. The benefits they offer to employees include:

Service awards

In recognition of service with the company, awards are given to both full-time and part-time staff with the following periods of service.

3 years service	A presentation pin plus a champagne dinner for two at any Stakis hotel.
5 years service	A presentation pin and gift plus an invitation to spend a complimentary weekend for two, at one of the Stakis hotels.
10, 15 and 20 years service	A presentation pin plus a presentation gift.
25 years service	Travel vouchers to the value of £1000

Discount Club

All members of staff are eligible to join the Staff Discount Club. Membership of the Club entitles the member to a range of discounts within Stakis Hotels and Restaurants.

Employee share scheme

Permanent employees who have at least three years continuous service are provided with the opportunity of becoming shareholders at no cost to themselves.

Pension schemes

Non-contributory

Permanent employees over the age of 21 and under 60 years of age, are eligible to join the Stakis Pension Scheme after one year's service. They do not contribute to the scheme and the company makes the contributions on their behalf. Linked to this scheme is a disability insurance plan and life assurance of twice annual wage or salary.

Contributory

Salaried employees aged at least 21 and under 60 years of age, with one year's service, will be eligible to join the Stakis plc Retirement Benefit Scheme. This is a contributory scheme and both the employee and the company pay contributions towards it. The employee contribution is five per cent of their annual salary. It is contracted out of the government scheme and therefore the employee pays lower national insurance contributions. This scheme carries with it disability benefits and life assurance of three times the employee's annual salary.

Death benefit

If an employee dies in service, their dependents will be paid a cash sum equal to one year's basic wage or salary. To be eligible, you must be a permanent employee and have completed one year's continuous service, and not be a member of either of the Stakis Retirement or Benefit Schemes.

Retirement Club

The Stakis Retirement Club organises regular outings, lunches and other functions for retired employees. They also receive special newsletters and are entitled to discounts within Stakis Hotels Ltd.

Suggestion scheme

All suggestions are acknowledged and considered once a month. Rewards are given for all suggestions used and there is the opportunity to win a Mini car.

Healthcare

All permanent employees having achieved ten years service are offered membership.

Live-in staff

Accommodation is provided for certain staff.

(With thanks to Alan Craig, Personnel Manager, Stakis Hotels, Glasgow, for permission to use the above information.)

DISCUSSION QUESTIONS 2.5

1 Do the employee benefits at Stakis Hotels encourage intrinsic motivation?

2 Do the employee benefits act as a good extrinsic motivation, encouraging people to work harder?

3 How could intrinsic motivation be increased for:

(a) shopfloor factory workers;

(b) a checkout operator in a supermarket.

4 What external factors have affected the work of the operators in the Royal Mail case study?

5 What external factors make the work difficult in the case study about Julie Brewer of United Way?

6 How does the Genus Opinion Survey help management to motivate their workforce?

CASE STUDY 2.4

Bisto Foods, Middlewich

Bisto Foods in Middlewich, Cheshire employ 350 people and make gravy and dried sauces as well as packing salt. Bisto Foods are part of Rank Hovis McDougal which is owned by the Tomkins Group, a British based industrial conglomerate. The majority of shopfloor jobs at Bisto Foods are semi-skilled or unskilled and the workforce are generally long-serving with many individuals having worked for the company for more than 25 years. The plant is fairly automated and the capacity of the machines, along with consumer demand, dictate the shift systems. There are several different types of shift systems operating in different departments. The company have a 'flexible year' during which working hours average 37 and a half. During the busy time of late summer to mid-winter, longer hours are worked and employees work a four-day week in quieter periods.

Rewards

Personnel Manager, Ken Barrett:

'Our levels of pay are relatively high for the food industry in the local area.'

Bisto Foods have no difficulty in attracting shopfloor labour when they require new employees, the only difficult area recently has been Packaging Engineers. Recruiting managerial, technical, finance and support staff, the situation is somewhat difficult, particularly in the sales and marketing areas.

Fig 2.9 Ken Barrett, Personnel Manager and Stuart Walton, Distribution Manager, Bisto Foods

CASE
STUDY
cont

Other rewards include 25 days holiday, plus bank holidays. A choice of three different pension schemes, sick pay and a share option scheme are available. The share option scheme entails employees saving with the company to purchase shares over a five or seven year period. If the shares are lower in value at the end of the time period, the scheme reverts to a savings scheme with interest so that employees cannot lose money.

Approaches to motivating people at work and improving performance

Money is not used as a motivator at Bisto Foods. There are two main grades of pay for shopfloor staff and piece rate systems are not used. Ken Barrett comments:

'There's no magic solution to getting good performance out of people. Having only two main rates of pay for the shopfloor makes it relatively easy for people to move from one job to another.

The overwhelming majority of people come to work to do a good day's work. If we're going to make business improvements, we've got to stop paying simply for hands and legs and realise that brains come free.'

Although around half the shopfloor employees have attended a team building course, the company have not formally implemented a teamworking system Ken Barrett says:

'We haven't called it anything; what we're doing is encouraging the culture that working together and encouraging ideas is beneficial to the company. We've got a very stable workforce who've seen a lot of ideas and senior managers come and go. Senior managers develop through the business, they go to different sites or pastures new. The workforce get used to new managers attempting to introduce new working methods. We need to take a long term view and look over a three to five year period.'

Bisto Foods has worked on improving quality over many years. Ken Barrett:

'The difficulty is not that it hasn't been followed through, but the name has changed. I can remember a discussion we had with an outspoken shopfloor worker who said, "What's happened to all this TQM? We had £160 worth of waste yesterday, that was more than the whole of last week put together." I pointed out that previous to the quality programme being implemented they never had such information, the very fact that she was quoting figures at me shows how much people have learnt and are using the quality principles.'

Ken feels that the quality approach to good performance has no end, as there is always something else to be done. He says:

'It has to be seen as a continual improvement, good performance today simply becomes the norm tomorrow.'

Stuart Walton, Distribution Manager: *'Instead of briefing down to people, we're saying "how can you contribute?" If you can get people on board with that, other things fit in.'*

Ken Barrett feels that the continued success of the business has been a barrier to change.

'If you're making a loss, drastic changes are easy. Change is seen as a risk when you are profitable. It's not change that kills businesses, it's lack of change. Competitors are

constantly investing in new processes and people. One thing people crave once they've achieved a felt-fair wage level is a degree of security and stability, and change is perceived to threaten that. If we stay exactly the same as we are people think things will go away. But we'll be passed by and the company will die.'

Stuart Walton, Distribution Manager: *'Resistance to change can affect the stability of the company, people start to move away from reality when they are convinced that everything can remain the same. Shopfloor people have got into the habit of being told what to do. We're just trying to get people to make the decision that they would have made if they'd had all the information they needed.'*

Ken Barrett: *'We need to get away from the situation whereby when shopfloor staff are asked by a manager for their opinion, they are shocked and say that they aren't paid to make the decisions. Many departments have got 700 or 800 years of experience amongst their workers, they don't need a manager with a lot of technical expertise – they need a manager with the ability to lead and motivate them. I think we've made a lot of progress, there's an acknowledgement that change has to happen and we don't have confrontational industrial relations. We're all working together to a much greater extent. It's a cultural issue of getting people used to being asked to contribute and managers used to asking for contributions.'*

Stuart Walton: *'In the past people looked around for someone to tell them what to do, but if I say "what do you think you should do?" They can give an answer and I say "well go away and do it", they then get used to coming to see you on a more constructive basis and are saying things like "I've done it this way, is that okay?"'*

Ken Barrett: *'It's getting away from the culture of people doing the job of the person who reports to them. That means a whole layer of people not contributing to their fullest extent.'*

Ken Barrett believes that any workforce possesses enormous talents and that taking a look at their leisure activities reveals 'active, switched on, highly motivated people – apart from the time they come to work for their employers'.

Stuart Walton:

'People assume that their working life is separate from their leisure time, but whether you are organising the local football team or coming to work, you need to come to everything with the same attitude.'

Ken Barrett: *'The principles that we're following are all about recognising people as an asset rather than an expense. For example, the work that the company is undertaking regarding the Investors in People programme is relating training directly to the business plan: as people's performance improves the company's performance also improves along the lines of the business plan.'*

NVQ qualifications for warehousemen

Stuart Walton has been Distribution Manager in the warehouse for five years:

'We carried out training assessments as part of our Investors in People programme. The scope for training in the department was very limited because everyone is fully trained to

carry out all activities. I went to a seminar on NVQs and took it from there. South and East Cheshire TEC gave us a talk here in the warehouse and I've had 70 per cent take-up of the qualification from the operatives. They are now two thirds of the way through NVQ Level 2 and it's getting more difficult. There was an initial flush as the Assessor confirmed that operationally they were already competent and the men all thought NVQs were great. Now they're finding that there's more to it. They're having to tell somebody else why we've got the procedures we have – which fire extinguisher to use for example. They need a greater understanding of why we have these things. Most things they can explain to the Assessor but they sometimes don't know how to follow through the procedure they are explaining. It's the difference between the tasks- and people-oriented approach. When the task is done there's no reflection as to why. NVQ encourages people orientation because of this reflection. If they don't understand why something happens, they are not demonstrating competence.'

Ken Barrett:

'I didn't want to make a big song and dance about NVQs; I wanted a line manager who was keen to try it and was dedicated to the principles of developing people. We are running it for six months and then we'll do a presentation at a management forum and ask who else wants to have a go at it. They can learn from our mistakes and successes. If you develop people, they'll develop their jobs themselves.'

DISCUSSION QUESTIONS 2.6

1 How does Ken Barrett approach the implementation of new management techniques such as teamworking?

2 Why did Ken and Stuart introduce NVQ qualifications in the warehouse without making it public throughout the company?

3 What rewards are offered to employees and do you consider that they would motivate the workforce to work harder?

4 How do Ken and Stuart attempt to improve individuals' performance at work?

Teams

3

From reading this chapter you will learn about teams, including:

1 the definition of a group;
2 group dynamics;
3 the significance of group size;
4 group behaviour;
5 decision making in teams;
6 team building;
7 stages in group development;
8 types of teams;
9 team roles;
10 internal influences on teams;
11 external influences on teams.

What is a group?

It is important to make a distinction between groups and a gathering of people. People queuing at a bus stop, for instance, have a common purpose to get on the next bus. But the bus queue does not act as a group – it does not have a structure or a set of rules.

People can be categorised together for statistical purposes. In market research, people can be classified as having the same characteristics and be grouped together in a social group. The National Readership Survey grouped people together according to social class, income and lifestyle. Lower middle class (C1) grouping includes people who work at supervisory, clerical and junior managerial positions.

Groups are distinct from associations of people because they have the following features:

◆ a clear membership
◆ people consider themselves to be members of the group
◆ the members have a shared purpose
◆ there is a hierarchical structure

◆ the members will interact with each other

◆ members of the group can change but the group will continue to exist.

 # Group dynamics

The study of forces operating within a group of people who interact face to face with one another is called group dynamics. Although small groups have existed since the first human family, the idea of making a science of looking at these social interactions is a relatively recent one.

Belonging to a group

Being a member of a group seems to be good for people, as groups:

◆ satisfy membership needs; people are not comfortable when they feel 'left out'

◆ provide a wide range of activities

◆ can provide support for members in times of stress

◆ are good at identifying problems

◆ are good at being innovative and creative

◆ often make better decisions than individuals

◆ are good at carrying out their decisions and gaining the commitment of members

◆ control and discipline members

◆ fend off the negative effects of size in large organisations.

Group norms

In order to be accepted by a group, a new member must trade some of their identity in exchange for the benefits of membership. The new member should dress and behave in ways which are acceptable to the existing members. A group of students dressed casually in jeans and trainers will not readily accept a new student who is dressed in a pin stripe suit and bowler hat. Similarly, a group of conscientious students would not feel happy with a new member who wanted only to socialise and do as little work as possible. Adherence to the informal rules adopted by groups is necessary for new members to be accepted and for existing members to continue to be accepted. These informal rules are the group norms and they constitute the correct ways of behaving for members of the group. A group norm is a shared perception of how things should be done, or is a shared attitude, feeling or belief. These norms have a very powerful and consistent effect on people's behaviour.

At work there will be norms which spill over from society and there will be those norms created and established in the workplace. The norms from society may include behaviour related to politeness and tact when interacting with others. The norms created by the group and established in the workplace will be concerned with:

The task. This refers to how the task should be accomplished, the time spent on it, the standards of quality and the units completed. Individuals who produce more than the group norm are sometimes referred to as 'rate busters'. Those who produce less than the group norm are sometimes called 'chiselers'.

Non-task activities. This refers to those activities which are not task-related but occur in the workplace and are concerned with group standards such as the standard of dress to be worn in the workplace, the time taken for lunch breaks, what people do after they arrive at work and before they get down to the job.

Communication. These norms establish how members of the group communicate with each other and the rest of the workforce – the type of language, whether it is abusive, or it may be a language which includes words and phrases only understood by the group.

Attitude. This refers to the members' general feeling about the organisation, the work and their behaviour to others, especially management. Anyone who says anything to management which would cause a problem for another individual in the group is sometimes known as a 'squealer'.

Norms only apply to behaviour and not to the thoughts and feelings of individuals. They tend to develop in relation to those factors the group deem to be important, such as pride in their work and organisation, supervision, teamwork, planning and profitability. Norms tend to develop over time and are difficult to change. No one individual has any great impact on norms but a dominant individual may well influence them.

There are two types of norms:

Positive. These norms influence the group behaviour which helps the organisation to achieve its goals. This may be that the workers take a pride in their work and the resulting output is of high quality and little waste is made.

Negative. These norms work against the goals of the organisation. Examples of negative norms include stealing, restricting output or the condoning of theft from the organisation such as inflating travel expenses.

The problem facing the new member of the group is that he or she will not know which behaviours are considered to be correct or incorrect, because there is nothing in writing to refer to and the rules regarding informal behaviour are unspoken. As time passes the new recruit learns, understands and follows the group rules.

One of the major problems facing management is introducing changes to the organisation which affect the way in which groups work. Many groups do not follow the rule book, but people carry out their jobs following customs and practices laid down over the years. If change is introduced which does not recognise the informal operations of the group, management will find the changes are met with reluctance, hostility and resistance. Managers may be able to change the working practices of groups by a shared power strategy. This process is a normative re-education strategy and is based on empowerment and participation. Change is brought about by involving people in examining personal needs, values, group norms, and encouraging people to work together to plan change and give them the power to make decisions which affect the way they work. By this method management can influence the setting of group norms.

Formal and informal groups

Informal. A collection of individuals become a group when members become dependent on one another, influence one another's behaviour and contribute to the satisfaction of one another's needs. Informal groups are often friendship groups and tend to be smaller in size than formal groups. For example, the Accounts Department may be a formal group within the organisation but they will probably not all sit together in the canteen at lunchtime, there will be smaller informal groups from the department who socialise with one another.

Formal. Those groups in an organisation which have been consciously created to accomplish the organisation's goals. These formal groups perform functions such as getting work done, generating ideas and liaising with others. The formal group has a task assigned to it and it is officially held responsible for the satisfactory completion of the task.

The formal group will have a strong effect on the membership of informal groups. Friends who start work together in the same organisation may become distanced by their formal groups. They may be in separate buildings and in different departments and may not naturally come across one another in their daily work. They will start to form friendships with those they work closest to and will therefore join separate informal groups. They may have to make arrangements to see one another outside work in order to keep their friendship going.

The shaping of behaviour

Conformity

People who belong to groups have to conform or agree to the behaviour of the group. However, individuals can conform by outwardly agreeing with the group, while inwardly disagreeing. A new recruit may join an all male department where an aggressive masculine behaviour is expected by the group members. The new entrant may also display the same behaviour but not agree with it personally.

Internalisation is a process of conforming in which the individual adopts group norms as their own. A person who felt that it was not important to dress very smartly at work may join a group who all wear very neat and expensive clothes. The new person will have internalised this norm when they come to believe for themselves that smart clothes are genuinely important.

Socialisation

This is the process where a group will modify the behaviour of an individual who joins, and at the same time the new entrant will influence the group's behaviour. Socialisation is a continual process of adaptation by the individual to their physical, psychological and social environment through interaction with other people.

Conditioning

People are conditioned into behaving in a particular way by the response of others to their behaviour. Behaviour which is accepted will be praised; behaviour which is unacceptable will be punished. The way an individual behaves in a formal group will be influenced by the conditioning the individual receives from the informal group. A person may prefer the praise from colleagues in the informal group rather than from the manager, so that the praise given by the manager may not have the intended effect. That person cannot be easily manipulated, influenced or controlled by rewards from the formal leader. The offering of incentives by management to individuals to work harder, improve quality, or produce more may have little effect if the individual operates in a group which does not value incentives.

Imitation

People learn how to behave by observing and imitating behaviour. Training is a form of imitation, i.e. being shown what to do. When a new person joins an organisation, how are they going to be shown what to do? Will they be taught 'off' or 'on-the-job'? Off-the-job training means that the entrant will be instructed according to the regulations laid down by the company or the formal organisation. On-the-job training means that he or she will be allocated an instructor who is working on the production process and the new entrant is shown how to do the job as it is being done. This means that the new recruit is expected to follow the instructions of the worker while picking up the values of the informal group at the same time.

In a situation where the group is task-oriented, with members working together and sharing skills and experience, the newcomer will imitate the cooperative behaviour of the group members. Wanting to be like the others will be the motivator to work in a particular way.

Identification

Identification is the acceptance of another person's values and attitudes. People see others behaving in a particular way and will imitate their behaviour. They will want to be identified with that person. For example, the manager who always wears a dark suit, whose desk is always clear, whose door is always open, who has time to talk to his subordinates, and who does the job efficiently may well have the values a junior wishes to imitate.

The holiday job

Clive is a university student working at a distribution centre of a large firm during his summer holidays. He started his holiday job full of enthusiasm and works hard at the task of loading lorries which come to the loading bays at the centre. Clive is shocked by the attitude of the team of men with whom he has been assigned to work. They do as little as possible and treat him as if he is an idiot because he works hard. When he is working, they sit about and make perfectly audible jokes at his expense. They go for a drink together at the pub across the road from the centre every Friday after work, but they never invite Clive. Clive is angry and hurt by their attitude and puts it down to a general dislike of university students. One day, when he is alone with Tom, one of the older members of the group, he complains about the way he is treated. Tom is not very sympathetic. He just comments, 'If you'd been here as long as me son, you'd be exactly the same.'

DISCUSSION QUESTIONS 3.1

1 Why isn't Clive accepted by the group?

2 Why do they make fun of Clive while he is working?

3 If Clive returned to the firm as a manager upon graduating from university, what steps do you think he should take to improve the performance of the men he has been working with?

Group size

Group size is a major influence on a group's effectiveness. Too few members to perform the task is likely to put the group members in a stressful situation: too many and members will get in each other's way or will be underperforming, often due to communication problems.

The ideal size will depend upon the task the group has to perform. Even with large tasks, a large group trying to organise activities can be ineffective. A smaller number of people may feel more committed and able to contribute to the group than when everyone involved is present. This is why companies and organisations have Boards of Directors or Senior Management Teams.

As a group gets larger there is always the danger that subgroups may form which have their own agendas and could be at variance to the formal agenda. The larger the group the longer it takes to reach a decision. The decision reached is normally after much debate and can be a result of compromise to appease conflicting views from subgroups in the formal group.

The size of the group will change over time as reasons for the group's existence change. For example, a small team might be brought together to work on a new project. As the project develops, so the membership may increase to meet the extra demands and this increase in group size will change demands on the leaders, members and group processes. Management must be careful about who to add to the group so that the group does not become unbalanced.

When organisations face an economic downturn, the problem managers have to face is who to remove from the group. The aim is usually to reduce costs. The organisation may have a policy on redundancy such as 'last in–first out', or those who stay are those the company has invested heavily in through education and training. Those who do stay are likely to experience disruption, and may have to take on additional duties which they resent or lack training for.

The optimum size of the group will include members who have a variety of skills and experience. The size of the group will influence the behaviour of those who participate in the group's activities. To some, a large group may appear intimidating and they may not want to be involved with group activities outside their own task. In meetings, they might not want to be involved in discussion. Others who have more self-confidence may contribute to the decisions and influence the group decisions just by their willingness to put forward their views. The group may reach a solution to a problem not based on the talents or experience vital to the decision but because of the dominating views of the more forthright people.

Problems of group dynamics

Hidden agendas

Group members may have objectives which differ from the formal group objective of getting the task completed. They may wish to score points off other members by making them look foolish, impress the leader, or they may wish to attempt to shelve the project they are working on as they have a better idea of their own. These hidden agendas are detrimental to getting the task completed and are causes of ineffectiveness in groups.

Blind spots

This is something of which one group member is unaware, rather like having a smudge on one's nose, and everyone else can see it except yourself. If a group member is considered unreliable by the rest of the group, they will not take his promises seriously. He is at a loss to understand why his suggestions are not taken up and he may stop contributing to the group. This may cause the loss of some good ideas. Personal disagreements between members may be unknown to the leader and he or she will be baffled by their reluctance to work together.

DISCUSSION QUESTIONS 3.2

What has gone wrong in the following group situations?

1   A large company wishes to involve the local community in their decision to relocate to their area. They invite 17 different local groups, five local councillors and have ten company representatives on a committee to discuss the effects of the move.

2   A group of pattern designers for a small fabric company have been working on a range of new designs. The marketing department have run a pilot test on the new patterns and informed the group that the public are less than enthusiastic. The group are annoyed by the negative attitude of the marketing department and continue with their work.

3   The Managing Director of a small manufacturing company has selected a young graduate engineer to be his deputy. This decision has annoyed other long serving members of the Board of Directors. The Managing Director cannot understand why simple tasks which he has requested board members to work on with his deputy have not been completed and why there is a deathly silence whenever he mentions how well qualified his deputy is.

4   The Purchasing Manager for a metal products firm cannot understand why he is not accepted by the rest of the management team. He explains everything in great detail at meetings and is always well organised with all the necessary paperwork, in addition to always being immaculately dressed. They, on the other hand, are casual not only in appearance, but with their short and informal progress reports. They greet his detailed reports with a depressed silence and he hears them laughing behind his back at the close of meetings.

Group think

This is a giant blindspot which involves all group members. Groups that are cohesive may be so anxious to agree amongst themselves that they become unrealistic and ignore outside evidence that their decisions are faulty. All group members are amiable and seek concurrence on every important issue, with no bickering or conflict to spoil the cosy atmosphere. Any critical thoughts are suppressed so that agreement can be maintained on all issues. The consequences are poor decision making and inadequate solutions to the problems under discussion.

Dependence

Individuals may feel that they cannot function alone after being used to the support of teamwork. Re-engineering and downsizing programmes which examine work processes and cut out many functions leading to redundancies may leave certain individuals without their team.

Stifling of creativity

Some team members may feel stifled due to having to work within a team, they cannot 'do their own thing' and feel that they have lost their independence.

◆ ACTIVITY 3.1

Hidden agendas committee meeting role play

Instructions

Objective: To illustrate the effects of hidden agendas on task accomplishment in a work group.

Materials

1   A copy of the committee meeting problem sheet for everyone.

2   A copy of the Hidden Agenda role play instructions for each role player.

3   A copy of the Hidden Agenda observation sheet for each role player observer.

4   A copy of the general observations sheet for general observers.

Setting

The five role players should sit in the centre of the room, preferably at a table. Each role player should be allocated an observer who sits outside the role play group but opposite the role player they are observing.

Process

1   The facilitator forms a committee of five people as role players and distributes to them a role description sheet and a copy of the Committee Meeting problem sheet.

2   Observers are chosen for each participant. The facilitator gives them their role play observation sheets.

3   The remaining members are instructed to note down general observations of what they think is happening generally within the group when the role play begins.

4   The role players begin the meeting under the Chairmanship of Martin Williams.

5   After 15 minutes the role playing is terminated, regardless of whether the group has completed the task.

6   The general observers are asked to report

7   The role player observers are asked to report

8   The facilitator asks the role players to read their roles aloud to the group. Matthew Davies reports last.

Fig 3.1 Hidden agendas can affect group problem solving

▶

9 The facilitator informs the group that the purpose of this activity was to demonstrate that 'what goes on underneath the table' interferes with task accomplishment. The following questions may also be discussed:

(a) How do hidden agendas affect group problem solving?

(b) What are some indications that group members have hidden agendas?

(c) When is it appropriate for group members to acknowledge their hidden agendas?

COMMITTEE MEETING PROBLEM SHEET

Alltown Leisure Centre, sub-committee meeting to decide on how to elect new unemployed members onto the main Leisure Centre committee.

Participants: Martin Williams, Leisure Centre Manager

Dean Talbot, owner of local sportswear shop

Matthew Davies, Rotary Club member

Joanne Rigby, Alltown Social Services

Alison Cooper, single mother and currently the only unemployed Leisure Centre committee member

The main Leisure Centre committee has already decided that more unemployed representatives are needed on the committee. The task of the sub-committee is to decide how to elect them. The alternatives are:

1 A one-year term of office

2 A three-year term of office (which current members enjoy)

The other possible topic for discussion is how to let people know that they can become committee members. The alternatives for this are:

1 personal recommendation from existing committee members;

2 advertise in the local press/job centre.

The meeting should make decisions on how to elect and attract new committee members. The meeting will be chaired by the Leisure Centre Manager, Martin Williams.

If no decision is reached, no new members will be elected to the committee.

HIDDEN AGENDA ROLE PLAY INSTRUCTIONS

(Not to be shown to the other committee members)

MARTIN WILLIAMS

You are the Manager of Alltown Leisure Centre and you are against having unemployed people on the committee. You consider that the Leisure Centre should be a place of excellence, where good players wearing correct sports dress can get the facilities to improve their game.

You were having a drink last night with your friend, Dean Talbot, and you both agreed to try and block the election of new unemployed members onto the committee.

HIDDEN AGENDA ROLE PLAY INSTRUCTIONS

(Not to be shown to the other committee members)

DEAN TALBOT

You are a Conservative councillor for the Alltown Town Council and the owner of 'Talbot's Sportswear', a shop in Alltown. You do not wish the unemployed to be elected onto the Committee and you have agreed with your friend Martin Williams to attempt to block this motion.

You feel that the subject of correct dress should be addressed at this meeting and try to get agreement on a dress code for the leisure centre.

You dislike Alison Cooper and feel that she has quite enough to do looking after her four children alone and that she should be at home with them instead of sitting on this committee. Try to get some digs in at her so that she will feel like resigning from the committee.

HIDDEN AGENDA ROLE PLAY INSTRUCTIONS

(Not to be shown to the other committee members)

MATTHEW DAVIES

You work as a Production Manager for the Alltown Times newspaper and you do charity work through the Rotary Club. You have no interest in the Leisure Centre or whether they have unemployed people on their committee. Your interest in being at this meeting is to impress Joanne Rigby who you would like to ask out for a date.

You will agree with Joanne on all points that she makes, support her and vote on her side, if a vote is decided upon.

HIDDEN AGENDA ROLE PLAY INSTRUCTIONS

(Not to be shown to the other committee members)

JOANNE RIGBY

You work for Alltown Social Services as a Social Worker and you are very enthusiastic about having more unemployed people on the Leisure Centre Committee. You know that Martin Williams and Dean Talbot are very good friends and are in favour of keeping 'riff raff' out of the Leisure Centre. You believe that it should be used by everyone and think that this objective can be better achieved by having more unemployed people on the committee.

HIDDEN AGENDA ROLE PLAY INSTRUCTIONS

(Not to be shown to the other committee members)

ALISON COOPER

You are a single mother of four children, unemployed and struggling to manage on benefit. You believe that more unemployed people should be encouraged onto the committee. You also believe that Dean Talbot is a snob who does not have the welfare of the community at heart, he wishes to sell more of his expensive sports clothing to the public.

You feel that the Leisure Centre would serve the community better if prices were lower and there were creches available so that people with children could use the facilities without having to pay babysitters.

HIDDEN AGENDAS ROLE PLAYER OBSERVER SHEET

1 Was your sub-committee member committed to having the unemployed on the Leisure Centre committee?

2 What do you think their objectives were for the meeting?

3 Did they achieve those objectives?

4 How did their behaviour affect the task of deciding how to elect more unemployed people onto the committee?

GENERAL OBSERVATIONS SHEET

1 To what degree were committee members cooperating with each other?

2 Did the atmosphere of the meeting change at various stages?

3 Who were the high and low participators?

4 Was there a relationship between level of participation and accomplishing the task of getting unemployed people elected?

5 To what degree were the committee members committed to a common goal?

6 What motives do you think each committee member had in attending this meeting?

Task and maintenance behaviours

If a group is going to work well together over time, there are two types of behaviours they need to display.

1 *Task.* Those activities which are directed towards reaching the goals of the group;

2 *Maintenance.* Those activities concerned with keeping the group together as a social system and making it operate as a group.

It is normally the job of the leader to carry out these activities but all members of the group can share in them.

Task activities

Initiating	Proposing tasks or goals and suggesting ideas and ways for solving the problem.
Seeking information or opinions	Seeking out information about the situation under consideration and finding out people's views, ideas and suggestions. Enables informed judgements to be made.
Giving information or opinions	People offer information, opinions and views on situations and are willing to make suggestions to help solve a problem.
Clarifying and elaborating	This involves the interpretation of ideas, clarifying points and proposing alternative ideas.
Summarising	This activity takes place after ideas have been put forward and discussions have taken place. It pulls together people's thoughts and ideas and offers solutions on the evidence offered.
Consensus testing	Making sure that the group accepts its decision.

Maintenance activities

Listening   Listening to other people's thoughts, ideas and suggestions. Giving full attention when someone else is speaking.

Harmonising   Reducing tension, bringing people together who are in disagreement.

Gatekeeping   Making sure that each member of the group participates in the discussions. Allowing relevant information to flow freely.

Encouraging   Supporting contributions from members, being warm and friendly to others.

Compromising   Looking for workable alternatives as solutions to problems.

◆ ACTIVITY 3.2

In groups of 4–8 people, discuss the setting up of a business by the group. Allow 20 minutes for this part of the activity. Decisions you need to make might include:

1 Decide on the product and how it will be manufactured.
2 What should your company be called?
3 Where and how will you sell the product?
4 Where will you get your raw materials from?
5 How will you market the product?
6 How could you raise funds, (e.g. selling shares in the company)
7 How should you keep the accounts for the business?
8 Who will perform the different tasks you have been discussing?

Assessing the group processes

1 Using the form in Fig 3.2 individually tick the boxes where you feel that each group member displayed the named behaviour.
2 As a group, discuss the results:
    (a) which behaviours do individual group members feel they exhibited?
    (b) were any behaviours lacking, if so, what effect did this have on the working of the group?
    (c) which behaviours were most helpful and which were most unhelpful towards both achieving the task and making people feel that their contribution was valued?
3 Discuss how the group could improve upon their use of task and maintenance activities at future meetings.

NAME OF GROUP MEMBER			
Task activity	Tick box	**Maintenance activity**	Tick box
Initiating	☐	Listening	☐
Seeking information or opinions	☐	Harmonising	☐
Giving information or opinions	☐	Gatekeeping	☐
Clarifying and elaborating	☐	Encouraging	☐
Summarising	☐	Compromising	☐
Consensus	☐		☐

Fig 3.2 Group performance form

Decision making in teams

We all have to manage our lives and every day we all make hundreds of decisions, for example, what to wear, what to eat, what to do, what to say to other people. The decisions we make are to allow us to reach certain goals. To keep warm, to stave off hunger, to get married, to get promoted at work. These decisions set us tasks to perform to achieve our goals.

In an organisation teams and workgroups have different tasks to do, a senior management team have to decide upon the objectives for the whole organisation and make decisions as to what strategies the company should pursue in order to achieve them; a simple factory floor workgroup also makes decisions as to how to divide the work between themselves and what to do when problems occur. Any situation which presents possible alternative courses of action requires decision making.

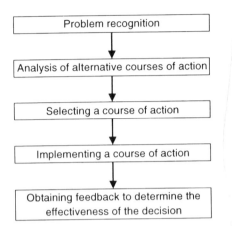

Fig 3.3 Decision-making procedure

Helen and George need to make a decision as to where to go on holiday this summer:

Problem recognition	They both feel that they need a break and have two weeks holiday from work booked in September. The problem is what they should do with those two weeks?
Analysis of alternative courses of action	Helen and George gather brochures from the travel agent and ask friends and colleagues about successful holidays they might recommend to get some alternative ideas.
Selecting and implementing a course of action	After taking into account what it is they both want from a holiday, the cost, the types of location they prefer and whether their choice is still available, they visit the travel agent and make the booking. They pay the deposit and as the time gets nearer they apply for passports, order currency from the bank, buy suitable clothing and pack their suitcases Eventually the appointed day in September arrives and they go on holiday together.
Obtaining feedback to determine the effectiveness of the decision	At the end of the holiday Helen and George discuss whether the holiday met their needs and what aspects of the holiday could be improved for a future trip.

Risk and uncertainty

Managers are always involved with making decisions which are normally to improve the performance of their organisation. Car manufacturers are continually updating the models of the cars. The new cars include new features which the public demand and the government require. The companies have to accept government regulations, they also have to decide how much to incorporate the wishes of the consumers because they need to achieve a balance between consumers' requirements and the selling price.

Most decisions involve conditions of *risk*. This is a decision situation in which sufficient information exists to estimate the likelihood of the outcome of each alternative. The car manufacturers may be aware that consumers would like airbags fitted into steering wheels but their market research tells them that consumers would also not like to pay the extra cost of the airbags. The information is incomplete as not all potential customers have been questioned in the market research and there may be on-going research into ways of producing airbags more cheaply. Decisions about the fitting of airbags will have to be based on predictions.

Major decisions facing the organisation typically involve conditions of *uncertainty*. An uncertainty decision situation is one in which insufficient information exists to estimate the likelihood of the outcome of various alternatives. The decision of recording artists to release their latest albums on vinyl only leaves record companies wondering whether this is a long-term trend or just a 'flash in the pan' which can be ignored.

Decision making at different levels in the organisation

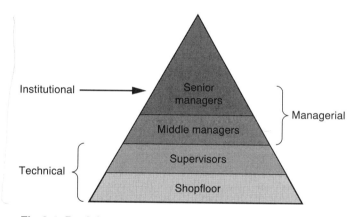

Fig 3.4 Decision making at different levels

Categories of decisions

Organisational decisions can be divided into the following categories:

1 *Institutional.* These decisions tend to be made by the Board of Directors and Executive Officers. They involve long-term planning and policy formulation. They concern such issues as diversifying into different product ranges, large-scale capital expansion, mergers, new research and development ventures.

2 *Managerial.* The task of managers is to coordinate and support activities within the organisation. They will make decisions relating to their function, e.g. Marketing Managers will make decisions about advertising campaigns and market research.

3 *Technical.* Those decisions concerned with the work of the organisation and how the inputs into the organisation (capital, labour and raw materials) are

changed into outputs (products and services). The decisions involve the operations of the organisation such as production. Quality circles often work on technical decisions.

Steps in decision making

Decisions may take moments or years to come to but the decision-making process always goes through the same procedure.

◆ ACTIVITY 3.3

List three decisions made today at work or at college. How long did these decisions take to reach? Are you involved in a decision-making group? How long has the group been working on their problem?

Identifying and diagnosing the problem

The team need to recognise that there is a problem as their first step in the decision-making process. The problem may be hindering the organisation in achieving its overall goal. The result of having this problem will be a performance gap, i.e. the difference in the expected performance compared with the actual performance.

Two inputs are needed for problem diagnosis:

1 primary and secondary information sources relevant to the decision maker;
2 managers' intuitive response to the problem.

Problem formulation

The extent of the problem needs to assessed. In their assessment, managers might have to consider the following factors:

◆ the nature of the problem
◆ the personnel involved
◆ the length of time the problem has existed
◆ time scale for problem solution.

Preparing a written problem statement

The fact that many problems are solved 'on the back of an envelope' indicates that the problem needs to be written down in some form in order to facilitate its solution. Stating a problem in written form has three benefits:

1 It forces decision makers to clarify their thinking and spend time identifying the problem. Decision makers may consider only the most visible *symptoms* of the problem, rather than its *causes*.

2 A well written problem statement acts as a foundation on which joint problem solving can be based and eliminates different perspectives and assumptions.

3 It provides a historical document of the decision-making process.

Identifying resources and constraints

Resources are anything which can be used to help solve a problem. Resources can include, for example, time, money, personnel, expertise, equipment and materials.

Constraints are barriers which impede problem solving or limit managers in their efforts to solve a problem. Lack of resources might prove a significant constraint.

The decision makers should list the major resources and constraints relevant to the problem under consideration. Budgets can then be drawn up for alternative solutions to the problem. Listing constraints makes the decision-making team aware of stumbling blocks which may affect the solution.

Generating alternative solutions

The decision-making team must generate a number of possible alternatives. The shortcut approach of identifying one or two alternatives and choosing between them often results in more effective alternatives never being considered.

A creative approach to finding alternatives can often prove helpful. Sometimes it is better to 'think around' a problem rather than attack it directly. A relaxed and lighthearted atmosphere, such as people joking about amusing solutions to the problem, can often lead to the actual solution.

Brainstorming is a problem solving technique which involves group members tossing out ideas to each other. Each idea is recorded for later evaluation. There are four rules in brainstorming:

1 there is no evaluation of any suggestion during the session;

2 quantity is the main objective, forget quality at this stage;

3 the stranger the idea, the better; and

4 modification or combination of existing suggestions are welcomed.

Evaluating alternatives and choosing a course of action

Up to this point, all the activities of the decision-making team have been preparatory. It is at this stage that the team finally decide what to do. This stage has three distinct phases:

1 determining which alternatives are feasible;

2 evaluating the quality of feasible alternatives; and

3 selecting the most appropriate alternative.

Determining which alternatives are feasible

Where a large number of alternatives have been generated, many of them will not be feasible. Often resources are unavailable or there are constraints on the implementation of many of the alternatives. Guidelines for evaluating feasible alternatives include the following:

◆ the solution should be of a *quality* to meet satisfactorily organisational goals

◆ the solution must be *acceptable* to those affected by it and to those who must implement it

◆ answers should be formulated for the anticipated responses from people

◆ the *risks* of each alternative should be considered. The choice of solution should focus on *present* alternatives, not past possibilities.

Quality

The quality of a solution has two dimensions:

1 efficiency – this refers to the ratio of outputs to inputs and compares the expected outcome of the solution with the cost of that solution;

2 effectiveness – a measure of the extent to which an alternative meets the stated objective (regardless of cost).

Before attempting to evaluate the quality of any alternative, the decision maker must establish the extent to which each of these criteria will be used.

Personnel affected by the decision

The chosen alternative must be acceptable to and preferably liked by those who implement it and those who live with the consequences of the decision. Failure to meet this condition is the single most likely reason for failure of the decision-making process to solve problems. A technically correct alternative may fail if implementation is half-hearted and badly communicated to those implementing it.

Implementing the decision

Implementing a decision is anything but simple. Managing the implementation phase involves several questions:

1 What should be done when and by whom? Everyone needs to understand their role during each phase of the implementation.

2 How should members of the organisation be rewarded for participating in the implementation of the decision? If the implementers have a stake in the success of the project, it is more likely to be successful.

3 How will the chosen solution be evaluated and modified during implementation? Minor adjustments are often needed when ideas are being put into practice.

Monitoring the decision

Monitoring involves collecting information to determine how well the decision is working. Feedback is needed for the decision makers to see how effective their chosen alternative has been in the solution of a problem. Several items are necessary for the evaluation of the effectiveness of a decision:

◆ a set of standards with which actual performance is compared

◆ performance data to be used in comparison with a set of standards

◆ a data analysis strategy must be developed. Teams who know exactly how the data is to be analysed can specify the types of data they need, the preferred format, and the time sequence in which they are needed. These advance specifications aid in reducing the amount of data collected that is never used.

DISCUSSION QUESTIONS 3.3

1 Name two ways in which a performance gap might occur.

2 What would be the best way to inform staff of a decision made about relocating the company to another part of the country in order to gain their commitment for the decision?

◆ Team building

The idea that you can bring people together and call them a team is misunderstanding of the term 'team'. A team is more than just a group of people who have been brought together for a common purpose.

The team concept

Put workers with different areas of expertise together, empower them with the ability to solve problems and make their own decisions, and together they will make better products, faster processes and more profitable companies. There are two things that distinguish a team from a group:

1 a team has common goals that everyone clearly accepts and there is a real need to work together to accomplish them;

2 a team has invested substantial time in learning how to work together.

The team has to be constructed into an entity which is separate and different from the individuals which make it up.

The team building process

The team building process involves various stages of development. We can compare the building of a team to the processes involved in building a house. These might be :

- the demand for a house of a particular design
- planning how the building will be constructed
- identifying the raw materials
- laying down the foundations
- the gradual construction of the building in logical steps
- using experts where necessary, e.g. electricians and plumbers
- before completion, checking for flaws or faults
- the family move in and house can function fully as a dwelling
- the family will make modifications during their stay in the house.

The construction is an investment by the builder in time, resources and money. The pay-off is when the house is sold. The builder will be most successful in selling the house if he has been in contact with the customer throughout the building phase.

Similarities between team building and building a house

The need for teams

Senior management may be aware that they need teams to help the organisation to meet its goals more efficiently and effectively. However, they need to know precisely how the team will function, for example there are different sorts of teams with different purposes: problem solving, quality circles, project teams.

Planning

Once the function of the team has been identified the management needs to plan the team building process to identify the requirements of the team such as how it will operate, the training and support required. This will give the management an idea how long the team building process will take.

The planning stage will identify the resources the team needs and who the people are who will make up the team.

The raw materials

Potential team members will be sought based upon their personal qualities and their technical expertise. Each team member will bring to the team different personalities, expectations, experience, education, skills and knowledge.

A problem facing anyone engaged in team building is one of individuality and self-interest. In our society, individuals have more experience of having to compete rather than working together. At school it is to come top of the class, to pass examinations, and at work it is to get a job, to get promotion, even sports teams playing together will often have an individual reward for 'Man of the Match'. Individuals will have been rewarded in the past on seniority or by gaining promotion, i.e. by their personal performance. However, teamwork means that they will be rewarded according to the performance of the team.

The environment the team is to work in and the tools which are required needs to be carefully thought out. If the management has been used to managing production by mass production and division of labour work flow, then a complete re-think may be required. The layout of the production process should be such as to encourage people to work as a team.

The typical high rise office block reinforces a hierarchical culture, especially if people aspire to gain promotion and work on the top floor, where senior management are located. In low rise buildings the layout of the office may hinder the development of the teams, if the work is carried out in a formal setting. If everyone is given a small and separate office, informal chats and meetings between team members will be hindered as getting together becomes uncomfortable. The team must have a say in the process by which they work, and the environment they are involved in.

Fig 3.5 High rise office blocks reinforce hierarchical culture

Fig 3.6 If work is carried out in a formal setting team development may be inhibited

Laying down the foundations

This is the important stage of the team building process. The whole team's success will depend upon the work which is done at this stage. Once the team members have been identified, the management must inform the team of their role in helping the organisation to meet its goal. At this stage the team needs to understand their function and their responsibilities. Team members need to be made aware that by performing as a team rather than as individuals the organisation will function more effectively and efficiently. Management need to explain to individuals how they as individuals will benefit from teamwork. It is a time to educate and train the team members. For example it should be explained to each member of the team the value of individual expertise to the team. Shopfloor team members may even need support in skills such as reading, writing and basic maths. Other team members might need help in how to participate in discussions or oral presentations. The management will have identified team leaders who may well have been supervisors in the past. The supervisor's new role will be one of support and coaching rather than checking. They may need training on managing people, managing and resolving team conflict.

This is an important time for managers because they have got to be able to give the teams the responsibility for their job, allowing the teams to make decisions. Managers should become more involved with strategic matters rather than day-to-day details.

Failure to let go at this stage will undermine the confidence of the team or reinforce old values of us and them with management keeping all the responsibility to themselves.

Construction

The building of the team is underway and will go through stages of development until the members are bonded into a team.

CASE STUDY 3.2

New Victoria Theatre

The Victoria Theatre Company was the first professional company in Britain to perform permanently in the round – that is, with the audience on all sides of the acting area. The theatre offers a very wide-ranging programme, and specialises in documentary plays which explore and reflect the life of the local community. The company moved to their new purpose-built theatre in Newcastle-under-Lyme in 1986. The new theatre has won the Royal Institute of British Architects' Award and has been nominated for the Most Welcoming Regional Theatre Award. They have won British Tourism awards and awards for the grounds which successfully combine a nature conservation area with the car park.

The New Victoria Theatre, which seats 605 people, has 57 staff, eight of whom are part-time. There are 150 volunteers and casual staff whom they can call upon to do a variety of tasks from putting playbills in envelopes for sending out to potential customers to looking after the audience during a performance. This may include checking tickets and showing the

Fig 3.7 New Victoria Theatre, Newcastle

audience to their seats. This team of paid staff and volunteers put on ten productions during 45 weeks of the year, with an average acting size of 13 actors. The programme is varied and includes modern classics, a Shakespeare play, documentary plays on local issues and a Christmas show for families. Actors are freelance, working on short term contracts.

There is also a restaurant in the theatre which is open from 10 am until the start of the performance, a bar and a shop in the foyer. Exhibitions, concerts, workshops and educational events often take place, in addition to the daily performances. Figure 3.8 is an organisation chart of the theatre.

There is a Chairman and Board who make policy decisions but they are not paid members of staff and are not involved in the day-to-day running of the theatre.

Maggie Saxon is General Manager for the New Victoria Theatre. She shares responsibility for the administration of the theatre with Peter Cheeseman, the Theatre Director, who is well respected in British theatre. Maggie looks after the administration whilst Peter is concerned with production. The running of the theatre requires close communication and co-operation between Maggie and Peter. Maggie says: *'There isn't an artistic decision that can be taken without financial implications and vice versa. You cannot separate out the two functions.'*

Peter has an Associate Director who assists him with programme planning, artistic administration, and casting. He also directs plays, visits new plays, and scouts for new talent in terms of writers, actors and new directors.

Judy Bowker, the Theatre Manager, is concerned with the day-to-day operation of the theatre. She is part of the Senior Management Team and is responsible for front-of-house areas and organises everything concerned with the public side of performances. Judy is responsible for the safety and comfort of the audience when she is on duty in the evenings. She works three evenings per week:

'There isn't a typical day, every day is different. The cleaners come in at 7 am and the ticket office and restaurant open at ten o'clock. Most of the administrative staff are in by ten o'clock, some earlier. Their hours are flexible, they can work nine till five, or ten till six.'

Judy also stocks and runs the shop in the foyer, organises the programmes exhibitions in the foyer, coordinates the rotas for the part-time staff, and forms a link for volunteers and the paid front-of-house staff. There must be at least one paid member of staff for every one hundred people in the audience. She also organises the selling of programmes, looking after the audience, the cleaners, security staff and car park attendants.

Maggie is very clear about the need for teamwork:

'Everyone has their own job responsibility but it interlinks. There's absolutely no point in an actor doing a one-person show with no audience. A theatre lends itself to having people there. We're making a spectacle, an event, costumes and props are needed to support that event. It also needs the Director's concept of how to portray it. Somebody once asked me "what's the unit of production you're making?" The production doesn't exist unless you've got an audience. You need people to get an audience into the theatre and then you need to water and feed the audience. It's like putting pieces of a jigsaw together, to put on

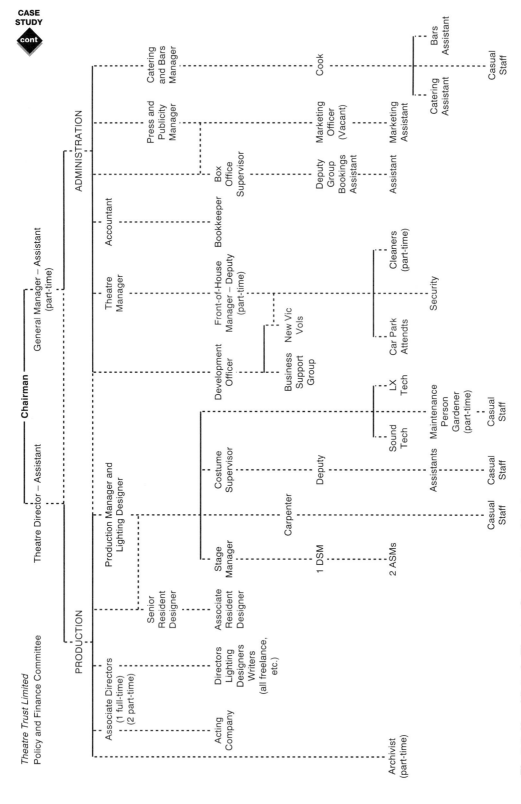

Fig 3.8 New Victoria Theatre Organisation Chart

CASE STUDY cont

an event as economically as possible and then to allow that event to continue on a regular basis.'

Other staff include Marketing Staff, a Production Secretary, Assistant to the General Manager, Assistant to the Theatre Director and the Accounts section.

Backstage the rehearsals usually start at about 10 am. Rehearsals are for a forthcoming production and therefore the Stage Manager has to organise the striking (or removal) of the set from the previous evening, depending upon where the rehearsals are being held. Sometimes there are two productions being rehearsed at one time and this double rehearsal necessitates the use of the auditorium. Judy explains:

'If the production being rehearsed is only a few days away the previous night's set will be struck and the actual set will be brought on. Before that props are used for scenery, such as a broom for a tree. If it's more than a week before the production is due to go on, the carpenter will still be working on the set.'

The actors continue rehearsing until lunchtime and continue after lunch until five o'clock, except if they appear in the scene being rehearsed, in which case they might only get a three hour break. Sound and lighting engineers are working during the day, checking equipment and making tapes. The carpenter, the design and wardrobe departments are all working on future productions and the maintenance man is busy doing repairs around the building. The bar is open at lunchtime from 12 noon until 2 pm. The restaurant stays open throughout the day. The bar opens again at 5.30 pm for the evening performance.

The Security and Duty Manager come in at 6 pm. The actors start their warm-ups and voice exercises at 6.30 pm. The performance staff are composed of permanent staff and volunteers and they arrive at 6.45 pm. The Auditorium opens at seven o'clock which is half an hour prior to the performance beginning, this allows the auditorium to be checked over by the staff to ensure that everything is in place before the audience enter. The ticket office closes at the beginning of the evening performance and the ticket office staff go home. At the interval of the play or concert all catering points open – the bar, coffee shop, sweet shops and occasionally additional sales points. The bar stays open after the interval. The actors and front of house staff go home after the performance. The Duty Manager will stay on when necessary, depending upon the activity in the foyers. The bar closes at 11.20 pm. Once the building is clear the security staff check around and lock up, usually at around 1 am. Judy also readily admits: *'We do work as a team, but everyone has their own role, I couldn't go down and help them sew the new costumes in the costume department.'*

The theatre staff work as a team through face-to-face communication and hold many meetings in order to plan and discuss problems. The Monday Morning Conference involves all departments and actors are invited to attend. Maggie: *'We all get to know what's going on, what we're doing, any problems on shows. Budgets and production are discussed and future meetings can be arranged. Maggie normally speaks about keeping costs down at these meetings. I remind them to put lights out and other matters like keeping the kitchen tidy. Representation from actors is encouraged at the meetings so that they too feel part of the team.'*

CASE STUDY cont

The Marketing meetings are for an exchange of information on the week ahead's bookings as well as longer term booking patterns. Maggie: *'We don't have a lot of bookings in advance. People mostly buy their tickets in the week they come.'* The team also discuss what is going well in terms of sales, marketing strategies which could be used for each production and stories about productions which may be of interest to the press. Maggie: *'We brainstorm for ideas and marketing strategies. Marketing is fundamental to the work that we do, we're all involved.'*

The Production meetings are weekly and the team involved are able to monitor how the plays are going. Maggie: *'We look at whether, for example, we've found the right props and ensure that we're going to get everything made in time for the first night.'* Other meetings include Catering meetings, Maintenance meetings and Events meetings.

On the subject of teamwork Maggie says: *'You can't have what we call "the personal pronoun syndrome" – on the one hand you want people to take responsibility for their work, but if it became "me, me, me" then that person is failing to take account of all the teamwork taking place.'* Everyone has to consider the implications of their actions. For example, if the audience is late and Judy, the Theatre Manager, decides to hold the show for them, she could put the actors into an overnight break infringement (union rules say that they must have eleven and a half hours break). That would mean paying the actors overtime as well as losing bar sales. Maggie: *'Communication is crucial so that people can place in context what they're doing and be part of the whole.'*

The season of plays runs from September–July each year. Maggie: *'The Theatre's Directors are looking at plays to do all the time, considering which would do good business.'* Twice a year the team have to focus on getting the playbill out. Maggie: *'Deliberations need to involve myself and the Marketing and Production Managers to look at feasibility – what resources are needed, finance, and whether it will be possible within resources.'* The Christmas show and Shakespeare play are usually the largest productions in terms of budget.

Fig 3.9 The Monday morning conference, New Victoria Theatre

Everyone working on creating a play calculates the cost of their contribution – designers, carpenters, costumes. Maggie: *'We have a group meeting, so that for example, Sound can have an insight into Wardrobe costs and so on. Everybody is as accurate as they can be with their own budget and in addition they can see the wider perspective. The aim is to get a shared commitment and responsibility. It's philosophically what we believe we're about, which is working with a group of people to make something creative happen. It's very satisfying when it works because people know that they've made a contribution. People will give that much more and get that much more out of it when they feel part of the team.'*

DISCUSSION QUESTIONS 3.4

1 How is the work organised at the theatre?

2 Why is it difficult to separate the artistic side of the theatre from the business side?

3 Why do you think the theatre has so many volunteer staff?

4 What costs could be saved if the theatre changed from being a repertory theatre to one which puts on visiting shows and plays from touring theatre companies?

5 How many teams can be identified?

6 What forms of communication are used by the theatre?

The organisation as a team

An organisation is a group of people working together towards a stated goal. The staff and volunteers at the New Victoria Theatre are all working towards putting on events every day for the enjoyment of the general public. No one person alone could achieve the standard of service given by the team at the theatre. The audience is looked after by car park attendants, booking office staff, volunteers who direct them to their seats, actors who entertain them, catering and bar staff who provide them with food and drink. There are also services provided by people they

Fig 3.10 Management teams

do not see such as cleaners, directors and administrators. The huge task of entertaining up to 600 people, often twice daily, needs very careful management. The team at the theatre carry this out successfully by giving every member of staff a definite role to play and through constant communication. The nature of the service they are providing is very perishable – if people do not buy tickets for today's performance, the revenue on the empty seats is lost permanently. Staff have to act quickly on a daily basis, both to put on the event and to inform the public of future events in order to fill as many seats as possible. Communication is therefore mostly face-to-face with daily formal and informal meetings. Written communication in the form of memos is only used for very detailed or technical instructions. A group of people acting together can achieve far more than if the individual members all worked separately.

Stages in group development

A collection of individuals who are unknown to one another cannot immediately function as an effective team. This takes time. The team members need to know and trust one another before they work well together. A group of people working together will have a relationship of their own, this is separate to the relationships between individuals in the group, and needs time to develop and grow. The various stages any effective group will go through in their development are as follows:

Forming

The group members may be new to one another or they may just not have worked together before. They will start to get to know one another, decide upon their objectives for working together, choose a leader and others to fill certain roles or do specific jobs and make other decisions as to how they are going to carry out the work. The group carries out their work according to these initial plans, all the time discovering new things about one another – who does what best, who is reliable, who gives the best advice, who is easy to get along with and who is hard working.

The leader's role

During this stage the leader will be concerned with helping the group with the task. The leader will help to clarify what the task is, set goals, and establish rules of operating, communicating and decision making. The leader must be able to demonstrate to the group the reason why each member is part of the group.

Storming

The storming stage is a period of conflict during which group members reveal what they really feel about the way the group works and what they want from the group. If this stage is gone through successfully by the group, members will know and trust one another to a greater extent, work roles will be changed to be more appropriate to the people suited to carry them out and the leadership and objectives will often be altered too.

Fig 3.11 Problem solving teams

The leader's role

At this stage the leader may be redefining goals, modifying procedures and clarifying roles. He or she will be encouraging individuals and will have to manage conflict. The leader must be prepared to listen to difficulties and encourage differences of opinion without causing conflict. He or she must be able to manage the group so that individuals participate, making sure that some do not dominate the group.

Norming

The group is now becoming much more cohesive, any hostilities and personality clashes have been dealt with and the group can focus on the task instead of on one another. The emphasis will be on co-operation and how best to get the work done. The group are learning how to work together and control their behaviour. The norms of the ways the group functions best are being established.

The leader's role

By this stage the group is becoming a cohesive unit and the leader needs to spend less time directing and so can become more of a team member, i.e. he or she has to 'let go' and allow the group to assume responsibility for its actions. However, the leader has to make sure that the group does not become too tightly knit so that it avoids conflict and disagreement. Too cosy an atmosphere will blinker the group from its own mistakes.

Performing

At this stage the group is performing effectively. The group members get on well together, they trust one another, they can be honest about their feelings within the group, all members participate in the work and decisions about the work and all members benefit from being part of the group. The quality and quantity of work the group are able to do is at its maximum at this stage. It may take a long or a short time to reach this stage in the life of a group, or it may never be reached. It depends upon many factors such as the size of the group, how much time they spend together, how well they get along together, whether they are prepared to be honest with one another and how important the task is that they have been given to do.

The leader's role

By this stage the group should be operating as a unit and there is less need for control and support from the leader. This means the leader can target her energies in other areas.

Not all groups complete the above stages to become an effective working team. Many groups find the storming stage too difficult to cope with as it involves everyone being honest and open about their feelings. Groups which do not meet very often, such as a committee which only meets every two months, will probably be able to avoid this painful stage of conflict and disruption. If the storming stage is avoided then group members will never be completely honest with

Fig 3.12 Quality circles?

one another and cannot function effectively as a group. Other tactics such as backstabbing and politicking behind the scenes may be tried by group members in order to achieve such things as recognition for their own efforts instead of the group's effort and trying to get an unpopular group member removed.

Some groups may be able to function effectively without a painful storming stage. Individuals who are trusting and naturally open about their feelings may get along well as a group as soon as they come together, their development as a group may merely involve getting to know one another better.

Fig 3.13 Work teams

Bass's stages of formal group development

In 1965 Bernard Bass suggested an alternative approach to the formation of groups. Bass put forward the idea that group development is a four-stage process influenced mainly by groups learning how to use their resources. The four stages of development are:

The acceptance stage

Members of a new group are usually very wary of other people and initially mistrust other people's views. Members are aware of their own strengths and weaknesses and tend to behave in a restrained manner so that they do not make mistakes or say anything that they might regret later. This stage of the group's development is typified by formal behaviour of group members.

The communication and decision-making stage

Once the acceptance stage has passed, people feel more confident with their own performance and about being in the company of their colleagues. People are more open and frank in their discussion. Standards of procedure are established and a mechanism for some type of group decision-making strategy is developed.

The group solidarity stage

This stage comes more naturally as mutual acceptance and confidence in group members increases. Communication and decision-making structures are clarified as members of a group work together rather than compete with one another.

Control and organisation

This final stage of the group's development is where group solidarity leads to group control. Work is distributed according to individual abilities within the group activities. Co-operation, flexibility and informality are accepted at this stage.

How well is your team working?

Answer *True* or *False* to the following statements:

		True	False
1	I feel part of the team all the time.	☐	☐
2	I feel perfectly safe to be myself, they don't hold mistakes against me.	☐	☐
3	I feel almost completely free to express myself with the group.	☐	☐
4	Everyone feels that his or her ideas, opinions and information are given a fair hearing before decisions are made.	☐	☐
5	I understand the goals the team is working towards and feel that they are worthwhile.	☐	☐
6	The team works well at its task and achieves definite progress at each meeting.	☐	☐
7	Our planning and the way we operate as a team is largely shared by all members of the team.	☐	☐
8	Each person accepts personal responsibility for getting work done.	☐	☐
9	Differences and conflicts are recognised and the team usually is working through them satisfactorily.	☐	☐
10	Team members respect the leader, but they work together as a unified team with everyone participating and no one dominant.	☐	☐

If you ticked 'True' for seven or more questions, your team is working extremely well together.

DISCUSSION QUESTIONS 3.5

1 Identify the problems within your group from those questions to which you answered 'False'.

2 Think of some suggestions for improving the functioning of your team.

Group needs during development

During the development stages the team will need continual support and training.

Team leaders may need training in:

◆ building trust

◆ inspiring teamwork

◆ creating a team identity

◆ help the team to make decisions

◆ expanding team capabilities.

Team members may need training in:

◆ the ability to persuade others to their point of view

◆ listening and effectively drawing information out of other team members

◆ learning how to create constructive conflict and manage the tension that arises as a result

◆ aligning personal objectives with team objectives, and understanding the individual's role in creating shared outcomes.

Completion

There will never be a completion phase in teambuilding because the team will always be striving for improvements in their operation and processes, team members will be developing and changing their views at various rates. There will often be outflows and in-flows of team members, which will keep the team in a dynamic state.

DISCUSSION QUESTIONS 3.6

1   What is the difference between a group and a team?

2   List all the teams you come into contact with.

3   What is the aim of each team?

4   How might the management communicate in the following situations:

   (a)   informing individuals the organisation is going to introduce teams;

   (b)   informing the team about the mission of the company;

   (c)   feeding back assessment on the team's performance?

5   What training might take place during the storming stage of development?

6   How might this training take place?

7   What problems is the team going to face during team building?

◆ ACTIVITY 3.4

The Belbin self-perception inventory

For each section distribute a total of 10 points among the sentences which you think best describes your behaviour. These 10 points can be distributed among several sentences, all the sentences, all given to a single response. Enter the points you allocate in the boxes on the right of each sentence.

1   What I believe I can contribute to a team:

(a)   I think I can quickly see and take advantage of new opportunities. ☐

(b)   I can work well with a very wide range of people. ☐

(c)   Producing ideas is one of my natural assets. ☐

(d)   My ability rests in being able to draw people out whenever I detect they have something of value to contribute to group objectives. ☐

(e)   My capacity to follow through has much to do with my personal effectiveness. ☐

▶

(f) I am ready to face temporary unpopularity if it leads to worthwhile results in the end. ☐

(g) I am quick to sense what is likely to work in a situation with which I am familiar. ☐

(h) I can offer a reasoned case for alternative courses of action without introducing bias or prejudice. ☐

2 If I have a possible shortcoming in teamwork, it could be that:

(a) I am not at ease unless meetings are well structured and controlled and generally well conducted. ☐

(b) I am inclined to be too generous towards others who have a valid viewpoint that has not been given a proper airing. ☐

(c) I have a tendency to talk a lot once the group gets on to new ideas. ☐

(d) My objective outlook makes it difficult for me to join in readily and enthusiastically with colleagues. ☐

(e) I am sometimes forceful and authoritarian if there is a need to get something done. ☐

(f) I find it difficult to lead from the front, perhaps because I am over-responsive to group atmosphere. ☐

(g) I am apt to get too caught up in ideas that occur to me and so lose track of what is happening. ☐

(h) My colleagues tend to see me as worrying unnecessarily over detail and the possibility that things may go wrong. ☐

3 When involved in a project with other people:

(a) I have an aptitude for influencing people without pressurising them. ☐

(b) My general vigilance prevents careless mistakes and omissions being made. ☐

(c) I am ready to press for action to make sure that the meeting does not waste time or lose sight of the main objective. ☐

(d) I can be counted on to contribute something original. ☐

(e) I am always ready to back a good suggestion in the common interest. ☐

(f) I am keen to look for the latest in new ideas and developments. ☐

(g) I believe my capacity for cool judgement is appreciated by others. ☐

(h) I can be relied upon to see that all essential work is organised. ☐

4 My characteristic approach to group work is that:

(a) I have a quiet interest in getting to know my colleagues better. ☐

(b) I am not reluctant to challenge the views of others or to hold a minority view myself. ☐

(c) I can usually find a line of argument to refute sound propositions. ☐

▶

(d) I think I have a talent for making things work once a plan has to be put into operation. ☐

(e) I have a tendency to avoid the obvious and to come out with the unexpected. ☐

(f) I bring a touch of perfectionism to any team job I undertake. ☐

(g) I am ready to make use of contacts outside the group itself. ☐

(h) While I am interested in all views, I have no hesitation in making up my mind once a decision has to be made. ☐

5 I gain satisfaction in my job because:

(a) I enjoy analysing situations and weighing up all the possible choices. ☐

(b) I am interested in finding practical solutions to problems. ☐

(c) I like to feel I am fostering good working relationships. ☐

(d) I can have a strong influence on decisions. ☐

(e) I can meet people to agree on a necessary course of action. ☐

(f) I can get people to agree on a necessary course of action. ☐

(g) I feel in my element where I can give a task my full attention. ☐

(h) I like to find a field that stretches my imagination. ☐

6 If I am suddenly given a difficult task with limited time and unfamiliar people:

(a) I would feel like retiring to a corner to devise a way out of the impasse before developing a line. ☐

(b) I would be ready to work with the person who showed the most positive approach, however difficult he or she might be. ☐

(c) I would find some way of reducing the size of the task by establishing what different individuals might best contribute. ☐

(d) My natural sense of urgency would help to ensure that we did not fall behind schedule. ☐

(e) I believe I would keep cool and maintain my capacity to think straight. ☐

(f) I would retain a steadiness of purpose in spite of the pressures. ☐

(g) I would be prepared to take a positive lead if I felt the group was making no progress. ☐

(h) I would open up discussions with a view to stimulating new thoughts and getting something moving. ☐

7 With reference to the problem to which I am subject in working in groups:

(a) I am apt to show my impatience with those who are obstructing progress. ☐

(b) Others may criticise me for being too analytical and insufficiently intuitive. ☐

▶

(c) My desire to ensure that work is properly done can hold up proceedings. ☐

(d) I tend to get bored rather easily and rely on one or two stimulating members to spark me. ☐

(e) I find it difficult to get started unless the goals are clear. ☐

(f) I am sometimes poor at explaining and clarifying complex points that occur to me. ☐

(g) I am sometimes poor at demanding from others the things I cannot do myself. ☐

(h) I hesitate to get my points across when I run up against real opposition. ☐

Scoring

Now enter the points you allocate to each statement in each section in the table below. So, for Section 1, write the points you gave to statement (g) in the first column, under the heading 'I' – 'Implementer', those you gave to (d) under the heading 'C' – Coordinator and so on. Then add up your total score for each team type.

Section	I	C	Sh	PI	RI	ME	TW	CF
1	g __	d __	f __	c __	a __	h __	b __	e __
2	a __	b __	e __	g __	c __	d __	f __	h __
3	h __	a __	c __	d __	f __	g __	e __	b __
4	d __	h __	b __	e __	g __	c __	a __	f __
5	b __	f __	d __	h __	e __	a __	c __	g __
6	f __	c __	g __	a __	h __	e __	b __	d __
7	e __	g __	a __	f __	d __	b __	h __	c __
Total	___	___	___	___	___	___	___	___

Now note down:

1   Your dominant team type (highest score). This will indicate how you can best make your mark in a team.

2   Other team types (your next highest score). This denotes the back-up team roles which you are able to take on if needed.

3   Your two lowest scores. These imply possible areas of weakness. (But remember you are not aiming to cover *all* team roles yourself, even if you are the team leader. These are merely areas where you should ensure you are complemented by another team member.)

◆ ## Belbin's team roles

The effectiveness of any group will be determined by the individuals in it. Individuals need to have the necessary skills, talents and experience to carry out their task as well as being able to work with others pursuing a shared idea and purpose.

In those groups which have individuals with a wide variety of skills and abilities, the strengths of one person can support the weaknesses of another. Meredith Belbin studied groups of managers attending various management courses. In 1981 he wrote a book about the different roles managers take on in teamwork. He identified people with different qualities who would be useful in a team. The eight roles are:

Coordinator	The controller and organiser of the group, ensures that the best use is made of each team member's potential.
Plant	The creative person with ideas, they are able to search for a different approach to a problem if the team gets bogged down.
Implementer	The practical person who puts the ideas into practice.
Shaper	The person who helps to give shape to the group's activities by standing back and seeing the whole picture.
Resource Investigator	The person with contacts or knowledge about where to obtain resources for the group's activities.
Team Worker	The person who supports other members and improves communication.
Monitor/Evaluator	The person who assesses ideas and progress.
Completer/Finisher	The person who looks after the details and makes sure the group meets its deadline.

The majority of people are capable of working alone and performing all the roles for themselves. However, everyone will tend to prefer a particular role or roles in a group. Some people will happily adopt two or three of the Belbin roles at once, others will have one dominant role.

Which Belbin role do you identify with?

Coordinator

◆ Prepares things beforehand. When they are in charge everything is well organised.

◆ Encourages individuals to play their part in the team by making sure each individual understands the objectives of the task and makes sure that they know the best way they can help.

◆ Can identify weaknesses in the team and takes action to rectify them. Notices if someone has a disproportionate amount of work and is able to reallocate the work.

◆ Able to coordinate the resources available to the group.

◆ Able to keep individuals working on the task.

◆ A role model for people to follow because of their qualities of commitment, self-discipline and perseverance.

◆ Able to delegate when appropriate.

◆ Knows when to move from discussion to decision making in meetings.

Plant

◆ Can concentrate on the main issues.

◆ Thinks of ways for the team to achieve its objective.

◆ Enjoys thinking out all the possibilities for a solution to a problem.

◆ Has good timing – can think of ideas exactly when they are needed.

◆ Can attempt to steer the team toward their personal interests.

◆ Can sulk if their ideas are rejected.

◆ Reluctant to suggest anything if the group if very critical.

Implementer

◆ Makes sure that people know what they should do.

◆ Sorts out the practical details from the plan.

◆ Does not get distracted from the task.

◆ Works hard to meet targets.

◆ Gives practical support, help and guidance to other team members.

Shaper

◆ Can see the need to set objectives and decide upon priorities.

◆ Can take an overview of what the team is doing and helps other team members to see their efforts in the bigger picture.

◆ Good at reminding the group about the direction they should be going in and summing up what they have achieved in terms of their original objectives.

◆ Can stand back from what is happening and assess the team's progress.

◆ Can intervene when the team is going off course.

Resource Investigator

◆ Able to get on with people easily. Has contacts and friends outside the team who may be useful in helping the team achieve its objectives.

◆ Interested in new ideas and new methods which they have experienced outside the group and is able to introduce to the team.

◆ Helps to maintain good relationships and is able to keep the peace.

◆ Enjoys other people's company and may distract group members from the work.

Team Worker

◆ Observes the strengths and weaknesses of members.

◆ Supports members in their strengths, i.e. building on their ideas and suggestions.

◆ Supports members in their weak areas by helping them.

◆ Improves communications between members.

◆ Sets an example in team spirit.

Monitor/Evaluator

◆ Can think critically in the interests of the team.

◆ Prepared to experiment.

◆ Good at taking other people's suggestions and building on them or modifying them.

◆ Good at convincing the team that certain ideas are not workable.

Completer/Finisher

◆ Good at seeing mistakes.

◆ Good at paying attention to detail.

◆ Helps raise the standard of the team's work by their vigilance and offers of help.

◆ Very keen to meet deadlines, reminds the team when the deadline is approaching and makes them feel that they need to get things moving.

Belbin discovered that the groups who performed best had a mix of individuals with different role preferences. When roles are missing within a group, this may contribute to inefficiency. Groups who fail often lack a Completer/Finisher role may be good at problem and solution generation, but never carry their ideas through.

If an important role is not being filled the solution is to bring someone into the group to do it. Often this is not possible in organisations, and the alternative is to find someone within the group who would be prepared to take on this role. Groups are often selected according to such criteria as the technical expertise of members and Belbin roles are not taken into consideration. A team full of Plants and Shapers may fight initially about whose idea should be adopted, but in the long run they may achieve very little. Similarly, a group of team workers will be very short of ideas and may

Fig 3.14 Virtual teams

start work on a project to which none of them feel very committed, they too will have difficulty in achieving an end. An awareness of the existence of these roles may help to point to possible solutions to problems.

 **Types of team**

The model team

Does your team, or a team with which you are familiar have these characteristics?

◆ The atmosphere tends to be informal, comfortable, relaxed. There are no obvious tensions. People are involved and interested and there are no signs of boredom.

◆ There is a lot of discussion in which virtually everyone participates, but discussion is restricted to the task of the group. If the discussion gets off the subject, someone will bring it back in short order.

◆ The task or the objective of the group is well understood and accepted by the members. There will have been free discussion of the objective at some point until the members of the group could commit themselves to it.

◆ The members listen to each other. Every idea is given a hearing. People are not afraid of looking foolish by suggesting a creative thought even though it seems fairly extreme.

◆ There is disagreement. The group is comfortable with this and shows no signs of having to avoid conflict or to keep things under the surface. Members who disagree are expressing a genuine difference of opinion, and they expect a hearing to find a solution.

◆ Sometimes there are basic disagreements which cannot be resolved. The group finds it possible to live with them, accepting them but not permitting them to block its efforts.

◆ Most decisions are reached by a kind of consensus in which it is clear that everybody is in general agreement and willing to go along. There is little tendency for individuals who oppose the action to keep their opposition private and thus let an apparent consensus mask real disagreement.

◆ Criticism is frequent, frank, and relatively comfortable. There is little evidence of personal attack, either openly or in a hidden fashion. The criticism has a constructive flavour in that it is designed to help remove an obstacle that faces the group and prevents it from getting the job done.

◆ People feel free in expressing their feelings as well as their ideas both on the problem and on the group's operation. There are few 'hidden agendas'. Everybody appears to know quite well how everybody else feels about any matter under discussion.

◆ The chairman of the group does not dominate and the group does not defer unduly to the chairman. The leadership should shift from time to time, depending on the circumstances. Different members, because of their knowledge or experience, are in a position to act as 'resources' for the group. This is little evidence of a struggle for power as the group operates. The issue is not who controls but how to get the job done.

◆ The group is self-conscious about its own operations. Frequently, it will stop to examine how well it is doing or what may be interfering with its operation.

The problem may be a matter of procedure, or it may be an individual whose behaviour is interfering with the accomplishment of the group's objectives. Whatever it is, it receives open discussion until a solution is found.

The winning team

Meredith Belbin's research highlighted the following characteristics of a successful winning team:

◆ The leader of the team will be patient, able to instil trust, and know how to direct and use the strengths of the team players. The leader will not dominate the proceedings but will be able to pull the team together to focus on issues, especially when decisions need to be made.

◆ A strong 'plant' – someone who is very creative and clever.

◆ A fair spread in mental abilities, i.e. having a mixture of intelligent and not so intelligent people. The latter, who recognise their own shortcomings, will look for alternative ways of fulfilling themselves.

◆ A spread in personal attributes, which offers wide team role coverage. Different types of team members provide a balance by offering varied skills and talents. This reduces tension within the team because individuals are not competing for the same role.

◆ A good match between the attributes of members and their responsibility in the team enables members to play to their individual strengths.

◆ The ability to recognise and counteract the shortcomings of the team, perhaps because it lacks a key player or has an individual who has a problem with his or her role. The team will help and support each other to reduce deficiencies.

The losing team

The teams which are most likely to fail to meet their objectives are those which, according to Belbin, lack the following features:

◆ Mental ability. There needs to be at least one member of the team who can analyse the problem or be able to suggest ways forward for the team.

◆ Negative selection. The organisation recognises a deficiency in a team, i.e. the need for someone with specific skills, and decides to recruit. However, it reduces the field of applicants by the restrictions it lays down, such as the salary being too low or there being an age or experience barrier.

◆ Personality. The culture of the organisation will influence the behaviour of individuals. This may well be restrictive for some people to the extent that they do not perform to their capabilities. Some organisations may encourage specialists to the extent that they see the world from a narrow, rather than a global viewpoint. This is a feature of the product-orientated organisation which concentrates on developing a product, then tries to sell it. Market-oriented companies first find out what customers want so that they can produce it for them.

◆ Composition of the team. The key players in a team have been identified as implementer, co-ordinator, shaper, plant, resource investigator, monitor/evaluator, team worker, and completer/finisher. Some teams may lack a key member such as a plant. They may have members carrying out a role for which they are unsuited or there may be a duplication of roles leading to competition. In some teams there may be those individuals who cannot operate well in a team because they are too individualistic or task-oriented. Some teams may have those individuals who have pushed themselves forward but are unable to live up to the standards set by the group and are incompetent and make mistakes. Unfortunately, the group is unable to help and support this person because perhaps they do not recognise their own shortcomings, or they cover up their trail so that no one can identify their mistakes.

Fig 3.15 **Problems of team building**

◆ Corporate cohesiveness. Managers are given responsibility for a specific function such as marketing, finance or operations management. Problems may arise for the team when the manager becomes more loyal to his area than to the organisation. This insular approach inhibits the ability of managers to see beyond their area and take an overview of the organisation.

◆ ACTIVITY 3.5

The interior design

Aim

To observe group processes at work

Instructions

1   In groups of no more than six, you are to make a scale model of the room you are in at the moment.

2   You have 25 minutes to complete the task, spend at least 10 minutes planning the model before you begin construction.

3   There should be at least one observer per group.

4   At the end of the 25 minutes, the models should be displayed and all participants should vote for the model they feel is most accurately to scale.

5   Observers give their reports.

▶

6 Groups reflect on the Observer's comments and discuss whether they could have behaved differently to improve the group's performance.

7 Groups attempt to identify which stage they are at in terms of group development – forming, storming, norming or performing.

Resources: Sheets of coloured card, Sellotape, paper, pens and scissors, Process Observer Sheets.

Process Observer Sheet

Group atmosphere

1 Are people involved and interested?

2 Are members getting satisfaction from being in the group?

3 Are people collaborating or competing?

4 Is the atmosphere friendly?

5 What happens when there is a conflict? Is it dealt with or ignored?

Participation

1 Did some members participate more than others? Who?

2 Who participated least? How were they treated?

3 Were contributions on target, or did they lead the group away from the task?

4 Was there a leader? Who carried out this function and what behaviours made you feel that they were taking the lead?

Influence

1 Who influenced proceedings the most?

2 Were there rivalries? Who handled them?

Procedures

1 How was the planning stage organised? Did the team stick to the plan?

2 Did the group discuss unrelated matters?

3 How were decisions reached? How did this affect the group?

4 Did anyone take control, if so, how?

5 Were subgroups formed? How did this affect the process?

6 What ideas were not dealt with because they were too risky?

Ground rules

1 How well did the group follow the instruction that the model should be to scale?

2 Did anyone call attention to the need for accuracy in scale when needed? What happened?

(The Process Observer Sheets can be used at every group meeting to monitor group processes.)

Team building using the outdoors

Companies employ the organisation Leadership Resources to help them build teams using outdoor training. Leadership Resources is run by Ken Minor, who employs his own staff of experts in outdoor training as well as buying in expertise from companies such as Avalon Adventure. Mick Jennings, a paramedic and ex-Parachute Regiment, owns Avalon Adventure and specialises in adventure training. Leadership Resources often use Stanley Head Outdoor Centre set in 65 acres of land near the Peak District, for their courses. Training includes personal interviews at the trainee's place of work, classroom modules, outdoor activities and debriefing sessions.

Working together as a team are experts from three different organisations, Ken Minor, Winston Rogers and Gill Steele from Leadership Resources in Warwickshire, Mick Jennings from Avalon Adventure in Devon and John Dodd from Stanley Head Outdoor Education Centre in Staffordshire.

Ken and Win prefer to commence their team training by visiting the individuals at their organisations. *'One of the first questions we ask is, "Who are your competition?" and they always name other companies in their market,'* Ken points out that that is not the only source of competitor. *'However the biggest competition is themselves. They know it's true. Fighting amongst themselves, politics, is the biggest problem. Getting people working together is a major task facing an organisation.'*

The team from Leadership Resources like to assess every individual who will be attending the outdoor team building course. Interviews last for an hour and a half and information is gathered on personal details, ambitions, responsibility in the job, their morale, morale of colleagues, positive and negative aspects of their jobs, how they see themselves, what training and development they have had and what training they perceive that they need. Each individual completes a psychometric profile and a Belbin self-assessment test.

Ken: *'When we've done the profiles for all the team, we write the programme.'* The team leadership and development programme devised for each group of people is not reinvented from scratch every time, but is considerably modified to suit the needs of the new team undergoing training. Ken: *'We've never run the same course twice, we are constantly evolving. The programme does not all take place in one weekend.'* For one team the research on individuals was carried out in May, classroom modules were completed in July, the outdoor programme in August and the final debriefing session in September.

Many people are afraid of outdoor training courses. Ken: *'We really have to reassure them that they're not going to die.'* Mick: *'The most dangerous thing they do over the weekend is drive home.'* The difficulty of the outdoor activities is altered according to people's abilities. Win says: *'We move the goal posts as we're going through the programme, if a team is not coping with a situation, then we make it easier. If a group are doing everything well and in good time, then we make the programme more difficult for them. We're aware of people's limitations.'*

Mick: *'We are fairly hard, we like them to bivouac out. If we bring them indoors because it has started to rain, the learning curve stops.'* However, Ken adds: *'The environment of rapid change, uncertainty and ambiguity is the same sort of thing as they get in business. Some hardship and discomfort really bonds people well. They remember the outside activities for life, it helps them recall the theoretical classroom bits, and helps the key issue which is of transferability of experiences back to actions in the workplace.'* John: *'We appreciate that we all have different personalities and there are some things that you shouldn't expect everyone to be able to do.'* Ken: *'If we've got someone who is unfit we'll find them a logistical role so that they remain part of the team. We might give them responsibility for the food or being a guide for the rest of the team. For example, someone not able to do hill walking may be taken to a position by a vehicle and have to guide the rest of their team with the use of a CB radio and a torch in the darkness.'*

Teams may have to compete with each other. John explains: *'It gives them something to compare themselves against.'* In smaller groups such as five or six people, everyone gets involved. *'In larger groups there are too many opportunities for the quieter ones to stand out and not contribute,'* says John. Sometimes the team has to cope with only one group to train. *'Sometimes if you've only got a smallish group of people you can put time pressures on them. Time is the most precious resource in business. Often in business people waste time and don't fulfil their objectives.'*

Getting people to work as a cohesive team within one weekend is difficult. Ken: *'To build a team takes two to five years. All we do is scratch the surface and help them become more aware of themselves and each other.'* John: *'It's not uncommon for the team to fragment off because of the actions of one or two people. The biggest problems occur when someone is completely dominant and believes they're never wrong.'*

Going through the developmental stages of forming, storming, norming and performing is important on the outdoor training course. Ken: *'When they are tired it helps storming. If they know they can go home at five o'clock it's difficult to get them storming; having them together for 48 hours continually seems to encourage them to get issues off their chests.'* Some groups get along so well together that they do not automatically go through the storming stage. Win: *'You set them a problem that you know they're not going to be able to solve to get them storming.'*

The storming stage changes relationships. Ken: *'I can speak to my team and tell them in an assertive manner things that they might not like. Going through the storming stage gets rid of aggressive and submissive behaviour. I have the right to say what I feel and I have the right to disagree, and so do they. Hidden agendas are released.'*

Ken feels that the Belbin roles are right 90 per cent of the time. *'If they disagree and say "I'm not like that at all", I just ask the rest of their team and they usually agree that the Belbin profile is about right.'* John: *'Once the activities are done, people can see that Belbin seems to work and that they do have fairly set roles. Some people are not natural team players – roles like the Shapers, the Resource investigators. The Shapers are prone to provocation and short bursts of temper. They feel that they've done their bit when they've thought of the ideas, and the Resource investigators feel the same when they have made the contacts.'*

The team encourage their groups to go through definite steps when attempting to complete a task: deciding objectives, planning, executing the task, reviewing and amending. Ken: *'This can be used for anything in life, from business problems to wallpapering the kitchen. All the tasks have a time limit as in business, people have to work together as in business, they need clear objectives as in business and when they've done the task they have to amend it – just like in business.'*

The team feel that they have really succeeded in their courses when people can transfer what they've learnt to their own jobs. Ken: *'The biggest issue is transferability. A delegate we had who thought he couldn't abseil managed to do it. He was emotional at the bottom and his team gathered round in support and congratulated him and gave him a cup of tea. He phoned me sometime later and said that he'd had to do something very difficult at work and beforehand he felt just exactly the same as when he had had to abseil. He knew he'd got through that and so it helped him at work.'*

Win: *'Life can get to be one big rut and for people to come out and do something they didn't want to do to start with means that they realise how easy it is for them to get out of that rut. What used to be a major problem now seems easy. Sometimes, as people, we blow trivial problems out of perspective.'* Ken believes that people are better at finding solutions to problems at work after they've been on an outdoor development course. *'They know that there's got to be a way out, so they now think "Let's find it".'*

Ken: *'People use about 30 per cent of their potential in life and if we can get it up to 31 per cent, we've succeeded.'* Win: *'They also realise their colleagues go through the same problems at work and they're not alone. They're aware by the end of the course that they've become complacent.'* Mick: *'They learn a lot about each other. We can possibly change people's outlook on work related matters and awareness. They find strengths and weaknesses in themselves and their colleagues that they hadn't known about before and they can take account of them.'* Ken: *'We cannot change anybody, what we do is provide an environment in which they question whether they need to change. One word is important – awareness – we raise their awareness.'*

After the activities the debriefing session is short, the main debrief comes four to six weeks after the programme. Ken: *'We find it's far more meaningful. People often have questions in the mini debrief, which if left for the main debrief just answer themselves.'* Win: *'You cannot take people up the hills and give them feedback immediately afterwards. Real meanings come from their hearts and minds.'*

One method of continuing the programme and ensuring actions are taken is for teams continue to meet at work for one hour per month in work time. At each meeting the team should address two questions:

1 How have we improved things since last month's meeting?
2 What are we going to do to improve things before next month's meeting?

Ken says that these meetings are 'holy meetings', they should always be the same time each month and no-one should be allowed to miss more than two consecutive meetings. There is no end to the process. Leadership Resources often go back to the company and do refresher courses to help integrate new members of staff into the team. This helps perpetuate continuous improvement.

John's idea of a cohesive team who work well together is: *'No one individual personality is too extreme, they will listen to each other – they can go too far the other way and spend so much time listening to one another that nothing gets done. They should be able to pick out the salient points quickly, be reasonably succinct, give themselves time to achieve the end. They should have the ability to learn from mistakes and put what they've learnt into practice the next time.'*

John Dodd's recipe for an effective team the team must:

1 share agreed goals, have clear objectives, common values and philosophy;

2 communicate openly and freely with each other;

3 have defined procedures for delegating, decision making and holding meetings;

4 review progress on route to objectives. Review processes used as well as tasks;

5 relate to other teams and groups;

6 demonstrate trust and support for each other;

7 handle conflict in a constructive and objective manner;

8 utilise leadership skills depending on members strengths. Recognise weaknesses. Reflect common aims;

9 search for opportunities to develop members continually.

Internal influences on teams

Teams are established to achieve particular goals. The goals set are the reason for the creation of the teams. The success of the team will depend upon:

◆ achieving the goal

◆ the resources required

◆ the time taken.

The effectiveness of the team will be influenced by internal and external factors. These factors help to determine the dynamics of the group. Internal factors include:

Individual differences

The personalities of individual group members will influence group effectiveness. A group comprising of quiet introverts may work very well together, a new member who is extrovert and dominating will change work patterns considerably. If most group members are confident and laid back, they will not worry about details which a more nervous group member may find a great source of anxiety. Managers often select new recruits to the organisation similar in nature to of skills and abilities, the team will operate more effectively and efficiently because these people will complement one another. The strengths of one person may support another's weakness.

Roles

Roles are patterns of behaviour which people expect individuals to perform. The behaviour reflects that person's position or function in society. We have expectations of how people should behave. There are some roles, such as supervisors, of which people expect different behaviours. The supervisor may have a manager who expects the supervisor to be a mentor and a coach, whereas the supervisor's subordinates may expect him or her to be someone who checks their work. At work a person usually performs more than one role; a store supervisor may also be the union representative as well as being an active member of the company's sports and social club.

Those group members who have too many roles to perform may suffer from *role overload*. The junior manager who has both her boss and her subordinates in the same group may face *role conflict* because she is unsure how to behave within the group. Conversely, *role underload* is when those individuals feel devalued because they are not performing the role they think they are capable of carrying out or because they don't have sufficient work to do. A person who has been passed over for promotion may feel rejected and their performance may deteriorate.

External influences on teams

Teams and work groups are one small group within the larger group, the organisation. Teams behave differently, according to the influences of the larger organisation to which they belong.

Business strategy

Strategy is the means for attaining the organisation's goals. Goals such as increased profits may be reached by such strategies as improving quality, increasing sales, reducing costs or growth. The strategy that an organisation is pursuing will influence the power and resources available to various work groups. An organisation that is selling off or closing down parts of its business will have fewer resources available to allocate to work groups and this will result in increased anxiety among team members, and the potential for conflict between groups competing for resources.

Authority structures

Organisations have authority structures that define who reports to whom, who makes the decisions and what decisions people are allowed to make. Work groups may be placed in different parts of the hierarchy, some groups may consist entirely

themselves to support the manager's own attitudes and beliefs. This cosy stabi
is often desirable as it leads to harmony within the group, but the group may]
the stimulus of conflict.

Age and gender also affect the work of a group. Groups who are used to wor}
as single sex groups will often reject a new member of the opposite sex. Simi]
groups with members all of a similar age will not feel comfortable with a
member who is much older or younger than themselves.

Education, experience and training

Group members' values and beliefs will be affected by their education, expe
and training. A well educated team may have a wider perspective on thei
they may be more flexible and creative than less well educated team me
Those team members who are well trained and experienced will have higl
of skill and knowledge of problems and solutions which have occurred in {
in the completion of specific tasks.

Attitudes and beliefs

People who have the same attitudes, values and beliefs find it easy to fo|
teams. The development of group norms fosters the development c
attitudes and beliefs. It seems that similarity promotes harmony and sa|
If others behave in the same way as ourselves, this reinforces our ow|
and view of self.

Motivation for work

Those groups whose members are all committed to the task will be |
effective than where there are differing motivations. For example, so
primarily work to pay their household bills and obtain money to li|
little interest in the job; whereas other members of their team may ge
satisfaction and accomplishment from feeling that they have compl<
The latter person will feel frustrated by the indifferent attitude of th

Career aspirations

Group members who are ambitious may wish to gain recogn
individual contribution to the work of their team and seek lea
group. They may engage in politicking behind the scenes to
reputation which could be to the detriment of the group.

Individual members' skill and expertise

The strength of the team will be dependent upon the individuals
team. Each individual will bring something unique to the tea|
able to complement other team members. Where individuals h

of directors while others consist of shopfloor workers. Teams may be made up of people from various levels of the hierarchy and certain members will have greater authority than others. The amount of authority that individuals and the group as a whole have will affect the way the group work. Those groups containing senior managers will be able to take decisions during their meetings, whereas groups containing lower level personnel may have to wait for the permission of their manager or senior management before they can put their ideas into practice.

Formal regulations

Organisations create rules to regulate employee behaviour. People working in organisations with very few rules will be able to use their discretion as to how they act, this will result in people behaving in very different ways. Those organisations with many regulations may impose rules or put their employees through stringent training courses in order to ensure that their behaviour is consistent and predictable. McDonald's ensure that their customers receive the same service at every branch. This is achieved by training employees to behave in a certain way.

Resources

Resources include money, buildings and equipment. Some organisations have sufficient money to equip their employees with modern high quality tools and machinery. They can afford to send their staff on training courses, allow them time during working hours to meet and discuss work related problems as a team, they can also reward their employees well in terms of salary and fringe benefits. Other organisations have very limited resources and can give little to their employees. The amount of resources available to a work group will affect its performance. Also, the allocation of different resources to different work groups may cause conflict and intergroup rivalries within an organisation.

Personnel selection

Recruitment of group members is rarely done according to whether they will fit in with the rest of the group or not but done on the basis of technical skill. The staff responsible for recruitment will be looking for people who can perform certain tasks such as operating computer systems. Their choices determine the kinds of people who will be in the organisation's work groups. Ideally, groups should undertake the recruitment and selection of new team members themselves.

Performance evaluation and reward system

It is possible to evaluate the performance of employees and reward employees in the following ways:

◆ as an individual
◆ as a group
◆ both as an individual and as a group member.

Organisations that evaluate and reward employees on an individual basis only, and yet expect them to work as groups, are not encouraging the development of team spirit or cohesive work groups. Companies such as Rolls-Royce Motor Cars encourage teams to develop ideas by allowing them time at work to meet and discuss solutions to problems. Those companies who also have Suggestion Boxes for employees to earn money from their ideas as individuals are not giving their wholehearted backing to the teamwork ideal. Few firms have performance appraisal systems for groups, but many do have group bonus schemes so that the whole team can benefit financially from working well together. The music store HMV (UK) Ltd gives a group bonus to all the staff in a store if they achieve sales above their target level in one week.

Organisational culture

Every organisation has a unique way of doing things which is their organisational culture. New employees soon learn what is acceptable to wear to work, whether rules are rigidly enforced, what kind of behaviours may get them into trouble and which are likely to be overlooked. A group's way of working will be strongly affected by the organisational culture. A culture which values teamwork and takes groups very seriously will encourage teams to recruit and select new members, will reward the whole group, promote the whole group, relocate the group together if they need to move, and dispense with individual job titles and salary grades.

Physical worksetting

The layout of the group's office or workstation is important for group interaction. If one or more group members are not located near the others, the work of the group will be affected. Teamwork done on an informal basis may often not include those working at a distance and sub-groups will tend to form of those group members who interact most frequently.

CASE STUDY 3.4

Iowa–Illinois Gas and Electric Company

This small investor-owned natural gas and electricity company is in the midst of preparations for a merger with a similar company. Iowa–Illinois Gas and Electric Company had just over 1300 employees and the merged companies will have 4000 workers. David Levy is Vice President of Human Resources and Corporate Services.

David: *'It is a happy merger because it is a merger of equals. Both organisations will no longer exist but the investors will own some percentage of the new corporation, according to what assets they owned when they came to the table. Our shareholders will end up owning something like 44 per cent of the new company.'*

The company is very engineering-biased and David feels that this has not encouraged them to make use of teamwork: *'We have discovered the drawbacks over the years of being very engineering orientated. The engineering stereotype is unfortunately true, we are very conservative in our thinking and not terribly creative, and often have difficulties in communication skills – the writing and speaking skills.'*

A US Army installation – The Rock Island Arsenal is a couple of miles away from the company and several employees at the gas and electric company have previously worked at this military installation. As a result, David feels that Iowa–Illinois Gas and Electric Company is particularly regimented and rigidly structured: *'Its not just the influence of the engineers, but as it turns out we have a history of having a military influence. So with the combination of engineers' direct logical view of the world and the military influence, we have become a command and control organisation. It makes it very difficult for us to move into teamwork.'*

The company's management believes strongly in the power of individuals rather than teams. Individual initiative has always been rewarded. David admits: *'Decisions are not made low down enough in the organisation, any teamwork effort has been limited to small departments.'* And yet after many years of believing that they did not subscribe to teamwork of any sort, the senior managers of the Iowa-Illinois Gas and Electric Company were surprised at how strongly they did work as a team when faced with the totally different ways of working of their merger partners.

David explains: *'Our senior management works as a team and it is stronger than we admit. We have discovered this more and more through the merger process. As we learn more about our partner we are finding major differences – their management is physically scattered in various locations and we are constantly amazed at the lack of communication which results.'* At the Iowa–Illinois Gas and Electric Company, five of the six Vice Presidents and the Chief Executive are on the same floor of their building. The other Vice President is one floor up. *'We do spend a lot of time interacting, more than we ever realised until we got into this merger and we saw how two companies which should have been so alike have such different cultures. They don't have a sense of the team at their top level. They are still very much isolated and operate as independent functions and departments. We are very much a team at the top level. We meet very regularly. We schedule a meeting once a week, but it probably runs every other week. There is no formal agenda, it's usually that a particular subject may be crucial at the time of the meeting and we will spend all of our time on that topic. Otherwise it's more of reporting of significant issues which are of interest to the others. Most of our communication takes place when one of us is walking past another's office and we will drop in and talk for half an hour.'*

The merger partners do not have these informal drop-in talks. The senior management team of the Iowa–Illinois Gas and Electric company are concerned that their teamwork will suffer after the merger. David is also worried: *'The merger will cause us to be more scattered over a larger geographical area and to be based in three different locations. In one city we will be located in three buildings on different floors. From the central location we will have managers 150 miles away both east and west. We will have video link connections, although its still not as good as someone stopping by your office.'*

CASE STUDY cont

David sees people working together in one form or another to be very important for the future: *'There is more competition which means we will have to act more like the rest of American industry. We will have to become much more efficient and human resource management will be more important. Our role is to coach people and then let go, we have to learn how to give people a broad base of skills so that they can work in teams or networks.*

Organisation charts are going to disappear and the organisation will be more of a network of connections between people. The network is already there, we do not draw them on paper, it is too complex. We have to allow people to make decisions.'

At present when mistakes are made David feels that there is a tendency to take the decision up to the next level of the hierarchy and say, 'Next time you do that, let me see it first.' David *'That just keeps ratcheting it up, the higher levels are making the wrong sort of decisions; top management should be making strategy decisions, not day-to-day decisions. What should be said is, "You made a mistake, here is where you went wrong, we don't expect that mistake to happen again. If you need some training we will help you with that."*

We plan, study and analyse, so in the end result we don't expect too many mistakes. We have worked over the last five years to reduce that cycle and do less planning. Now we make a decision and modify as we go along. Our merger partner is where we were five years ago, they plan to death, they study forever, they cannot move any faster than they do at the moment. Speed will be one of those characteristics of the future.'

Fig 3.16 David Levy, Vice President, Human Resources and Corporate Services, Iowa–Illinois Gas and Electric Company, USA

DISCUSSION QUESTIONS 3.7

1 Why didn't the Iowa–Illinois Gas and Electric Company senior management team notice that they worked very strongly as a team?

2 What difficulties will the merger bring to the operation of the senior management team?

3 What conditions does David Levy identify as making teamwork easier?

4 How do the Iowa–Illinois Gas and Electric Company senior management team manage to implement their decisions much more quickly than their merger partner?

5 How does David Levy see the future of teamwork?

Performance at work

4

From reading this chapter you will learn about performance at work, including:

1   the learning organisation;

2   coaching skills;

3   training and development;

4   employee and management development;
5   counselling;

6   discipline; and

7   monitoring and reporting individual and group performance.

The learning organisation

For individual and group performance at work to be enhanced, people in organisations need to be learning all the time. The idea of the Learning Organisation is that an environment is created where behaviour which contributes to continuous improvement is encouraged. Learning happens all the time and is not just about sending people on courses or organising training. A learning organisation is one in which people share creative ideas and help one another by building on those ideas, implementing them and learning from them whether they succeed or fail. Behaviour that prevents continuous improvement includes things such as covering up mistakes, blaming, being deferential to senior people, acquiescing, being cautious, looking busy and filtering bad news.

Peter Honey had identified several examples of 'wanted behaviours' for a learning organisation, these can vary according to the needs of the organisation, 'wanted behaviour' is:

◆ asking questions

◆ suggesting ideas

◆ exploring alternatives

◆ taking risks/experimenting

◆ being open about the present situation

◆ converting mistakes into learning

◆ reflecting and reviewing

◆ talking about learning

◆ taking responsibility for own learning and development

◆ admitting inadequacies and mistakes.

These behaviours need to be 'triggered' by such means as inviting questions, seeking ideas, asking people how things could be done differently, managers taking action themselves and groups evaluating how their projects are going. It is also important to have reinforcers for the desired behaviours, so that people will feel motivated to continue questioning, coming up with ideas, etc. Honey believes that managers need to go to great lengths to ensure that people take continuous improvement seriously. When people support one another and take responsibility for their own learning, everyone in the organisation can learn and move forward.

 # Coaching skills

Coaching involves two or more people sitting down together to discuss situations and events which have taken place during an individual's recent experiences at work and analysing how these were handled and how similar situations could be dealt with more effectively on future occasions. Coaching transfers skills and knowledge from one person to another in an on-the-job setting, so that the work experience of the coach is used to advise and guide the individual being coached. The coaching activity aims at helping the individual review the consequences of different actions and behaviour and evaluate which option would be like to be the most relevant and effective. It also means influencing the learner's personal development, for example, their confidence and motivation. Mentoring is for the guidance of new members of staff, whereas coaching can take place at any time during an individual's career. Coaching is intended to assist individuals function more effectively.

One-to-one coaching is a powerful learning model. It begins where skills based training ends and helps individuals to incorporate formal learnt knowledge into day-to-day work and management situations. The individual being coached is in an actively demanding situation with their coach which requires them to analyse themselves and practise greater self-awareness. The coach professionally assists the career development of another individual, outside the normal manager/subordinate relationship. The coaching relationship does not necessarily provide solutions to all problems, but provides a space for discussion and feedback on issues such as people management, interpersonal skills, behaviour patterns, assertiveness and time management. Successes and failures can be evaluated in a safe environment. Through coaching an organisation can meet skill shortages, discuss dips in performance and support employees in dealing with challenging situations, all at short notice.

Effective coaches

Effective coaches are usually those who get satisfaction from the success of others and who give time to the coaching role. Giving people coaching responsibilities can support their development; either nurturing management potential through small scale one-to-one assignments, or by providing added job satisfaction to managers who feel that they are stuck in their present jobs. A coach is a confidential advisor and sounding board, accustomed to identifying areas for individual improvement and to developing positive and effective approaches to management, organisational and change problems, many of which can be controversial.

Managers need to be developed so that they have the coaching skills they will need to bring out the best in people, and improve company performance. Coaches need to develop skills such as flexibility and the ability to appreciate the perceptions of others. People are not born mentors or coaches. Mentors and coaches must have excellent communication skills including the skills to question, to listen, to reformulate, to challenge and to provide feedback. Coaches need to be able to:

◆ build rapport

◆ diagnose need

◆ achieve an outcome

◆ test the solutions reached.

Some common uses for coaching:

◆ *when someone is new to a job or project,* e.g. a young manager who is promoted to the head of a team can gain guidance and support from the coaching relationship.

◆ *to learn from success,* e.g. when a key sale has just been closed or a project successfully completed, the factors contributing to success can be identified.

◆ *to learn from mistakes,* e.g. when a person's department is not meeting its targets, or a customer has been lost.

◆ *when someone has a specific problem,* e.g. if a senior person's management style is seen as insensitive.

Building rapport

Coaching can also be beneficial in forging a relationship between a senior employee and a more junior member of staff. The building of relationships can help break down hierarchies, increase communication and generate innovative ideas.

Non-verbal communication is vital to building rapport. It can account for between 75 per cent and 95 per cent of the meaning when a person is communicating. Matching, or mimicking, the other person's posture, gestures and tone of voice helps to establish rapport. Once learned, this technique can enable people to avoid misunderstandings and overcome barriers to agreement. The meaning of any communication is the result achieved, therefore coaches need to learn ways to adjust their behaviour to get the results they want.

To diagnose need

The professional coaching environment ensures personal and corporate goals are articulated and planned. Individuals can combine assessing how to handle situations and change with the opportunity to improve continuously their own effectiveness. The coach needs to:

◆ understand the individual's present situation in order to lead someone to their desired future result

◆ view the situation almost as an outsider to see the intentions lying behind a person's behaviour.

The coach can then clarify his or her understanding and lead the person towards ways of overcoming difficulties by asking precise questions. For example, if someone complains 'She thinks my work is no good', the coach could respond by asking 'How do you know she thinks that?' to get at the real facts of the situation.

To achieve an outcome

'Stepping down'

Working with outcomes is a vital area. In this part of the process the coach helps the person become clearer about his or her own objectives. While many people do have plans for their career and their future in the organisation, others are unsure of what they want and what they are capable of achieving. If a person comes to a coach with a big goal, such as wanting to be the best salesperson in the company, the coach can help him or her to 'step down' from this outcome. For example, the coach might ask 'What stops you from reaching that goal?' They might then discuss how these obstacles can be overcome. From these sorts of questions the coach encourages the person to imagine the future steps that need to be taken in order eventually to achieve the goal.

'Stepping up'

On the other hand, if a person complains to a coach about having to do a seemingly pointless task, like tackling a big pile of paperwork, the coach can help in the process of 'stepping up'. This time, the question would be 'If you did that job, what would it do for you?' the person might reply along the lines of feeling better, satisfying others, and these in turn can be 'stepped up' ('If you achieved that, what would it do for you?') until the task is identified as a worthwhile step in the achievement of a challenging goal.

Testing solutions

The coach learns to help a person to test any solution reached in the coaching session and, from training in reading non-verbal behaviour, the coach is able to search for signs of doubt or objections, when the imaginary future is being created. New behaviours and solutions to problems can be tried out in the workplace and discussed and analysed with the coach in the coaching session.

The individual will benefit from the reflection, feedback and counselling which the relationship with their coach provides. The learning process is speeded up when compared to an individual who is testing out new behaviours alone and has no-one to talk to about whether they are the right behaviours. When solutions have been tested, modifications can then be made to the action plan agreed between the individual and their coach.

Types of development relationship

Robin Evenden has identified three types of development relationship which can be likened to the leadership styles of autocrat, democrat and laissez faire. The three types are Usurper, Sharer and Abdicator. The Usurper takes an autocratic approach to the coaching relationship and directs the individual as to how to behave. The Sharer is more democratic and shares the decision-making process with the individual so that they might together decide on the best course of action in the various situations under discussion. The Abdicator adopts a laissez faire leadership style and participates very little in the individual's learning. Each type of relationship is appropriate for learners with different experience in the job, confidence and learning skills (see Fig 4.1 below).

	Usurper	Sharer	Abdicator
Values and behaviour of the manager	'Your needs are . . .' 'This is good for you' 'My experience is . . .' 'This is what you do . . .' 'My way – no risk . . .'	'Let's discuss your needs' 'What is important?' 'What is our experience?' 'How should it be done?' 'Try it out . . .'	'What needs?' 'Important?' 'Experience?' 'Do what?' 'Risk!'
Appropriateness for which learners? In terms of experience, confidence and learning skills?	Low	Average	High
Dependence and security	High	Independent and secure	Very low
Outcomes	Fits some who are new to the job	Fits most learners	Fits self-directed learners
	May reinforce dependence, insecurity, low confidence, etc.	Integrates organisational and individual needs	Will it be what the organisation wants?

Fig 4.1 Three different types of development relationship in coaching

Training and development

Training is the process of learning a skill or skills related to a job. The definition according to the Manpower Services Commission is:

> **'A planned process to modify attitude, knowledge or skill behaviour through learning experience to achieve effective performance in an activity or range of activities.'**

Development is a more generalised type of learning and does not involve job-specific skills. Taking an HND or HNC course or enrolling for evening classes to improve your assertiveness would count as development. Organisations may be interested in developing their workforce so that they are more flexible in the tasks they are able to take on and the problems they are able to solve. This equips the firm with a workforce better able to respond to changes in the future and to contribute to the organisation in the present.

Training and the labour market

The labour force (which includes the unemployed, as well as those in work) stood at 27.8 million in 1995. The average age of the labour force is rising and women are taking up an increasing proportion of the workforce. The workforce is also becoming more qualified. In 1995, 79 per cent had some qualifications (60 per cent in 1985) and 20 per cent had higher qualifications, such as degrees or HNDs (13 per cent in 1985).

Yet while many employers are doing a considerable amount of training, they do not usually train all employees and some employers do not train any employees at all. A third of employees have never been offered training by their current employer.

Some training is intended to meet needs, while other types of training represents planning for the future, building a more flexible and competitive workforce for the firm. The Department for Education and Employment's research on employers shows that they provide a mixture of these two reasons for training their employees:

◆ immediate needs training: 81 per cent provided health and safety training and 49 per cent induction training.

◆ future needs training: 60 per cent provided management and 53 per cent supervisory training, and almost two out of three (64 per cent) provided training on new technology.

The demand for new skills is in occupations which are growing. However, even where jobs are in decline there is still a need for newly qualified entrants because of job changes and retirements.

The service industries saw major growth in the 1980s, and there are now three million more jobs in service industries and 1.4 million fewer in manufacturing compared with 1981. By 1994, less than 30 per cent of employment is in manufacturing, primary and construction industries.

A shift of employment towards the managerial, professional and technical occupations is taking place, and is projected to continue. In 1994 these high level occupations accounted for about 36 per cent of total employment, and by the year 2001 they are projected to account for almost two in every five jobs (39 per cent).

Training is disproportionately concentrated on:

◆ those already in high level jobs

◆ those already well-qualified

◆ those in particular industries

◆ those aged in their twenties.

People working in establishments with 25 or more employees are up to four times more likely to receive training than those in smaller establishments. Women, on the whole receive training as frequently as men, but tend to have less time devoted to it. Some organisations employ highly skilled and well trained workers without actually doing any training themselves. This is because they may poach them from other firms, for example, by offering greater rewards than the firms who have originally provided the training.

In addition to the growth in the number of higher skilled jobs, the general skills needed in most jobs is growing. In 1995, almost three out of four (71 per cent) of employers reported that the amount of skills needed by their employees was increasing. The increase in skill demands within jobs is not restricted to specialist skills in specific jobs. New work organisation, the introduction of new technology, greater emphasis on quality, innovation, and customer care are leading to jobs which demand a wider range of skills.

The need for training and development

There are many advantages to organisations of having a well trained workforce. Advantages include:

1 *Meeting strategic aims.* Corporate strategy is a way of achieving organisational objectives. This may include improving customer service, improving quality, increasing productivity or reducing waste. These strategies can be implemented by training the workers in the appropriate techniques. The workforce who can contribute to the achievement of organisational objectives will provide a competitive advantage to their organisation.

2 *Meeting the challenge of change.* The trained workforce will be more flexible in their approach to changes in product, production methods, new working practices and the restructuring of the organisation. Employees who are slow to accept change and resist management's efforts to compete in the market may cause productivity and organisational effectiveness to fall.

3 *Integration of new employees into the organisation.* New recruits need to be introduced to the organisation and its ways of working, as well as to their actual job. They therefore often need both induction training and job-specific training.

4 *Motivation of employees.* Training and development activities are expensive and time consuming for an organisation to undertake. If management are prepared to spend the time and money ensuring that the workforce is well trained this communicates to the employees that they care about the people who work for them.

Types of training

Training methods are generally divided into 'on-the-job' and 'off-the-job' training. Both methods are effective for meeting different requirements.

On-the-job training

This is the most common type of training and can range from informal arrangements whereby an experienced employee demonstrates their job to the new recruit to organised and highly structured training packages for the new recruit. The observation of the experienced employee is often referred to as 'Sitting by Nellie' and many workers still learn their jobs in this manner. Although this method appears to be the least expensive form of training, often 'Nellie' is not usually trained herself in the skills and methods of training others. The new recruit may pick up Nellie's bad habits or take longer than necessary to understand the explanations. In some organisations this approach is used for all training when other methods might prove to be more effective.

It can be more successful to use a senior or experienced worker who has been trained as a trainer. The move towards multi-skilling and autonomous teams has encouraged organisations to train more workers to become trainers so that they can pass on their skills to others.

Mentoring

A senior or experienced employee takes charge of the training and development of a new employee. This is a much closer relationship than the trainer/new recruit relationship as the trainer is acting as an adviser and protector to the trainee.

Shadowing and job rotation

This method usually aims to give trainee managers knowledge of the whole organisation by giving them experience of working in different departments. Often, not every department can be included in the training programme as greater understanding is provided by a longer placement than many short placements. The trainee may be allowed to follow specific managers and observe them working, or they may be given special projects or tasks to complete for the departmental manager which enables them to get a good insight into the department. Rolls-Royce's training programme for potential managers allows the trainees to have some choice in the department to which they are finally attached and this decision is aided by the trainee's experience gained during the training programme.

Another version of training is job rotation which became popular in the 1970s to help relieve boredom and raise the productivity of shopfloor workers. It can be a good learning experience for workers as they gain understanding of the work of their colleagues and become multi-skilled in the process.

Off-the-job training

Off-the-job training is sometimes necessary to get people away from the work environment to a place where interruptions are eliminated. This enables the trainer to study theoretical information or be exposed to new and innovative ideas. The study of theory enables the trainee to take a different perspective on their work situation and re-evaluate what they already know.

Some off-the-job training is done in-house by organisations with their own training school. Trainees are trained at work, but away from their workstation. This enables the trainer to give instructions away from noise and distractions and to implement activities such as discussion and role plays for training. This type of training is very organisation-specific, in that it often does not apply to other jobs in other firms. The organisation's culture (the way things are done and the type of attitudes held by staff) is transmitted in these training sessions.

Off-the-job training may involve courses conducted off-site. Some courses may be very specific, for example, to develop teamwork or negotiating skills, while others develop the individual and improve his or her general level of education, such as HNC or part-time degree courses. Some organisations are reluctant to finance these types of courses as it makes the individual more marketable as far as them finding another job elsewhere is concerned.

Induction training

This is the most important first step in the training of new employees. New employees often experience an 'induction crisis' as their new work environment is often perceived by the new recruit as perplexing and even frightening. An unwelcoming reception by the existing staff may make the new recruit feel that it was a mistake to begin work there.

Many organisations try to reduce uncertainty by presenting their new employees with lots of information which can result in the induction trainers feeling that they have carried out their responsibilities towards the new recruits, and the new recruits feeling totally confused and blaming themselves for not being able to take in all the information. The induction programme should be planned around the needs of the new employee and the imparting of information should be given at designated times spaced over the first few weeks or months of employment. Explanations of details such as customer or supplier links will be much more meaningful to the new employee when they have several weeks of experience of working in the organisation. The intensive induction course can result in the new recruit feeling 'lectured at' and dissatisfied with their initial treatment in their new job. New employees often want to have a go at the job to see if they can do it. An induction spread over a greater period of time gives variety and a break from the job. The various stages of the programme need not be carried out in the training school with the same trainers but can be organised so that the new employee's own manager or team leader goes through specified information.

CASE STUDY 4.1

Customer service training at Asda stores

Asda Stores in Wolstanton, Staffordshire is a large modern superstore and has 450 employees, the majority of whom work part-time. The store has sales of around £700 000 per week with between 20 000 and 25 000 customers each week.

Fig 4.2 Lisa Statham, Deputy Customer Services Manager, Asda Stores, Wolstanton

Customer services

Lisa Statham is Deputy Customer Services Manager at the store: *'I would say that in the last three and a half years Asda has changed a lot in its attitude towards customers and the type of customer service that we give. Because of the intense competition between supermarkets we've tried to do something different. The Chief Executive, Archie Norman, has changed the organisation around with the main emphasis on value and fresh food. He has tried the American way of looking at customer service: the customer is always right. We give a bit extra, our people are helpful and friendly and go out of their way to help customers. We are, without doubt, progressing towards world class customer service. It's interesting to see how other countries develop their customer service and to learn from them. It makes us different from the competition to have such good customer service. We've got more competitive prices, but also when customers enter the store with a problem, a query or complaint and you deal with that efficiently, then they'll want to come back. People are very good at passing on your bad qualities rather than your good qualities. Our staff have got more responsibility and are able to deal with customers' problems on a one-to-one basis, people tell their neighbours, friends and family that they've received a very good service here. We have Customer Suggestion boxes in which customers can recommend changes in the store or products. We get back to those people to acknowledge their suggestion and let them know what we can do. Our policy is good customer service, no excuses. If customers don't like a product, they can bring it back and get a refund or get it exchanged. There's no quibble, no passing them on to someone else, they get it done officially and professionally at the desk. We don't keep the customer waiting.'*

As well as efficient staff interactions with the customer, customer services include:

◆ Concession shops to improve the range of services offered under one roof. At Wolstanton these include: a chemist, newsagency, Thorntons Chocolates, a flower shop, hairdressers, a travel agent, jewellers and a 30-minute photographic processing shop.

◆ Customer Service Desk, exchange service, National Lottery facility, Royal Mail post box, telephone, toilets with baby changing room, customer information board – customers can advertise items for sale on postcards free of charge, trollies with seats for toddlers or babies, mother and toddler parking, Big

Shopper Service which includes bag packing and taking the shopping to the customer's car, umbrella service, jump leads for customers whose cars have flat batteries, Asda Club Card which enables customers to choose gifts from a GUS catalogue according to the number of points they have accumulated one point is allocated for every £1 spent in the store, free bus service, bank cash points, cheque cashing facilities at Customer Service Desk, in-store events such as magicians, jugglers, balloons, face-painters and bouncy castle, cafeteria, and a passport photograph booth.

'We try and cater for children as much as for parents. If we keep the children happy, then the parents feel free to do their shopping and hopefully those children will become our customers of the future. The First Aisle Greeter says 'Hello' to people, gives leaflets out and tells people what the star buys are. Its important to have a greeter at the entrance because it provides a friendly atmosphere as soon as customers walk in.'

Recruitment

Lisa: *'We know how many people we need to staff the store because we also have Colleague Scheduling which involves timing the completion of a particular task, from this the number of colleagues needed is calculated and we know there will always be at least one person available on each department. Lunch breaks and collecting stock is covered so that there is always someone available for the customer to ask if they have a question.*

To have good customer service we need the right sort of people. It's very important to recruit people who are open and friendly and have the potential to work well as part of a team. We hold group interviews to see how people work together and how open and friendly they are. They have to introduce each other and sell each other by telling everyone about their partner's good points. They have to work as a team to make something such as an Asda uniform or a cornflake box. We give them a bin liner, tissues, Sellotape and a pair of scissors so that they can make a uniform together and we see how they work together and what sort of ideas they come up with. We can see who would be the leaders and who would be the followers, whether they share ideas with each other rather than saying "we'll do this", how they interact with people. We bring them down into the store and have them doing various activities such as bag packing or greeting people so that we can find out whether they listen to people's views, whether they ask customers questions, whether they say hello. Some people might find the interview situation unreal and would be uncomfortable behaving as they normally would. If you give them a real life situation, you can assess how they get on with people, how open they are, whether they are good listeners and how they interact.

We tell them about the company and take them to the department they want to work in and show them what goes on in that department. When they've gone we assess them according to our criteria for customer service. The criteria include such things as the asking of questions, eye contact with people, listening skills and whether they are good at mixing. If they do well on that they are invited back to a second interview which is individual and very informal. We discuss what hours and days they would like to work, we'll take them downstairs again and show them where they'll work.'

CASE
STUDY

cont
Induction training

Induction training takes place the week before employment starts. The new recruit attends a four hour induction session to learn more about the company; this includes talks and videos.

On-the-job training

The trainee is taken to their place of work and is met by the Team Trainer (team leader). There are many different tasks associated with checkout work, and for new checkout operators, the trainer demonstrates how a checkout works and explains the procedure for scanning, taking cheques and credit cards, dealing with cash, using the intercom and the cash register. The new trainee will then be given a basket of shopping to process and scan so that they get their first practice of operating the checkout. The Team Trainer then explains the monitoring system Asda uses which involves 'mystery' shoppers employed by Asda who report on the customer service they receive when visiting the Wolstanton store. These weekly shoppers are employed by Asda. Monthly 'mystery' shoppers also visit the store and these work for a separate company who are engaged in monitoring Asda's customer service. The one-to-one practice sessions on the checkouts for new part-time staff will last for 11 or 12 weeks. They will go onto a checkout to serve customers within four to six weeks of the training period starting.

Lisa: *'We don't push them to go onto the checkouts, if they do need extra training, they'll be given it. Not everyone picks things up as quickly as others.'*

During the training period, the new starters from all sections within the store go to the Training Room once a week for a two hour training session. There are seven training sessions which cover:

1 customer care matters;
2 customer care communication part 1;
3 customer care communication part 2;
4 working together;
5 dealing with difficult situations;
6 solving customer problems;
7 measuring customer satisfaction.

Each session has a workbook which outlines the module and has space for the trainee's own notes. Sessions begin with an introduction from the Team Trainer who encourages suggestions from the trainees as to the best course of action in certain situations. The trainees also take part in role play to illustrate how customers should be dealt with.

Lisa explains: *'It gives them an insight on what customers can be like when they come into the store, what to expect and how to deal with the situation. When they are actually on the shopfloor, if they have that scenario with a customer they'll know how to deal with that situation. Hopefully, they'll come up with a good answer. You're always learning, I've been here seven years myself and I'm still learning. Each customer is different and has different needs. Its a matter of reacting to what they want. The training is very in-depth on how to deal with a customer, because if a customer doesn't come in again we're losing money and losing jobs. We try to make the training interesting and enjoyable, it helps to get the point across and the trainees are happy to take part. They remember more if they've enjoyed it and have actively participated in it. We split up the various modules so that there isn't too much to remember.*

Examples of the subjects covered in the dealing with difficult situations module include:

◆ Introduction
◆ If we receive no complaints why should we be concerned?
◆ Make it easy for customers to complain
◆ Every complaint is an opportunity
  – to avoid harm caused by dissatisfied customers
  – to improve things for the future
  – to learn what is important to our customers
  – to increase the loyalty of the complainant
◆ So what are the do's and don'ts of face-to-face complaint handling?
◆ The Seven Steps to good customer contact
  1 Acknowledge
  2 Respond
  3 Question
  4 Listen and check
  5 Agree action to be taken
  6 Take action
  7 Follow up
◆ How can the Seven Steps help you?
◆ How will the Seven Steps help the customer?

Lisa: *'In the long run colleagues' jobs are more enjoyable because we give very good customer service. They feel that they can interact with customers and help the customers. They are not just there to fill shelves or process goods, there's more to it. The staff have more responsibility and more interest in the company. We tell our colleagues how much money we take, what the waste is like, all the information we can.*

We have teamwork and this gives the customer the feeling that the staff are working together well, and it looks more professional to the customer. We have autonomous working teams and this gives colleagues ownership of their area. This provides better customer service because colleagues think "If I were a customer, would I like this?" and they have the power to change it if they think it would look better displayed differently. We're all customers ourselves and colleagues can identify with customer needs. Customers often work full or part-time and they want to get everything done under one roof. If we've got everything available for them and the service is good, they're going to come back each week.

I enjoyed being a Team Trainer; seeing someone progress and learning new tasks and skills gave me a buzz. I thought "I taught that person to do that". You see people working in a different way and enjoying their work and taking on extra responsibility. They can work in various parts of the store. We're trying to get everyone multi-skilled, it's an on-going process. We don't push people into it because we've still got people who want to come and do a particular job on a permanent basis. For those who would like to learn new skills, the opportunity is there for them. It all affects customer service, because if a department is short staffed for some reason, there's always another member of staff who can fit in and do the job.'

Employee and management development

Employee development is more future oriented and more concerned with education than employee training. Employee development activities attempt to teach reasoning processes – to enhance one's ability to understand and interpret knowledge – rather than imparting a body of facts or teaching a specific set of skills. Development focuses more on the employee's personal growth.

Successful employees who are prepared for positions of greater responsibility will have analytical, human, conceptual, and specialised skills. They are able to think, understand and evaluate. Management development helps an individual's cognitive skill development enabling them to understand cause-and-effect relationships, to conclude from experience, to visualise relationships, or to think logically. Potential managers need good listening skills, interviewing competence, and the ability to read, analyse, and classify types of employee behaviour.

All employees, at no matter what level, should have the opportunity to receive support other than training for specific skills or tasks. In the past, development was reserved for potential management personnel. The use of teams, reduction in the number of supervisors, allowing workers to participate in the design of their jobs, and even giving employees the right to stop a production line if they see a problem, have changed the way training employees is viewed. Individuals need to know how to plan, organise, lead, control and make decisions. Those methods used to develop employees in general are the same as those used to develop managerial personnel.

The process

Efforts towards developing employees begin by looking at the organisation's objectives. The objectives give an idea of where the organisation is going and provide a framework from which employee development needs can be determined. The second step is an appraisal of current resources. From the details of the background and qualifications of employees, combined with a statement of organisational objectives. A third step involves identifying development activities necessary to ensure that there is enough talent in the organisation to fulfil future organisational needs.

This comparative analysis shows the potential obsolescence of some employees, the inexperience or shortage of individuals in certain functions and highlights skill deficiencies for future needs. The next step is to determine individual development needs, skill development, changing attitudes, and knowledge acquisition. Most development work will centre on the changing of attitudes and the acquisition of knowledge in specific areas.

Once development needs are known, it is necessary to identify the types of development programmes which will meet the specific needs of each individual. No one development method is the most effective in all situations. Lectures, role plays, case studies, coaching, or any of the techniques can be appropriate or inappropriate depending on the employee, his or her present skills, and future responsibilities.

Finally, once employees have participated in development activities, the process should be evaluated – looking for changes in behaviour and managerial performance. Just as with employee training programmes only through performing this final step can a programme's effectiveness be appraised, its weaknesses highlighted, and the information developed to determine whether the development should be continued or how it can be improved.

Development should not just be a one-off affair, but continual development should be offered to enable the employee to grow as an individual. The organisation will benefit from the increased potential and abilities of each employee. The individual may benefit from increased job opportunities and promotion and will be helped in the short term by the increase in motivation.

In summary, employee development depends on knowledge of the organisation's objectives, development of management inventories, and evaluation of programmes to appraise their effectiveness.

 # Counselling

Counselling is an exchange of ideas and feelings between two people, the counsellor and the person being counselled. It is intended to help employees cope with problems and it should improve organisational performance, because the employee is more cooperative, worries less about personal problems, or improves in other ways. Counselling also helps the organisation be more human and considerate with people problems.

Counselling may be performed by both professionals and non-professionals. Counselling is usually confidential, so that employees feel free to talk openly about their problems. It also involves both job and personal problems, since both types of problems may affect an employee's performance on the job.

The general objective of counselling is to help employees develop better mental health so that they will grow in self-confidence, understanding, self-control, and develop the ability to work effectively. The counselling objective is achieved through one or more of the *counselling functions.*

Functions of counselling

◆ *Advice.* Telling a person what you think should be done.

◆ *Reassurance.* Giving a person courage and confidence to face a problem.

◆ *Communication.* Providing information and understanding.

◆ *Release of emotional tension.* Helping a person feel more free of tensions.

◆ *Clarified thinking.* Encouraging more coherent and rational thought.

◆ *Reorientation.* Encouraging an internal change in goals and values.

Managers are important counsellors because they are the ones who have daily interaction with employees. If managers ignore the emotional problems of employees and refuse to discuss them, it appears as if they are saying to employees, 'I don't care about you, just your work.' Managers cannot, when an emotional upset arises, say, 'This is not part of my job. Go and see a counsellor.' Emotions are part of the whole employee and must be considered a part of the total employment situation for which a manager is responsible. Managers need training to help them understand the problems of employees and to be able to counsel them effectively.

Types of counselling

The amount of direction or guidance that a counsellor gives the person being counselled varies from full direction (directive counselling) to no direction (non-directive counselling). Between the two extremes is participative counselling.

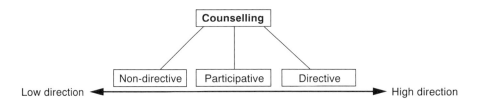

Fig 4.3 Three types of counselling methods

Directive counselling

Directive counselling involves listening to an employee's problem, deciding with the employee what should be done, and then telling and motivating the employee to do it. Directive counselling mostly accomplishes the counselling function of advice, but it also may reassure, communicate, give emotional release and can clarify thinking.

Non-directive counselling

Non-directive counselling is also called client-centred counselling. This is the process of skilfully listening and encouraging the person being counselled to explain troublesome problems, understand them, and determine appropriate solutions. Throughout the counselling relationship, it is important for the counsellor to accept feelings – rather than judge them offering blame or praise, because judgement may discourage an employee from stating true feelings. The basic idea is to get the employee to discuss feelings, to explore solutions, and to make wise decisions.

Ways in which non-directive counselling differs from directive counselling

Counselling method. In non-directive counselling the employee primarily controls the direction of conversation and does most of the talking. In directive counselling the emphasis is on the counsellor advising the employee.

Responsibility. Solution of the problem is the employee's own responsibility in non-directive counselling. However, in directive counselling the counsellor is responsible for the advice given to the employee.

Status. The employee is equal to the counsellor as a person in non-directive counselling, while the directive method implies that the counsellor is superior and knows what to do.

Role. The employee is psychologically independent as a person in non-directive counselling. He chooses a solution and grows in ability to make choices in the future. In the direct counselling relationship the employee is less psychologically independent as advice is given and he is told what to do.

Emphasis. Emphasis is on deeper feelings and problems rather than surface symptoms in the non-directive relationship. Adjustment of a person, rather than an immediate solution of a current problem, is of greater importance. In the directive relationship the solution of the problem at hand is of greater importance.

Participative counselling

Participative counselling is a mutual counsellor–counsellee relationship that establishes a cooperative exchange of ideas to help solve a person's problems. The counsellor and the person being counselled both apply their own knowledge, perspectives, and values to problems. The ideas of both participants are integrated in this counselling relationship.

Summary

Counselling is occasionally necessary for employees because of job and personal problems that subject them to excessive stress. The conditions that tend to cause stress include work overload, time pressures, role ambiguity, financial and family problems. Stress affects both physical and mental health and results in burnout when it occurs over a long period of time. Excessive stress reduces job performance, although a moderate amounts may help employees respond to job challenges.

Discipline

Managers are dealing with discipline when they issue warnings to persistent latecomers or individuals who have been absent on several occasions. The manager is attempting to control the performance of his or her staff through providing rules. Discipline should not only be seen in a negative light – involving punishment or prevention – it can also be a positive process and be the key to the production of excellent results and performance. As well as self-discipline, which enables individuals who have expertise, training and self-control, to work alone to produce a good performance, there is team and managerial discipline. Team discipline allows a perfect performance to be contributed to by all group members. Optimal performance comes from all team members being dependent upon one another and from their commitment to the task. Managerial discipline involves the leader guiding performance, the carrying out and completion of the task depends entirely upon the leader.

Rules

At work discipline is a question of devising appropriate rules of behaviour for employees and providing fair and consistent means of enforcing them. Rules should be clear and readily understood. The number of rules should be sufficient to cover all normal disciplinary matters. Employees should have ready access to the rules, through the employee handbook and noticeboard, and the personnel manager will always try to ensure that the rules are known.

Rules fall into six categories, relating to different types of behaviour:

◆ negligence
◆ unreliability
◆ insubordination
◆ socially unacceptable behaviour
◆ theft
◆ safety offences.

Keeping to the rules

Just having rules is not sufficient, they must be conformed to by employees if they are to be effective. It is illegal to drive without wearing a seatbelt, but no-one checks up on every driver each time they take the wheel. Drivers, in the main, voluntarily comply with the law in the wearing of seatbelts. Means of making rules more likely to be obeyed include:

1 information about the details of the rules to ensure that everyone understands them;
2 induction training is a period of time when rules can be introduced to all employees;

3 placement of a new recruit with a team that obeys the rules avoids the risk of rules being broken;

4 training increases new recruits' awareness of the rules;

5 review of the rules occasionally ensures that they are up-to-date;

6 penalties – if the rules are broken then management need some form of penalty they can impose on the subordinate concerned. Some typical forms of penalty:

(a) *rebuke* a straightforward telling of the employee not to do certain things. For example, telling the employee that further lateness will not be accepted;

(b) *caution* a caution is slightly more serious and formal and is recorded. This does not trigger the procedure for dismissal, it is just making a note of a rule being broken and an offence being pointed out;

(c) *warnings* these are part of legal disciplinary practice and can lead to dismissal. There should normally be a formal oral warning, or a written warning, specifying the nature of the offence and the likely outcome of the offence being repeated. Further misconduct could then warrant a final written warning containing a statement that further repetition would lead to a penalty such as suspension or dismissal;

(d) *disciplinary transfer or demotion* this involves moving the employee to less attractive work, possibly carrying a lower salary;

(e) *suspension* being suspended is a serious matter but avoids the disadvantage of being long-lasting, like demotion. Employers have a contractual obligation to provide pay, but not to provide work, so it is easy to suspend someone from duty, with pay, either as a punishment or while an alleged offence is being investigated. If the contract of employment permits, it may also be possible to suspend the employee for a short period without pay;

(f) *fines* there are infrequently used, because of contractual problems, but the most common is deduction from pay for lateness. Sports people are sometimes fined for bringing their game into disrepute;

7 procedural sequence should be well known and trusted, so that the steps of a grievance or dismissal procedure do not vary with individual cases.

Disciplinary procedure

The law requires that managers should not normally have the power to dismiss their immediate subordinates without reference to more senior managers. The disciplinary procedure within an organisation should ensure that disciplinary action is not taken until it has been established that an offence has been committed justifying the action. If there is the possibility of disciplinary action, the person to be disciplined should be told of the complaint, so that an explanation can be made, or the matter denied, before any penalties are decided. If an employee is to be penalised, then the reasons for that decision should be explained to make sure that cause and effect are understood.

Steps in the disciplinary procedure

1 for minor misconduct, the Supervisor will give a verbal warning;

2 for a repeated minor misconduct, or serious misconduct, a written warning should be issued by the Departmental Manager;

3 a third incident of a minor misconduct, or a second incident of a serious misconduct, should entail the issuing of a final written warning by the Department Manager or the Human Resource Manager;

4 any repeats of the misconduct after the final warning should entail dismissal or transfer, or demotion or suspension. These penalties should come from senior management or the Personnel Manager.

The model features of a disciplinary procedure suggested by ACAS includes the following guidelines. The procedure should:

◆ be in written form

◆ specify to whom it applies

◆ provide for the speedy progress of disciplinary hearings

◆ indicate the various form of disciplinary hearings

◆ indicate the various forms of disciplinary action that may be taken (warnings, dismissal, etc.)

◆ specify appropriate levels of authority for exercising disciplinary action

◆ ensure that individuals are informed of the disciplinary charges made against them

◆ permit such individuals to state their case, and to be accompanied by a friend or trade union representative

◆ ensure the proper investigation of every case before disciplinary action is implemented

◆ ensure that individuals are informed of the reasons for the action being taken against them

◆ ensure that no individual is dismissed for a first offence except in cases of gross misconduct

◆ provide for a right of appeal.

Whether or not an offence is the cause of disciplinary action depends upon the nature of the circumstances, on management's previous attitudes and on the culture of the organisation generally. What in one firm would be a dismissable offence, could be far less serious in another firm.

Monitoring and reporting individual and group performance

In order to control activities, managers need to monitor and evaluate progress. This is the final function which managers need to carry out. Managers should plan the task, organise how it will be carried out and then monitor the work to check that it is going according to plan. The ideal situation is to monitor continuously the work and to report this back to the operatives, operations management and senior management as the work is happening. This can keep managers informed so that they can take corrective action if work is deviating from the norm set. Sometimes this is not possible and the work has to be checked only at certain times, or at the end of the production period. Retail outlets such as Top Shop/Top Man have weekly computer printouts from head office, showing their sales of each item of clothing, these are rank-ordered in terms of quantities of sales, so that the best sellers are at the beginning of the list. These printouts enable the manager to monitor sales and plan for future stock requirements and immediate layout changes to the shop.

Group performance

When managers wish to encourage teamwork, they will monitor the performance of a group of workers together. Having the production figures of a team fed back and reported on will have a motivating effect on the group and encourage group members to help one another, particularly where a group bonus is awarded according to production. Monitoring can easily be done in the case of sales teams and production workers as their output is easy to quantify. In some teams where solutions to problems or innovative ideas are called for, people may sometimes feel that certain group members do not contribute sufficiently and that management is unaware of this. In these cases, a different form of monitoring is called for such as individuals appraising group members on their contributions and observation of the group working together to identify non-contributing members.

Electronic devices or computers can be used to monitor the performance of individual workers and check that the individual's work conforms to the group norm. In factories where Total Quality Management has been adopted, teams and team leaders have a great deal of discretion in the way the work is carried out and who does what. Multi-skilling is encouraged and work rotation is allocated by the team. Within the team individuals are encouraged to improve personal performance and make innovations to improve productivity and product quality. Team meetings provide forums where such issues are debated and information shared.

Quality is controlled by visual inspection and electronic tests which also trace the individual responsible for the fault. This information together with data on absenteeism, conformity to standard times and production planning targets can be displayed for all the team to see. The information can form the basis for much discussion between team members. In turn this creates a situation where the team will 'discipline', through the use of peer pressure, those that they feel are not conforming to the norms, a situation where the group acts as the controller of the individual and the team. In some factories in Japan team lists are posted on notice-boards. Any individual who is underperforming, in the opinion of the other team members, has a black mark put against their name. This means that the individual has to work harder to get the mark removed.

Individual performance

Until recently, there was an emphasis on the workers as a collective body, all receiving the same rate of pay for the same job. The membership of trade unions has been declining and the idea of a 'going rate' for a job is fading with pay becoming more of an individual issue. Rewards are more likely to be linked to individual performance, as well as to company performance through profit sharing.

There are various ways of monitoring people's performance at work. For those who work in manufacturing, it may be possible to monitor their performance very accurately. Someone making bread rolls in a bakery may produce 100 in half an hour, and so it is very easy to tell whether he or she is performing better or worse by measuring output. For those who are not directly connected with production, such as maintenance engineers or people who work in service industries such as nurses or shop assistants, performance is more difficult to measure.

Where performance is easy to measure, payment systems such as piece rates or bonus payments for exceeding given targets can be used. Piece rates involve linking pay directly to the amount of production. The fastest workers will earn the most in a week. Bonus payments are given on top of a basic salary, so that employees earn more if sales or production figures are exceeded. In situations where performance is more difficult to monitor, the following systems can be implemented:

◆ performance appraisal
◆ performance-related pay.

Performance appraisal

A performance appraisal is normally a one-to-one interview between supervisor/manager and subordinate, carried out annually. The objectives are:

1 to decide whether people are suitable for particular jobs. The manager may have vacancies or plans for re-organisation of the department and can use the appraisal system to discuss new opportunities for individuals on a one-to-one basis. The appraiser can use the time to discover what tasks the appraisee enjoys and with which people they like working;

2 to decide on the training, education and job experience needed by the individual. The appraisee can state what tasks they have difficulty with or aspirations they have for the future, and training can be provided to meet their needs. It is easy for the appraiser to dismiss the below-average performer as not worth bothering with, yet it is this individual who is the very person who needs development;

3 to identify people suitable for promotion. Monitoring and assessing people as they carry out their work and then discussing their likes and dislikes, training needs and future aspirations assists managers in identifying those who would be suitable for more senior positions in future;

4   to give feedback on the individual's performance and provide an opportunity for the subordinate to discuss various aspects of his or her job. In order to assess performance, many organisations use rating scales. If, for example, it has been decided that the top ten per cent of managers will receive a salary increase of five per cent, this can be calculated from the ratings given by their bosses. Alternatively, if evidence is required for not renewing someone's contract, the relevant poor ratings can be produced in evidence. If the object of assessment is to improve performance, ratings are not required. In order to improve performance, the manager should discuss specific incidents with the subordinate and how these could have been handled more effectively. Ratings are too general to be used for discussion of improvements;

5   to motivate employees and increase their commitment to the organisation. The time and effort taken over appraisals indicates concern for individuals by managers and the organisation. Discussing the likes and dislikes about the job and having goals set will have a motivating effect upon individuals.

Many companies also use the appraisal system to give pay awards. This can have a dramatic effect on the interview as people will be more interested in the pay award than the discussion about how they are doing at work.

The appraisal may consist of the supervisor informing the subordinate about written comments or gradings against specific job competencies. Ideally, if the subordinate has been making mistakes or doing badly generally, he or she should not hear about it for the first time during the appraisal interview. An employee should be informed on a day-to-day basis if his or her performance is unsatisfactory. The appraisal interview is then more likely to be positive and motivating rather than a 'telling off' session. Many supervisors are reluctant to carry out appraisals as they find them embarrassing and time consuming. There are benefits for everyone of doing appraisals:

Appraisees:

◆ receive feedback on their performance
◆ learn what is expected of them
◆ can say what training they think they need.

Appraisers:

◆ have a monitoring mechanism to measure the performance of their staff
◆ have the opportunity to find out more about the aspirations and needs of each member of staff
◆ can motivate and encourage better performance from staff in order to improve their area of responsibility.

Appraisal interviews can improve communication in the organisation, improve employees' understanding of the organisation's goals, and assist with manpower planning by identifying staff suitable for particular promotions or shortages of staff suitable for more senior positions.

Performance related pay

This is increasingly being introduced, both for white-collar and blue-collar employees. In those organisations operating systems of performance-related pay, the amount of a person's salary which is awarded for performance is normally around five per cent. It is therefore a very small proportion of a person's salary, but is generally considered by workers to be welcome, important and motivating. Instead of giving salary rises some organisations sometimes reward people with a choice of gifts such as a ride in a hot air balloon or a meal at a local restaurant.

Managers are given a budget by the organisation for performance-related pay. The budget may mean giving a proportion of workers a certain percentage rise. In Marks & Spencer plc, the budget is for 30 per cent of the employees in a department to receive an award. The manager has the discretion to award more than 30 per cent of employees, as long as he or she stays within budget. If 60 per cent of employees are awarded the performance-related pay, then the manager could give them all half of the five per cent, or whatever the amount o the 30 per cent the figure may be.

◆ ACTIVITY 4.1

Devise a list of do's and don'ts for appraisers. In groups of three, carry out an appraisal interview, with one appraisee, one appraiser and one observer. The objective of the interview is to discuss the student's performance at college over the past few months.

With help from the observer, discuss your individual emotions during the interview and how the interview could be improved in future to increase student motivation.

QUIZ
4.1

How do you rate on performance appraisal?

	Yes	No
1 Whether I have two employees or 200, I have a formal, written, performance evaluation system.	☐	☐
2 I enjoy the appraisal process because it gives me an opportunity to work closely with my employees on their personal development.	☐	☐
3 I complete my evaluations on time and I insist that managers under me do reviews on a regular basis and complete them on time.	☐	☐
4 I do not use an appraisal form that judges people on traits such as aggressiveness, cooperation or leadership ability.	☐	☐
5 I meet with my subordinates regularly throughout the year to talk about their performance and to help them improve.	☐	☐

	Yes	No
6 I always praise people when they do something well. I do it immediately; I don't save it for the annual review.	☐	☐
7 When someone makes a mistake, I discuss it with them immediately, with the aim of getting them to improve. I never shout, and I never punish mistakes.	☐	☐
8 I involve my subordinates in the review process by having them evaluate their own performance in writing before we meet.	☐	☐
9 I work with my subordinates to set measurable goals for the coming year. I use these goals as a basis for evaluating performance.	☐	☐
10 I ask subordinates to give me feedback on my performance and suggest ways that we can work together better.	☐	☐

If you wish to be a top performing business owner or manager, you should have answered 'Yes' to all 10 questions.

DISCUSSION QUESTION 4.1

1 List the things a boss might do that would make a performance interview very uncomfortable for an employee.
2 List the things which could make a performance interview very constructive and helpful for an employee.
3 Combine the individual lists to make a group list that everyone agrees upon.
4 What experiences have you had with performance appraisal? Which ones were most and least useful?
5 Which areas covered in performance appraisal are likely to be most sensitive?
6 What are some of the common prejudices which influence performance appraisal?
7 Are there advantages to getting subordinates to evaluate their manager?
8 How can all employees be persuaded of the value of a performance appraisal?

CASE STUDY 4.2

Crewe & Nantwich Borough Council

The Borough Council spent approximately £38 m in the financial year 1994–95. The Council's income comes from a number of sources such as government grants, income from trading accounts, payment for the provision of services on an agency basis and is spent on such things as housing, provision of sport and leisure facilities and refuse collection. The council employs approximately 1000 people, 750 of whom are on permanent contracts. John Williams, Head of Personnel:

'We provide a range of quality of life services. We are, though, more than service providers. The Council also acts as a focal point for the community, seeking to represent the public interest and influence other organisations such as health authorities, police, water

companies, etc. We also work with the voluntary sector through the provision of grants and by helping them the work together. The Council initiates a number of strategies concerned with such issues as creating safer communities, addressing disadvantage, creating a safe and sustainable environment. This broader role is about governance and is legitimate because many of the organisations which affect people's lives are no longer directly accountable to the public, whereas the Council is an elected body.

We are an organisation that values the people we employ. We recognise the quality of services we provide depends greatly upon the quality of the people we employ. Effectiveness of our management is a matter of great concern, therefore not only from the point of view of the development of management skills but also the appropriateness of management style. In particular, we have spent a lot of time over recent years addressing the issue of effective communication. We have developed a clear vision for the future of the organisation and the development of our role within the community. We have also prepared a Staff Charter which embodies the obligations that managers feel toward their staff.

Fig 4.4 John Williams, Head of Personnel, Borough of Crewe and Nantwich

The performance appraisal system

Prior to the beginning of each financial year we prepare our Corporate Key Tasks. As part of the process the Management Team consult employees. The Corporate Key Tasks are the steps that we intend to take that year towards achieving the aims of the Vision Statement. Once agreed, Corporate Key Tasks are confirmed by Council and published.

Next, each division prepares a service plan which sets out in detail how the division is going to contribute towards the Corporate Key Tasks. The service plan is circulated throughout the organisation. We then undertake Performance Development Interviews with individuals. The purpose of the interview is to look back on the previous year's performance and identify any development needs and to look forward to the coming year to identify the individual's contribution. In looking forward, additional development needs may be identified.

The actions that follow from this process are not only concerned with attending training courses but may involve such things as coaching on the job and representing the division on inter-divisional working groups, etc.

Like many organisations we have had a number of false starts at introducing appraisals. I suppose the difference with this approach is that it is directly linked to the Council's overall performance management system, and therefore, reflects far more accurately 'the needs of the business'.

The public sector is under a microscope nowadays. Employees feel far more accountable than perhaps they did in the past and want effective feedback from their managers about things they are doing well and the areas where they need to improve. Employees then feel more in control of their own destiny. In an ideal world, managers would be having this kind of conversation with their staff on a continuing basis. The beauty of the appraisal process, however, is that both the manager and member of staff can prepare thoughtfully

Staff Charter

Your managers will, at all times, attempt to live up to the following:

Be visible and accessible and give 'quality' time to staff to answer questions, consider concerns and frustrations and generally talk about areas of work and related problems.

Recognise ability, acknowledge achievements and generally give credit where credit is due, both personally and where appropriate publicly.

Listen - be open to new ideas and suggestions and respond constructively.

Be prepared to give and accept criticism constructively and to act upon it.

Communicate openly and regularly, keeping people in touch with what is happening both within and outside the organisation which has a bearing upon their work.

Provide leadership and accept responsibility for subsequent actions.

Provide support when things go wrong and demonstrate fairness and understanding.

Seek to continually improve the working environment in consultation with staff.

Provide opportunities and help people to develop so that they can fulfil potential.

Provide fair and equal treatment for all and protection from harassment on any grounds.

Signed _____

Set in Corel Draw 3 by Computer Services

Fig 4.5 Crewe & Nantwich Borough Council staff charter

CASE
STUDY
cont

in the context of the general performance and direction of the whole organisation. Employees are also encouraged to comment upon the way they are managed or supervised; this also helps the manager to develop.

We may consider introducing a 360 degree approach for managers to formalise this feedback process so that everyone who comes into contact with an employee can give feedback on their performance. Such a system can only work in a mature organisation where managers do not regard self-knowledge as threatening. We are currently working with consultants on the prospect of introducing a competency based management development process to increase further our effectiveness as managers. Our aim is to become a learning organisation. Performance and Development Interviews form an important part of this process. They enable employees and managers to identify learning experiences through the performance of individual tasks which can then be transferred to other areas of the job. If the individual is capable of doing this then collectively the organisation will become stronger and more effective.

Fear and blame can inhibit this process. A local authority, by its very nature, attracts attention from the media. Much of what we do also requires decisions to be made that affect people's lives directly. For instance, in dealing with planning applications giving consent to one person may cause annoyance to another or conversely, denying planning consent may frustrate someone's ambition. When determining housing benefit applications, an individual may feel aggrieved at not being granted benefit, even though the Council and the individual employee have no discretion. The local radio and press may criticise the Council from time to time and staff are clearly affected by negative publicity. Managers need to understand this and seek to keep employees informed so that they can deal with these issues. They need to develop the ability to counsel staff who are upset by individual contacts with the public or by working in particularly contentious areas.

Training and counselling

I have to accept that in the past training was often 'done to people'. A lot of money was devoted to sending people on courses without sufficient preparation and follow up. Often frustration was caused when employees came back with new skills and knowledge and were not given the opportunity to apply them fully.

It is also fair to say that most of the effort and expenditure was devoted to professional and technical training and not enough attention was applied to what I would call the softer skills of communication, teamwork and general behavioural aspects of the job. An effective manager can help increase the performance of staff by being aware and supportive in these areas. Coaching and mentoring are important skills to the modern manager. It is important for managers to say 'well done', but it is more important to help employees to identify why things go well and sometimes go badly.

There is a danger of presenting many of these new approaches to management as new initiatives. Many managers today will complain of initiative fatigue. New philosophies intended to create a more effective future imply at the same time that employees had previously been ineffective and had somehow failed. This is particularly true of managers who are often given unrealistic charismatic examples of effective leadership. For instance, Tom Peters is a good performer, but has he really tried putting into practice his own message? The kind of thing I am talking about includes such philosophies as TQM, customer care, etc., all aimed at making the manager more effective. My experience has been that this can undermine managers' confidence making them less, rather than more, effective. Coaching and counselling skills, regularly giving feedback to staff and transferring learning experience, are basic common sense rather than earth-shattering philosophy. They deal with the realities of the organisation rather than trying to create some ideal set of aspirations.

Counselling skills are particularly useful for managers in that it encourages individual problem solving rather than imposed solutions. I draw a distinction between managers helping staff to identify and solve problems relating to the work and those relating to their personal and domestic life. What we seek to do with the latter is to accept that an employee's personal life affects life at work and vice versa, but offer external counselling support rather than dive in ourselves. Employees should be able to retain their dignity and privacy.

It is worth mentioning as an aside the importance of knowing who the real managers are. Traditionally, in local government, jobs are defined by words such as senior, principal, team leader. These titles were often applied without much thought. We now seek to define managers by identifying management tasks and competencies in such areas as preparation and management of budgets, direct staffing responsibilities, for instance, within disciplinary procedure and so on. This helps to create a flatter structure with fewer links in the managerial chain.

Induction

There are two significant and distinct areas of induction. First, there are the practical things that employees need to know concerned with the physical environment at work, pay arrangements, how to apply for leave, etc. Second, there are the cultural aspects of the organisation such as its collective vision, appropriate management styles, methods of communication and expectations of behaviour.

We have introduced a system for gradually introducing a new employee to the organisation based on self-help and support from managers. Even before the employee starts they are sent a booklet raising certain questions which they may wish to consider in preparation for the new job. After starting the job the second phase comes into play, where staff are encouraged to locate and understand conditions of service, any rules that may exist and procedures and systems concerned with sickness absence. There are a series of booklets which pose questions and require staff to find answers as well as a checklist of actions for managers. At a later stage employees are introduced to the cultural aspects of the organisation by having the opportunity to speak to senior managers and members of the Council about what the organisation stands for, what service it provides across the whole organisation and aspirations for the future. The system is based on the belief that people need to feel physically secure in the workplace before addressing cultural issues.

Teams

Teambuilding courses used to be more a feature in training programmes. We now seek to integrate the principles of creating effective teams into the everyday experience of work.

The performance management system clearly identifies targets for teams as well as individuals and by encouraging discussion and by increasing understanding through better communication, team effectiveness has increased. When problems occur we provide support through training in the use of techniques in problem solving. Again we are seeking to achieve transferable learning rather than imposing solutions.

Personnel and training professionals have the terrible tendency of imposing courses on people aimed at creating effective teams. From time to time we now employ an external consultant to work with teams aimed at integrating processes into the day-to-day work routines. For example, the staff who had the job of collecting the poll tax and introducing a new Council Tax and housing benefit system, became very stressed. By introducing quality circles and techniques such as forcefield analysis, SWOT and transactional analysis, the work groups began to confront many of the causes of stress themselves. One of the greatest sources of stress is not feeling in control – through empowering the individual and the group in this way, much of the stress was removed.

The management team

In a local authority the management team reflect the range of services and professions for which it is responsible. It is not surprising that the members of the team are very different in terms of their background and personalities. This has the potential to be a great weakness or great strength. Our objective is to concentrate on the latter to build on the differences by encouraging effective communication between the members and the team. It also is important to concentrate on identifying appropriate behaviour within the group and the management team has spent a lot of time talking through the steps necessary to create an effective management team. External consultants are currently helping us in this process and we have to listen to constructive criticism and learn from it.

Some members of the team work in the centre and are concerned with such things as policy development and providing political support whilst others are concerned with the day-to-day pressures of providing services directly to the public. It is important that we are aware that these differences create different perceptions and can create conflict. Individual members of the team have to take responsibility in this area for making sure that such differences are used positively to strengthen the decision making process. I suspect that the most valuable skill is the ability to listen.

There is a growing recognition of the need to develop a more systematic approach to the development of managers. The Management Charter Initiative and an increasing use of a competency based approach is long overdue. There has been a tendency in this country in the past to allow managers to stagger from experience to experience in the hope that along the way they become an effective manager. The effect of this on both managers and staff is destructive. Most of the exciting work done on competencies relates to the 'softer' skills such as influencing, providing leadership, effective communication, etc. Understanding the need to create a climate within an organisation within which people can succeed and develop is probably the most critical competence of all.

Work planning and organisation

5

From reading this chapter you will learn about work planning and organisation, including:

1 organisational planning;
2 SWOT analysis;
3 planning the operation;
4 network analysis;
5 planning break-even;
6 operations management;
7 effectiveness and efficiency;
8 work study;
9 re-engineering;
10 work measurement; and
11 changing and amending plans.

 ## Organisational planning

Planning is the process of organising activities to meet a goal. Planning must involve organising the best course of action to meet future demands. The planning process also includes decision making and should answer:

Fig 5.1 Questions to ask during the planning process

If the family summer holiday is planned to take place in August, that is the objective. The next stage is to identify what should be done: getting time off work, visiting travel agents, collecting brochures, deciding on a destination within the

OUR VISION

After many difficult years of change there is a growing confidence in the future of local government. During this time Crewe and Nantwich has established a reputation as an innovative Council that is not afraid of change.

The public value what we do and how we do it. We must maintain that trust and build on it by making sure that everything we do is of a high quality and relevant to the lives of the public.

We have earned and will maintain the right to represent the community through our dealings with central government and other local and regional organisations that influence the future quality of life for the inhabitants of the Borough.

We will, therefore:

- continue to provide quality services

- aim to be a leading example of good working practice amongst local authorities

- provide community leadership and represent the interests of the public

- be responsive to changing circumstances and sensitive to the needs of the community

- develop partnerships with the local community to enhance the economic and physical environment

- aim to be a model employer with an informed and committed workforce

Vision Summary

Fig 5.2 Crewe & Nantwich vision statement

time scale allowed and the amount budgeted for. Once agreed, a visit to the travel agent is necessary to confirm dates, the resort, hotels and transport. The tasks seem endless. Who should collect the brochures? Who decides upon the budget? Who makes the final decision on the destination? Planning therefore involves making decisions about the activities to be performed.

Planning occurs at all levels in the organisation and takes various forms.

Strategic planning

Strategy is the result of decisions taken about what to do. Strategic planning is the process of defining the primary objective, and selecting activities and allocating the resources necessary to achieve that objective. This is carried out at the highest level, usually by the Board of Directors. The ultimate objective is normally stated in the vision or mission statement such as in the Crewe & Nantwich 'Our Vision' (*see* Fig 5.2).

However, there are usually secondary strategic objectives set which, if achieved, will meet the overall strategic goal. The secondary objectives tend to be long term – over three to five years – and involve clear measurable goals, for example, to increase market share by x per cent, to increase sales by y per cent, or to enter a new export market.

Tactical planning

Tactics are how the strategy will be implemented. Tactical plans identify those activities which will achieve the secondary strategic objectives. These are usually put in place by senior or middle managers. For example the organisation may want to increase its market share in France. It may decide to do this by increasing its advertising budget, retargeting its advertising or changing its advertising medium.

Operational planning

This is carried out at the supervisory level and involves planning for specifics, or example, setting targets or quotas for individuals or groups. A section of an organisation might be set a target by the middle managers, and it would be up to the supervisors of small units to devise plans to make sure their unit contributes to the overall target.

Objective	Strategic plan	Tactical plan	Operational plan
To have a rest	◆ To have a holiday	◆ Where to go	◆ Planning the route
	◆ To have a holiday within a budget	◆ How to get there	◆ Planning the stop-overs
		◆ Who to go with	◆ Planning the hotel stay

Fig 5.3 Planning a holiday

Planning is done at each level in the organisation. The higher the level the more planning is done. Planning is not just about achieving some major objective. Operatives on the shopfloor plan their work standards. We have to plan our daily lives in order to be organised. Many people plan their day and know that certain tasks have to be completed by certain times. Time management is concerned with managing time effectively which requires thought and planning. Some tasks have to be completed before others. Some tasks require inputs in the form of resources. All tasks have to be completed by a deadline. To operate within the constraint of meeting deadlines, a person needs to plan ahead. Some deadlines are more immediate than others. The more distant deadlines need to be planned for so that known events do not suddenly arrive and cause organisational problems.

An organisation which pays close attention to planning and priorities encourages individuals and organisations to focus on relevant results rather than endless tasks. Managers who do not plan are those who say they haven't got the time because they are too busy. Yet the activities and tasks they are doing are probably because they have not planned. Work becomes a forest fire, out of control and consuming all in its path. Planning however sets a tone, focuses attention and encourages action. Planning also provides a means for individuals to cope with change.

Contingency planning

Contingency planning is being prepared for unforeseen problems. These usually occur when the organisation is not in control of events. This means plans sometimes fall through and the organisation has to react to the new situation. In some cases an organisation's product is found to be defective and the organisation must respond quickly. It must decide whether to recall the product to rectify the problem or recall the product and stop production. In both cases the organisation must decide how it is going to reduce the adverse publicity. Companies such as Perrier, Unilever and Ford have found themselves in this position.

Recalling a product to correct a defective part needs planning: is it all the products that have to be recalled or just a certain batch number? How is the recall going to take place? How are the customers going to be notified? Who is going to receive the faulty goods and if they can't be repaired how are they going to be disposed of? What is the time frame for this to be done? Exactly how will the company respond to adverse publicity?

In cases where accidents occur, crisis management takes over to implement crisis management policy and use the procedures laid down to deal with the problem. If the accident is in a factory planning might be needed to keep production going as far as possible and communicate with interested parties of progress being made to deal with the accident. In some routine health checks the wrong diagnosis has been made and the hospital has to plan how to deal with the problem: how to correct the diagnosis; how to inform the individuals concerned; how to respond to their reaction; and how to keep the public informed in order to restore public confidence. In this situation there are different deadlines: the immediate deadline of correcting the diagnosis procedure and informing the individuals; and a longer term deadline of bolstering the public confidence. The authorities also need to plan to find out how the problem arrived in the first place and how to make sure the problem doesn't happen again. This will involve investigating and reviewing all procedures until the weakness in the procedure is identified and rectified. New plans to change the procedure will have to be devised and implemented as a corrective measure.

 # SWOT analysis

Some organisations plan for the future using a SWOT analysis to take stock of where they are at a moment in time. Using SWOT analysis the organisation can assess the following:

Internal Factors:

◆ **S**trengths, i.e. the strong points of the organisation.
◆ **W**eaknesses, i.e. the problems it has at present.

External Factors:

◆ **O**pportunities which may arise in the future.
◆ **T**hreats which may arise and should be avoided.

On the completion of a SWOT analysis the organisation can decide what action needs to be taken whether it be to remedy a weakness or threat, or to enhance its strengths and exploit opportunities.

Factors in a SWOT analysis tend not to operate in isolation, for example, if an organisation can harness its strengths it may capitalise on an opportunity. An example of this is the concern relating to the depletion of the ozone layer which means that ultra violet rays will damage our skin and perhaps ultimately cause skin cancer. Organisations which produce sun tan lotion to help the tanning process may identify an opportunity by producing a lotion which completely protects the skin from harmful rays. This opportunity could perhaps be widened further by advertising companies extolling the virtues of having pale skin colour rather than one which is sun tanned.

Opportunities for some organisations may become threats to others making them vulnerable in the market place. For example a company may identify that there is an opportunity to exploit a situation but is constrained by being unable to meet this opportunity by being strapped for cash. An organisation faces problems when it identifies weaknesses to external threats and has limited means to respond to these threats. For instance, a rival company may have launched an unexpected new product which is taking sales away from its own product, and the organisation is not in a position to respond. The ultimate threat is loss of market share. From carrying out a SWOT analysis, an organisation may wish to reassess its strategy in the market place and take appropriate action.

Apple Computers – searching for a strategy

Apple Computers was started during the 1970s and came to fame with the Apple Macintosh. However, during the first quarter of 1996, Apple Computers made a record breaking loss of $740 million.

Two-thirds of Apple's yearly revenue comes from low profit-margin products sold primarily to the home, small business and education markets. The remaining third comes from sales of top-of-the-line computers like the 7500, 8500 and 9500, as well as most PowerBooks and servers (powerful computers accessible on the Internet). These high profit-margin products are complex to design, difficult to build and require skilled dovetailing of software and hardware. Apple has to spread the profits from these machines over a product line covering low profit-margin items. This cross-subsidisation results in a lack of finance, which means that innovation and product reliability have been stunted.

Apple has made the mistake of wanting to be in both the hardware and software businesses at the same time. In contrast, Microsoft have always been in the software business and are now the largest software company in the world. Apple have also suffered from several changes in leadership. Their original visionary leader and co-founder, Steve Jobs, was chief executive officer until 1985. He had been in charge of the development of the Macintosh and had saved the company with its launch. Since Steve Jobs, the company have had four different chief executive officers, whereas Bill Gates continues to lead Microsoft as he has done from its inception. Apple have 47 different models and their latest CEO, Gilbert Amelio, intends to simplify the product line as well as build on key markets and promote brand awareness.

Apple have suffered from extravagancies in the past. In 1984, they showed a television advertisement during the Super Bowl which appeared once, lasted for 60 seconds and cost $1.05 million. Apple's expensive headquarters are in Cupertino, California and consist of six buildings in a university campus-like setting. It is all designed to make employees feel special.

Mr Amelio, the CEO, has impressed Wall Street by taking some tough decisions to trim Apple's workforce, laying off 1500 people, bringing the total job cuts to 2800. Another possible solution is to license out manufacturing. By moving less profitable products to licensing partners, Apple could focus on what it does best – developing new technology, especially for the Internet.

DISCUSSION QUESTIONS 5.1

1 Using the information in Case study 5.1 carry out a SWOT analysis and discuss reasons for your inclusion of certain factors in the analysis.

2 Using the SWOT analysis, suggest what action Apple now need to take.

3 What differences do you think there are in strategic planning at Apple and Microsoft.

4 To what extent does it help an organisation to have a 'visionary leader' such as Steve Jobs?

Planning the operation

Whenever an activity has to be carried out there is always a time constraint. The timeframe is the time from starting the planning of a project to its completion time. The activities which have to be planned include estimating, planning and co-ordinating resources such labour, materials, machinery, and deciding which procedures should be involved in order to complete the activity. The manager's responsibility is to bring all these factors together when required, without shortages or surpluses, and to ensure that they are fully employed during the production time. Managers commit plans to paper to ensure the balance of factors is right and eventualities are planned for. The written plan can also act as a means of communicating information about a project to others.

As projects become more complex and there are a range of activities which are interdependent it is important that the sequence of these activities is planned. The sequencing of activities can be recorded on timetables or charts which indicate dates the planner has calculated. Questions the person planning the operation will need answered are:

◆ What is the start date?

◆ What is the completion date?

◆ Where exactly are we on the plan now?

◆ Where should we be on the plan now?

Gantt charts

Gantt charts are based on bar charts and are easily constructed and interpreted to show activities planned and completed at each stage of production in a timeframe. A Gantt chart shows the project broken down into activities. These are listed on the left hand side of the chart. The timeframe is indicated at the top or bottom of the chart. The duration and the scheduling of each activity is shown by a bar.

The example of the building of a house shows the major activities under headings: job, items for payment and payments due. The activities shown for April indicate the roof will be tiled between Monday 1st and Sunday 14th. This allows roof insulation to take place on Monday 15th and 16th. The roof insulation is expected to arrive on site on Friday 12th.

A Gantt chart is a relatively simple, visual and effective management tool for planning and controlling a simple project. It is possible to check each of the planned stages of the project and their planned completion against their actual completion. However it does not clearly show the level of interrelated and

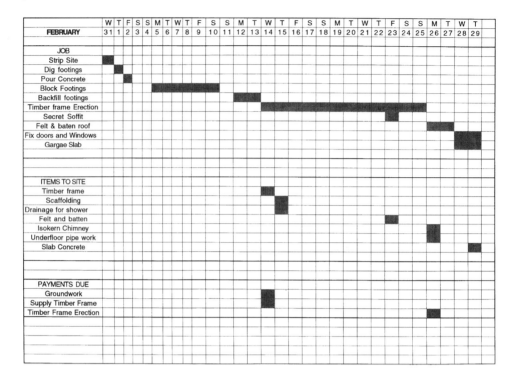

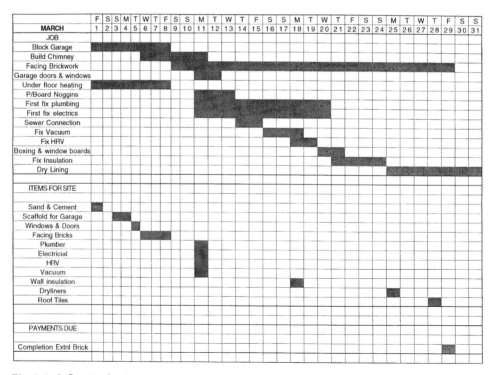

Fig 5.4 A Gantt chart

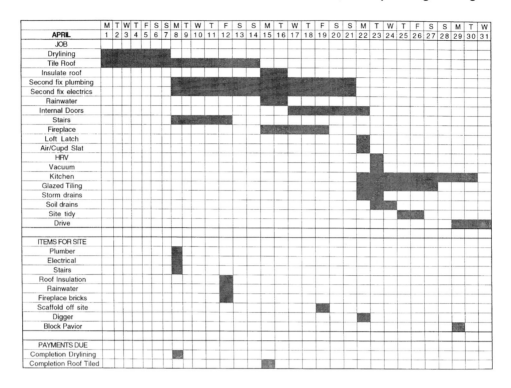

APRIL	M 1	T 2	W 3	T 4	F 5	S 6	S 7	M 8	T 9	W 10	T 11	F 12	S 13	S 14	M 15	T 16	W 17	T 18	F 19	S 20	S 21	M 22	T 23	W 24	T 25	F 26	S 27	S 28	M 29	T 30	W 31
JOB																															
Drylining	█	█	█	█	█	█																									
Tile Roof	█	█				█	█	█	█	█	█	█	█																		
Insulate roof															█																
Second fix plumbing							█	█	█	█	█	█	█	█	█	█	█														
Second fix electrics							█	█	█	█	█	█	█	█	█	█	█														
Rainwater															█	█															
Internal Doors																		█	█	█	█	█									
Stairs							█	█	█	█	█	█																			
Fireplace														█	█	█	█	█	█												
Loft Latch																						█									
Air/Cupd Slat																							█								
HRV																															
Vacuum																															
Kitchen																						█	█	█	█	█	█	█	█	█	
Glazed Tiling																						█	█								
Storm drains																															
Soil drains																								█							
Site tidy																									█						
Drive																													█	█	█
ITEMS FOR SITE																															
Plumber							█																								
Electrical							█																								
Stairs																															
Roof Insulation											█																				
Rainwater																															
Fireplace bricks											█																				
Scaffold off site																		█			█										
Digger																						█									
Block Pavior																											█				
PAYMENTS DUE																															
Completion Drylining							█																								
Completion Roof Tiled														█																	

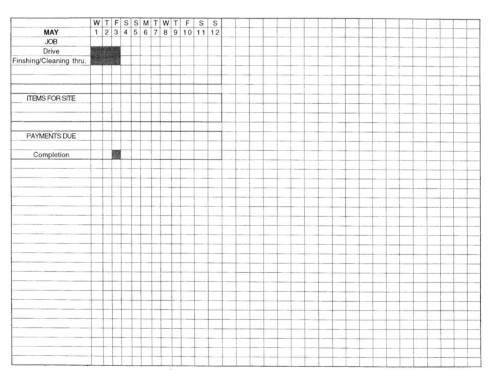

MAY	W 1	T 2	F 3	S 4	S 5	M 6	T 7	W 8	T 9	F 10	S 11	S 12
JOB												
Drive	█	█	█									
Finshing/Cleaning thru.	█	█	█									
ITEMS FOR SITE												
PAYMENTS DUE												
Completion		█										

(With thanks to Peter Cuthbert, Senior Lecturer, Manchester Metropolitan University.)

interdependent activities required by some projects. It is merely an indication of the times required for each stage of a project, the project itself is more complex and has more constraints on it.

 # Network analysis

Many projects are extremely complex, for example the building of the new Severn Bridge. It takes time to plan and organise the inputs into a process and an organisation does not necessarily want to have all of its raw materials, labour and capital available at the start of the project but when required. The project needs to be broken down into separate activities, the length of time for each activity determined, and when these activities can take place identified. This can be done by the use of a network analysis method.

Network planning methods involve breaking projects down into activities and determining the required length of time for each. They are more complex than Gantt charts because they consider the interrelationship between activities. There are two main network analysis methods which can be used:

◆ **PERT** (Programme Evaluation and Review Technique)
◆ **CPA** (Critical Path Analysis)

The Project: Making a cup of tea

This is a complex project which is performed every day. To make a cup of tea in the shortest time possible the activities are broken down on the basis of which activity takes the longest time to complete if the activities are analysed.

◆ boiling water
◆ obtaining cups/saucers
◆ obtaining ingredients
◆ putting the teabag in the pot
◆ pouring the water into the teapot
◆ letting the tea stand
◆ pouring the tea into the cups.

Of these activities, boiling the water takes the longest time and it should be started first. It is not dependent on the other activities being completed. Some activities are dependent on others, for example pouring the water into the teapot is dependent upon having boiled the water. Boiling water must come first. Other activities need to be sequenced to ensure the project is completed through its logical stages. It would be illogical to get out the cups and saucers before putting the kettle on.

CPA uses a shorthand system of letters of the alphabet to represent each event or activity. It is quicker to say that E is dependent upon A, rather than you must boil the water first before you can pour the boiling water into the teapot.

The next step is the construction of the network diagram. The main features of the diagram are:

Events

These are the events or the start or finish of a task. They are represented by circles called 'nodes'. The node contains information in the left-hand-side semicircle is the node number. The top right segment is the **E**arliest **S**tart **T**ime and the bottom right segment is the **L**atest **F**inish **T**ime.

Arrows which connect the nodes show the order in which the tasks must take place. Above the arrow will be a letter to represent the task and the number below the arrow will represent the time taken to complete that activity. A dotted arrow may represent slack time – the difference between the end of one activity and the start of the next activity.

Activities
$$\xrightarrow[24]{A}$$

The following activities are the breakdown of a project. The time taken for each activity to be completed can be estimated either in terms of minutes, hours or days. For example,

Activity	Duration in days
A	7
B	2
C	15
D	8
E	10
F	2
G	5
H	8
I	2
J	3

If the activities for the project were taken in sequence it would take 62 days to complete. This means that resources would be standing idle wasting money. Therefore, by constructing a network, it is possible to identify the relationship between activities – those activities which are independent of others and those activities which must precede others. The sequencing will help with the scheduling of the activities and shorten the time to completion. The relationships between the activities are as follows,

A

B

C

D must follow E

E must follow A and B

F must follow D and G

G must follow E

H must follow G

I must follow C and F

J must follow I

The network can be constructed from the data given or it is possible to order the activities in tabular form to ensure the order of sequence of the activities. Clarifying the relationships between activities can be done in stages, for example:

A

B

C

D must follow E

E must follow A and B

F must follow D and G

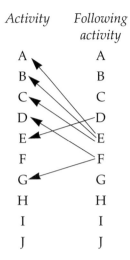

This shows that A, B, C, are independent activities and the network can start to be constructed as

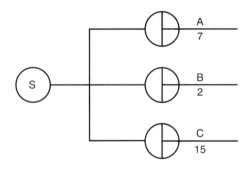

If the sequencing is continued,

D must follow E

E must follow A and B

F must follow D and G

G must follow E

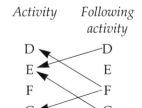

Although E is dependent on the previous activities A and B it precedes the other activities. The network can be extended to

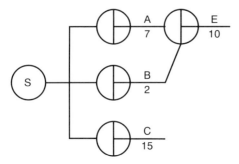

The next relationships can include

F must follow D and G

G must follow E

H must follow G

Activity   Following
*   activity*

At this stage D is the next activity which can be completed and the network can be extended to

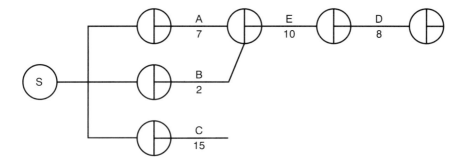

This sequencing continues until all their relationships between the activities are shown and the network can be completed. In some cases activities have identical predecessor activities and successor activities such as with activity F. The relationship here can be shown by drawing a dummy activity: this is depicted by a dotted arrow. The dummy solves any logical difficulties when drawing networks.

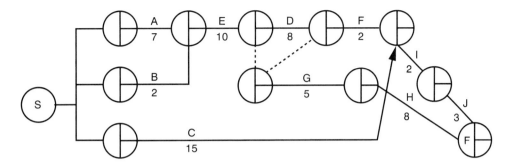

 ## The timing of the activities

The timing is important in critical path analysis because timing will not only show how quickly the project can be completed, but also it will show activities which may have slack or 'float' days. This means the activity has spare time and if it is delayed for any reason the delay will not affect the project or, if the float is of long enough duration, resources which have been earmarked for this activity may be used elsewhere until needed.

The earliest start time

The calculation is made from the start of the project.

A, B, C all have 0 start times,

E can only be completed after A so the earliest start time for E is 7.

D can only be completed after A and E and the earliest start time is 17.

This calculation is done for each pathway and the calculations are placed in the top segment of the node.

The latest start time

The calculations for each pathway are made from the end of the project and worked backwards. For example, to calculate the latest start time for C would be, finish 32 days, less 3 days for J, less 2 days for I and less 15 days for the completion of C, means the latest start time for C is 12 days.

The calculations are then shown in the bottom half of the node.

Activity	Earliest start time	Latest start time	Float	Activity	Earliest start time	Latest start time	Float
A	0	0	0	F	25	25	0
B	0	5	5	G	17	19	2
C	0	12	12	H	22	24	2
D	17	17	0	I	27	27	0
E	7	7	0	J	29	29	0

Identifying the critical path

The critical path is the longest time it takes to complete the project. This can be calculated by adding the times it takes to complete each pathway. In the example, the critical pathway will be

pathway   A   E   D   F   I   J

days   7 10 8 2 2 3

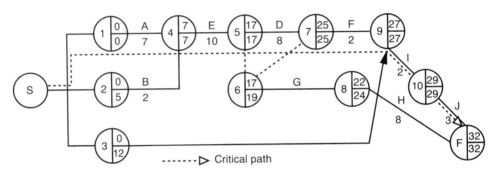

- - - - - - ▷ Critical path

The time to complete the project will now take 32 days.

It is also possible to identify the path by those activities which do not have a float.

Once the critical path has been analysed and the project is implemented the actual time taken to complete the activities should be recorded against the estimated time to identify any discrepancies in order that adjustments can be made. Thus network analysis helps managers to plan and control projects.

 # Planning break-even

Organisations need to be able to estimate how many units they have to produce before they make a profit. This analysis is important for those organisations which are setting up and need credit from a bank. They will have to show the bank manager that their organisation is financially viable and is projected to make a profit at a time in the future.

Break-even analysis is calculated by comparing costs over a range of outputs with the expected sales revenue from the sale of these units. An organisation breaks down its costs into:

- *Fixed costs* Those costs which do not alter as output changes, for example, the cost of buying equipment.
- *Variable costs* Those costs which do alter as output changes such as, the cost of energy.

Expected profit can be calculated by:

Fixed costs + Variable costs = Total costs.

Total sales revenue − Total costs = Profit.

However this does not inform the organisation how many units to produce and sell to break-even. Therefore to calculate output required by the organisation to break-even the following arithmetical calculation can be done:

$$\text{Break-even} = \frac{\text{fixed costs}}{\text{contribution}}$$

Contribution is the value of a product which goes towards paying for an element of fixed costs and profit. Contribution is calculated as selling price – variable cost.

Assume:

Fixed costs   = £10 000
Variable cost   = £8
Price per product = £12
Contribution   = £12 – £8
                          = £4

$$\text{Break-even} = \frac{\text{fixed costs}}{\text{contribution}}$$

$$\text{Break-even} = \frac{£10\,000}{£4}$$

$$= 2500$$

The organisation needs to produce 2500 units all of which need to sold at £12.

The break-even point can also be shown graphically:

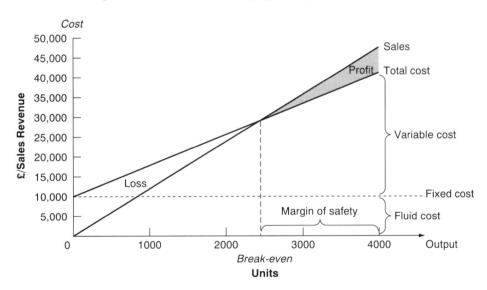

Fig 5.5 Break-even chart

If the organisation plans to produce 4000 units it will make a profit as shown in the break-even chart. The distance between producing 2500 units and 4000 units is known as the 'safety margin' and will allow for discrepancies in actual production. A break-even chart enables planners to see:

◆ the number of sales required to break-even

◆ what the planned effect of a price change would be on profit

◆ how planned changes in output may influence profit

◆ how the purchase of a fixed asset will change the relationship between total costs, sales revenue and profit

◆ how a planned change in variable cost will change the relationship between costs, sales revenue and profit.

Operations management

Operations management refers to the planning, organising, coordinating and controlling of all aspects of an organisation's operations, especially production. Production processes all differ to meet the needs of individual organisations. The processes can be categorised according to the variety of products produced, the number of repetitive orders and the quantity of the product produced. There are two types of production: intermittent and continuous. The characteristics of the intermittent production process include producing goods to individual requirements, for niche or segmented markets. The continuous production process is concerned with manufacturing identical products for a mass market.

Intermittent production

Jobbing

At the one extreme of the intermittent production process is 'Jobbing'. Examples of this method of production include the construction of ships, submarines and office blocks, the cleaning of windows or the servicing of a car. Output is determined by demand for the particular product. The scale of operations will depend on the product being built, for example to build submarines will require large investment in capital equipment, a specific location and a large area for the submarines' construction and launch. An organisation making driveways out of ornamental bricks will be much smaller, will require less investment in equipment and can operate from a smaller location. Some jobbing operations may be repetitive, for example cleaning windows on a housing estate where the houses are similar. However, the demands of the householder might vary slightly such as one having all windows cleaned, another might want their windows and glass in doors cleaned, and someone else only wanting the upstairs windows cleaned.

Job production is suited to meeting the demands of the individual customer. Usually the customer will already have the design or will be closely involved with the design of the product. The close working arrangement with the customer enables the design to be changed during production. For example, the production company may come forward with new suggestions, or because costs are rising more quickly than expected, the customer may change their specifications.

The organisation has to be flexible to produce different designs. This may be an advantage for the people involved with the construction of the product as they may have more job satisfaction compared with those on a production line. They are not tied to the speed on the 'line' and there is less chance of the workers suffering from job alien-ation. For example, those construction workers who built the Channel

Fig 5.6

Tunnel will be able to see and recognise the contribution of their efforts, whereas someone working in a car factory will know that they helped in producing only a small part of hundreds of thousands of cars.

The need to be flexible and responsive to the demands of the individual means the organisation will use more general purpose machinery. When costing a new job one of the important factors which has to be taken into account is the requirement to purchase new machinery which might only be used for one specific job. The tunnelling machine used for the construction of the Channel Tunnel has limited uses! It is the estimation of costs in times of uncertainty which is a drawback to jobbing production. If a price is agreed based on costs, and, if during construction costs suddenly rise because of inflationary pressures the production company could face financial difficulties.

Batch production

Combining intermittent production with repetition is called 'Batch' production where a variety of similar products can be made with production runs depending on the product and the availability of raw materials. For example, a wallpaper manufacturer will produce a particular design, and will mix the colour dyes to the specified shades. The production run will last until the dyes are exhausted. The wallpaper produced will be given a batch number to ensure that all the wallpaper from that run are kept together. To continue the design more dye will be mixed but because there might be slight difference in the dye shades this production run will be given a different batch number.

The feature of batch production is that many different products can be produced at the same time, it relies on general purpose machinery which can be used in a variety of ways, and machines can be grouped according to the process they fulfil. By being able to change production methods the organisation can be flexible in meeting different customers' specifications. This flexibility means that the workforce need to be skilled in their particular area and that there be sophisticated costing, planning and control systems to manage this flexible production.

Continuous production

This is a highly repetitive type of production, in which identical products are made for a mass market, for example the manufacture of cars, TV sets and washing machines. This type of production includes ensuring raw materials and components are always in stock, and that machines are always maintained to guarantee the flow of the product along the production line.

The work is divided into its simplest components so that workers concentrate on a simple task which is relatively easy to perform. By continually performing the same task each day, the worker becomes an expert in that task. Continuous production also allows specialist machinery to be employed to carry out tasks. The use of technology operated efficiently in the mass production continuous process makes products to the same standard irrespective of the numbers produced. The standardised product produced on the standardised production line enables the managers to monitor performance more clearly. Continuous production methods are suitable for large scale production and gains are accrued from this, such as bulk buying. The gains from large scale mass produced products mean unit costs will be low compared with job production products.

This method of production has drawbacks, the speed of the production line is set by management which can incite conflict causing workers to lose interest in their job so that they become bored and alienated from the product they produce. Each worker is dependent on the previous one in the line and payment is by output. Therefore in this process the quality of the product can be affected by the input of labour and for many years to maintain quality, management installed quality checks at different stages of production. This is labour intensive and may add little to the value of the product. The response of management to these problems has been to review the production process and mechanise the process as much as possible and look at different ways to enrich the work experience for labour. Schemes such as teamwork, job rotation and quality circles have been introduced which has enabled the workforce to do its job better. By breaking down the process into teams this has enabled the team themselves to monitor their own standard of input. They have been able to review and monitor their own progress and, where necessary, implement changes.

The impact of changes in technology on the production process has been to facilitate the monitoring and control of the production process, and the use of Japanese production methods has changed the way in which many organisations now operate.

CASE STUDY 5.2

Production at Morley's Bakehouse

There are ten Bakehouse bakeries/shops in Cheshire and Stoke-on-Trent. The production process covers just a few metres, with bread and cakes being made at the back of the shop and sold over the counter to customers. The baker working at the back of the shop can be seen by the public, as can the ovens and newly baked produce. Chris Morris is the Baker/Manager and Craig is his Assistant.

Chris Morris:

'We arrive at 5 am, the first job is to put the ovens on to warm up, then we switch the radio on, have a cup of tea and get changed. The first mix of dough is 32 kilos, the large and small loaves, bloomers and cobs all come out of that first mix of bread. It takes about two hours from starting the first mix to it coming out of the oven. You mix the first mix, take it out of the bowl, chop it into the sizes that you require, drop it into the tin and place it into the prover, that's a steam cabinet which proves the yeast and makes the bread rise – that takes about half an hour. You have to take everything into account when you're making the

Fig 5.7 Chris Morris, baker and manager of Morley's Bakehouse

dough: water temperature, flour temperature, the temperature outside, that affects how fast things work. You have to make major adjustments when the season changes, on warm days you can have bread proving over the tins and the quality suffers.

After that, you start again with the wholemeal. Craig and I work as team, I mix and divide it up, Craig puts it into the tins. We have to work as a team to achieve maximum production. As soon as the mixer stops, the next mix goes on, wholemeal and granary. You stick to a regular routine so that the bread which needs the highest temperature is baked first because after that batch, the oven is cooler. It's an electric oven but the energy is absorbed by the cold metal tins. The oven temperature can drop between 100–150 degrees during one baking. The oven has to recover or you can follow on the first batch with things that need less heat. We then move to french sticks, baps, finger rolls and what we call morning goods – iced fingers and fruit bread. We make all our own icing and custard and fresh cream cakes. We also have some items which are pre-baked and readymade such as chocolate eclairs and pastry case shells.

There's no particular target, the target is whatever we sold last week. We need a crystal ball to forecast what people will buy, if things sell well we make them again.'

Bread production normally consists of 150 loaves, made in large and small sizes, and various types of flour: white, wholemeal and granary. In addition to the bread loaves Chris and Craig make around 420 rolls and baps. Unsold bread is thrown away at the end of the day, the staff are allowed to take home one loaf each per day. As well as Chris and Craig who work full-time, there are eight part-time staff who work in the shop. Chris:

'If the owner could get away with it, Craig and I would be part-time, it's so competitive in the present climate. We can't calculate for exact production, it's "how long is a piece of string". Somebody could turn up with a coachload of old age pensioners who might buy every cake we've got – how do you account for that? It's happening all the time like that on a lesser basis. We'd finished baking this morning and someone rang for 12 french sticks. They're in business themselves and they knew that they should have asked me earlier. I have to decide what I'm going to make early on in the morning. Part of the staff's job is to pack and present the produce, make sandwiches and serve the customers. We get visited by the Health Inspector, he comes in for his lunch every day. It's another thorn in the side, we're on show all the time, if he saw anything untoward he could step in at anytime. The customers judge you anyway. If a customer doesn't like what he sees he won't come in again – the public are unforgiving. I'm under pressure in a wider sense in that people are going to supermarkets and shops where they've already got these things prepared at very competitive prices. If things are not quite ready and not on display, people will walk out and it's your own fault. If your doughnuts just aren't ready they may call back in a few minutes, but you can't calculate what you win or lose. You've got to have what other people don't supply. You need to have something special which people like, such as our honey and sunflower loaf, it's difficult to get the sunflower seeds but people often ask if they're available. I'm not supposed to make my own decisions. Head Office tells me what to make, but it's no good making things that won't sell.

Head Office are in contact every day or every other day, they check on stock – amounts of ingredients used. I place an order once per week straight to the wholesaler which is part of the company – Morley's Importers, they import flour and fruit. This ties us to where we buy our ingredients from. The General Manager is always in conflict with the company because things are cheaper elsewhere. But if we tried to shop around we could end up with so many suppliers that we might not win out eventually anyway. We might save money on jam from somewhere else, but it takes time running around and we might have to buy a whole pallet load of it.

Head Office set prices, we have to do the costings, and then we ask ourselves, "would I pay that?" Supermarkets are a big problem, everything is at very competitive prices. Takings fluctuate, it's uncontrollable, it's up and down too much. We don't know what people are doing, there are so many opportunities to go elsewhere that it's getting more and more of a slippery pole. At one time there used to be a cobbler on every street corner, but now people buy a new pair of shoes instead of getting them mended. We're a dying trade too.

My main target is to cut down waste. It's a difficult balance, if you don't make enough you sell out too soon. We do burn things, the chances of burning things are quite high because we do so many different products. If you're working alone and you're mixing a dough, it needs concentration to make the best quality dough, you've also got to put things in the oven and walk away. There are five ovens and you've got to remember what's in each and how long its been in there. It comes down to skill, a chef wouldn't have an alarm on his sauce and I don't have them on my ovens. The counter staff don't help out. It's a bit sad because if we had a bit more co-operation things might be better. It works the other way, we're so engrossed in our work we don't help them. It could be construed as interference if we started doing one another's jobs. Craig and I work as a team, but not with the shop staff. If we're all working hard and things need to be done, something might have been sitting on the shelf at the back for too long, but it's difficult to say "can we have this packed?" because that person is working flat out. We feel short staffed quite often.

It's an advantage having the retail outlet so close. Everything is very fresh and if customers want a particular item, they ask the counter staff and they can ask us immediately, we can then say that it will be five or ten minutes. I can't chat to customers because I lose my concentration, I forget what I've done, it's very important to keep my concentration. There's no staff training for customer service, the knowledge is passed on from one person to another. The manageress of the shop interviews the new shop staff. I'm not convinced that we should have younger girls working on a Saturday, because they're not quick enough. At the same time I do feel that you should give people a chance.

Head Office don't advertise, it's difficult to advertise. People's habits are changing, more go to the supermarket than ever, children copy what their parents do, they think everything comes from one shop. Each generation is having a toll on the business due to the change in shopping habits. We have a high percentage of older customers who shop in the village. Younger people all seem to have cars and trips are made out to the supermarket because so many factors make the trip worthwhile.'

DISCUSSION QUESTIONS 5.2

1 What difficulties does Chris Morris face when planning production levels at the Bakehouse?
2 What advantages are there to small-scale production?
3 Why does Chris feel that small bakeries are a dying trade?

Work planning and organisation at British Steel

British Steel plc, Shelton Works, situated in North Staffordshire, is part of the Sections, Plates and Commercial Steels (SP & CS) business organisation. Shelton Works manufactures 400 kilometric tonnes per year of universal beams and columns, collectively referred to as sectional steel products, and employs 380 people, 330 of whom are shopfloor. The products are used in the construction of all types of steel-framed buildings such as high rise office blocks and out-of-town shopping complexes. SP & CS has other plants in Teesside and Scunthorpe which make similar products as Shelton but in different size ranges. Unlike these other plants, Shelton has no steel making facilities on site, it relies on the supply of semi-finished product in the form of bloom (blocks of steel) from either of these two plants. Derek Tate, Mill Manager:

'One of the features of the domestic construction industry, our main customer, is that it is one of the first industries to feel recessionary pressure. It tends to suffer large peaks and troughs in activity which in turn affects demand for our products. SP & CS, in an effort to keep volume up and their plants loaded during this low domestic activity, look to their export markets. Europe is the most important market, others include the United States and the Far East.'

Fig 5.8 Derek Tate, Mill Manager, British Steel, Sections, Plates and Commercial Steels, Shelton Works

The international market for steel is very competitive, as there are sectional steel producers similar to British Steel in almost every country worldwide. Profit margins in the export market are continually being squeezed and are often lower than those gained by domestic sales. Shelton typically exports 70 per cent of its production, but this can increase up to 85 per cent when domestic market demand is very low.

The Production Control Department handles customer orders and employs 23 people. It links with the two operating sections: Hot Rolling and Cold Finishing. To minimise the times they are lying idle due to line changes i.e. product change, both operating sections, collectively referred to as 'the mill', require the products to be manufactured in batches of 800 tonnes. This is determined by the time the mill is operating in the manufacture of one product whilst preparation work is ongoing for the next product. The ideal time for the rolling (where hot steel is passed between rollers) of one batch of production is between 16 and 24 hours, but this is only possible when demand is high and customers are ordering large batches. The mill produces 80 or so different products and the grouping of customer orders according to product is an important part of the Production Control Department's work. Each product is manufactured once every two or three months.

In order to achieve a line change, the production process must cease. As this incurs cost without producing revenue, Production Control attempts to plan the production so that downtime is minimised. In addition to various sizes of steel section, the sections can be made from different chemistries of steel. Derek Tate:

'When customers request non-standard chemistries, we will often ask to look at their application and where possible advise them to use a standard chemistry. Non-standards tend to be small batch sizes. In the case where the customer's needs necessitate non-standard chemistry, then the smallest economic batch size will be produced. The customer will be supplied and the remaining tonnage will be stocked awaiting further orders. This is an expensive way of doing business but it ensures customer satisfaction. The first tactic, of advising the customer to take a standard product, is the most cost effective.'

Good customer service is vital in a highly competitive market. Derek Tate:

'The business competes on price and our customer service gives us the competitive edge. We are reducing our manufacturing costs progressively and we believe that British Steel is as cost competitive as any world manufacturer. We promise to deliver on time every time

and we work closely with customers to try and give us an edge over our many competitors but basically the war is won on price.'

When a different product is to be manufactured it takes around eight hours for a team of men to prepare a set of standby rolling stands. These are made ready for the production of the next size in the production schedule. During these eight hours, the mill continues to roll the previous size in the production schedule. At the end of that production run the mill ceases. Large overhead cranes lift away the used rolling stands and replace them with the standby units. This operation takes 50 minutes and represents lost production time. The mill produces for 15 shifts per week, which is a five day week, three shifts per day. There is a capability of producing for 20 shifts per week but increased shifts mean less time for maintenance. This is currently done at weekends. Derek Tate explains:

'In terms of production planning, we operate on a soft production schedule which is a three month look ahead at the order requirements. This is refined to a hard production schedule two weeks in advance of the rolling mill. Our ability to stick rigidly to the hard schedule depends very much on the commercial scene at the time. When fewer orders come in that hard schedule needs to be much more flexible and by necessity we will undertake line changes more often to roll smaller batch sizes.'

The manufacturing operation at Shelton is divided into two sections.

1 *Hot Rolling.* Highly automated employing 100 people, comprising of two processes, reheating and rolling.

   Reheating prepares the raw material for hot rolling. Seven metre long rectangular blocks of steel (blooms) are heated to a temperature of 1300 degrees centigrade. This renders the steel soft and ductile. The steel, at this high temperature, is transferred to the first of three milling processes. Each milling process in turn progressively changes the shape of the steel until finally the 'H' shape is produced.

   Rolling is the process whereby the shape is achieved by the action of large steel rollers between which the heated steel passes. The steel rollers squeeze and deform the material passing between them until the final desired shape emerges.

   These two milling processes are controlled by operators aided by computer. The operators are situated close to the mill in purpose-built control boxes known as 'pulpits'.

2 *Cold Finishing.* Labour intensive with low levels of automation, employing 200 people and comprising of four processes: sawing, cooling, straightening and dispatching.

   The rolled steel leaving the last of the milling processes can be up to 85 metres in length. This requires sawing to length, according to customer requirements. Customers generally order sections between 12 and 15 metres, therefore, the cold finishing section must deal with seven or eight times more pieces than the hot rolling sections. This fact, combined with the more labour intensive nature of the work, explains why twice as many people are employed in the cold processing compared to hot rolling.

CASE STUDY cont

The temperature of the steel being sawn has fallen to 900 degrees centigrade. It is necessary, before cold straightening, to reduce this to 50 degree centigrade. To achieve this the bars are passed over a series of cooling banks where they are air cooled to the desired temperature.

The cooling process has the effect of inducing bends and twists into the product, a result of uneven cooling along the surface. Because of this it is necessary to cold straighten the product by once again passing the material between a series of steel rolls. This process straightens the cold product to the exact requirements of the customer. The product is now ready for delivery to the customer, either by road or rail.

Efficiency and performance measures

Three indicators of efficiency and performance are recognised by all hot rolled steel product producers:

1 *Mill availability* The number of productive rolling hours achieved per week. World best mill availability is recorded at 82 per cent compared to Shelton's 79.5 per cent. The lost production time includes line changes as well as production and engineering failures.

2 *Yield* The difference between the weight of the steel as raw material going into the reheating process compared to the weight of the steel being sold to customers. World best yield for a mill producing Shelton's product range is 95 per cent, compared to Shelton's current performance of 93.8 per cent. Yield loss is accounted for by the weight loss due to:

◆ Oxidation during heating and rolling 1–2 per cent

◆ Waste resulting from imperfect manufacture 1–2 per cent

◆ Failure to utilise all available rolled product length into customer orders 3–4 per cent

3 *Speed* The weight of material or number of blooms rolled per hour. Speed is a measure of how fast the mill is operating, and is dependent not only on the capability of the mill equipment, but also on the skill and motivation of the people operating that equipment. Operators are encouraged, through financial inducements, to work as fast as possible, whilst ensuring that the product is of good quality.

Using these indicators rolling mills can benchmark their performance against competitor mills worldwide. The Japanese, are acknowledged as world leaders in steel rolling practice, and provide the world's best performances.

SP & CS business introduced TQM some 15 years ago, shortly after the 13 week steel strike. The idea then was to develop trust between management and shopfloor and improve working relationships. Derek Tate:

'We have progressed towards the Japanese idea of total quality, adopting as the norm quality circles, empowerment and the development of self-managed teams. We have moved through the stage where TQM was seen as just a tool to get us to work together to solve problems. It is now a culture.'

CASE STUDY cont

There are many examples of proactive process improvement teams in all parts of Shelton Works. For example, a team working in the cold straightening process area has been effective in reducing customer complaints by 90 per cent. The teams firstly agree the right way to do the job, then apply those methods across all three shifts, giving consistency with all teams carrying out the work in the same way.

Failure analysis has been adopted, getting rid of the negative 'blame culture' and adopting a positive attitude of 'what do we need to do to put things right?' Learning from others has been an important part of the drive for continuous improvement, for instance, members of the straightening team recently visited Nippon Steel Corporation's mill near Tokyo. The Japanese, in turn, have visited Shelton, an experience found to be very valuable by all participants as they shared ideas and learnt from one another.

The TQM programme has improved efficiency in all areas of the works. Three years ago the Mill had an availability of 72 per cent and and yield of less than 91 per cent compared to today's figures of 79.5 per cent and 93.8 per cent. Improvements have also been achieved by adopting an analytical approach to problem solving. Each failure is analysed thoroughly to determine the true cause and then, where possible, to introduce preventative measures. From the adoption of these total quality measures, availability and yield performance has gradually improved. Derek Tate:

'If we have an incident or failure on the Mill, we brainstorm as a team and try to find the true cause. Having got agreement as to the true cause then we put our minds around how to prevent it from occurring again in the future. In the last three years we have had an injection of capital to improve the operating pulpits: sound proofing, air conditioning, ergonomics and more computerisation. The Mill is a hostile environment – noisy, hot, dangerous and dirty – we believe by improving the operator's working conditions we improve their concentration, motivation and efficiency.

If there is an opportunity to invest capital in the business, we start with a clean sheet of paper and think creatively how we could best use the money. Cost reduction is the driver, we will only invest where we can reduce costs.'

Flow of work

Computers are used throughout the works to measure, control and monitor the flow of work. Computer systems work at three levels:

◆ Level 1 Micro computers. Dedicated to a single process, controlling and monitoring the operation of that single processing unit, for example, one of the three milling processes.

◆ Level 2 Mini Computers. Continually reading and linking the micros. Acting as a short term storage facility for data gathered from the micros and for data required by the micros.

◆ Level 3 Mainframe Computers. Situated at Teesside, continually reading and linking the two mini computers via a dedicated telephone link. This computer acts as 'big brother' for Shelton Works, providing on-line a wide variety of services to every workplace.

The mainframe provides on-line and immediate details of delays, yields, speeds, as well as week by week production schedules. It also provides a word processor package used extensively throughout the plant for shift reports, passing messages or just general information flow. Derek Tate:

'At any point in time the operator can check his own and his shift's performance. He can see at a glance what is left to roll and what is completed. He is also able to see what we are rolling tomorrow or next week. We have an expediter on each shift, his primary function is to check actual progress against the plan. This man is paid to check other people's performance. He's an expensive guy to keep but we think he's worth it. He is able to monitor the process from a centrally located operating pulpit, the computer systems continually providing him with the operational detail. He simply manages the process by ringing around, talking to key people, checking that things are going to plan and on occasions he will need to step in to take corrective action. As mill performance improves and operators are more certain, these interventions become less frequent.'

Changing plans

Derek Tate:

'For example, a need to change the plan would occur when equipment is damaged or fails in service. Dependent upon when this occurs in the rolling batch, the decision to repair the damage and complete the batch, or, line change to the next product needs to be made. For example, if we have planned to roll a batch of 1000 tonnes and having completed only 500 tonnes, part of the mill becomes damaged. The decision is a commercial one – change to the standby mill and lose the ability to complete that product size, in so doing we fail to meet customer delivery dates, or stand the mill to fix the fault and so incur a large financial penalty but ensure that the customer orders are completed. This decision needs to be taken quickly and very often in the middle of the night. Who makes that decision depends mainly on the consequences. In the 500 tonne example, the consequences could be drastic, with many customers involved. For this reason the decision would be referred to me, or my boss.

Fig 5.9 Controlling the production process from computerised 'pulpits' with closed circuit television at British Steel, Shelton Works

If the tonnage left is as little as five tonnes, then the Shift Manager is authorised to act. An outcome of the overall process improvements already mentioned is that we need to make these changes less often. We are working in a more certain environment. Five years ago, we would be changing the plan 10 times a week, now it's once a month. Decisions taken in the middle of the night are now an unusual event. The message is "plan the work and work the plan".

However, we need to have the flexibility to respond to our customers' late order requests. If we get urgent orders it is important that we are flexible enough to inject these orders to the mill programme at very short notice. The computer systems are configured to make this possible. If a customer rings

CASE
STUDY

cont

us saying that he knows we are rolling this order today and has ordered 100 bars and now he'd like 120, we do everything we can to give him the 120 bars. It's an important part of customer service.

There are just so many improvements, not least is the change in the mill, its surroundings and the workforce changed from a gloomy, demotivated place with no visible evidence of any improvement activity, to a bright, clean, colourful workplace that greets visitors and customers daily, and it is all due to the people at Shelton who do the work, the manager is just the catalyst for change.'

DISCUSSION QUESTIONS 5.3

1 What similarities are there between the Bakehouse and British Steel in terms of demand for product and competition?

2 Are both firms using batch production methods? How does their production planning differ?

3 What problems do both firms experience when changing the product being made?

4 Why has the Bakehouse got greater flexibility in its production process than British Steel?

5 How does the use of heat in both production processes cause problems in forecasting precisely the volume of production?

6 How does the use of teamwork improve production planning at British Steel?

7 What constraints are there on the Bakehouse staff working as a team?

8 Why is the plan changed less frequently now at British Steel than it was in the past?

Effectiveness and efficiency

Effectiveness is the ability to select goals and to achieve them, whereas efficiency is the ability to make the optimum use of resources available in the process of achieving goals. Both are performance criteria and can be used to compare internal and external performance.

Effectiveness enables the organisations to measure its performance against its goals. For example, a company might have achieved a 40 per cent increase in sales over the last five years and now has 12 per cent of the UK market. Its goal might have been to take 10 per cent of market share. In some circumstances objectives and outputs might be difficult to measure and the effectiveness of organisations might be expressed in subjective terms saying for instance, the effectiveness of Northfield Hospital has improved lately but Westfield Hospital has deteriorated.

Efficiency refers to the ratio of outputs to inputs, i.e. the amount of resources needed such as the amount of raw materials, money and labour required to produce a given volume of output. Comparability can be made between organisations or within organisations. For example, the number of cars made per man hour can be compared between companies and also between plants within a company. Efficiency usually enables a quantitative measure or performance to be made. Organisations come under pressure to increase their efficiency because of the competition they face, the rewards their owners expect through dividends and the need to compete for resources. Organisations can become more efficient by investigating saving measures which could be made through its operations.

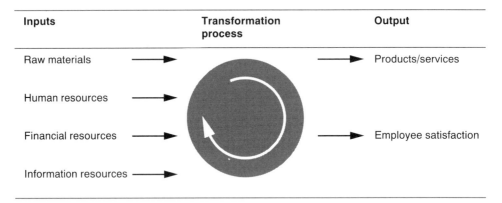

Fig 5.10 Efficiency refers to the ratio of outputs to inputs

Measures of efficiency

The measures of efficiency can relate closely to performance indicators and include, for example, the number of suppliers, financial ratios, time to complete the transformation process and delivery times to the customer.

Increasing efficiency

In the 1980s organisations pursued efficiency by introducing changes in the production process, the use of labour and the introduction of technology. Some firms have made particular efficiency gains through process re-engineering where all the procedures of an organisation are investigated to see whether it is possible to reduce those procedures which do not add value to the process as a whole.

Employing lean production techniques such as JIT, Total Preventive Maintenance and TQM cuts down on waste and will enable the organisation to reduce costs. Employing work studies such as method study will reduce non-added value activities from the production process and procedures. Work measurement may indicate changes in the standard time to produce the product. Ultimately, there then may be major changes in the organisation so it may become leaner. There may also be a delayering of management.

Organisations may invest in labour saving machines to increase efficiency with the most obvious example being the computer. Increased investment in machinery will, in the long-run, improve efficiency because machines are being continually updated to improve their performance as is the case with computers, cars and telephone systems.

Plant layout

Effective layout of factories and offices provides the opportunity for maximising efficiency in the production of goods and services. Having necessary equipment located in distant or inconvenient places makes the production process less efficient and more time consuming. Plant layouts in organisations are determined by factors which include the location of the organisation, for example in a city, or in a rural area. Factors also to be considered include the process and the product involved, for example generating electricity or building computers or offering a service such as fast food or insurance will all require different layouts due to the way the product is made. The actual manufacture will determine the layout of the plant. For example, one of the most efficient methods of manufacturing steel on a large scale is by linking all the processes. This saves on costs because the steel does not have to go through the expensive process of being reheated at each stage. The heat from the furnaces also determines the location of machinery raw materials and labour.

The factors which have to be taken into account when planning plant layout include:

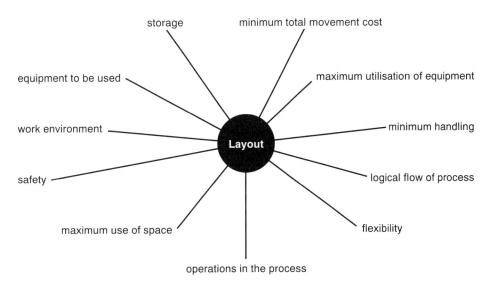

Fig 5.11 Factors to take into account when planning plant layout

Plant layouts can be categorised as follows:

◆ fixed layout
◆ process layout
◆ product layout
◆ cellular layout.

Fixed layout

Building an oil rig will determine the location of the organisation as well as the plant layout. The raw materials need to arrive at one location and there needs to be an area large enough for the launch. Specific machinery needs to be located for their best possible usage because it will be difficult to change once construction has begun. Building office blocks or constructing houses have to be in the position of sale. Materials will have to be brought in for the construction such as bricks and cement. Other parts of the construction can be prefabricated and be brought in to be fitted as a unit. Restrooms can be made off site and brought in and fitted as a unit. Curtain wall building has speeded up the building of office blocks, for example by being partially prefabricated with windows already in position and glazed. Machinery such as cranes will be brought in and removed after use.

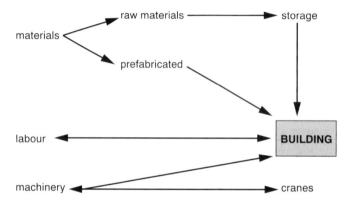

Fig 5.12 Building construction site

Process layout

Facilities and equipment are grouped according to the different functions carried out. For example, in supermarkets all the checkouts may be located together, and in an insurance company all the claims will be located together. Locating

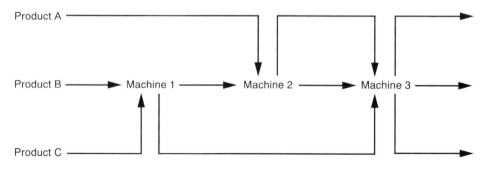

Fig 5.13 Process layout

machines and people in a designated area brings economies of scale and reduced costs.

Process layout is used in batch processes enabling different lines to follow different paths through set processes in accordance with the the processing requirements. This may cause problems because the actual path a product takes can be long and complicated as it passes through several different processes before completion; some production lines can be three or four miles long.

Product layout

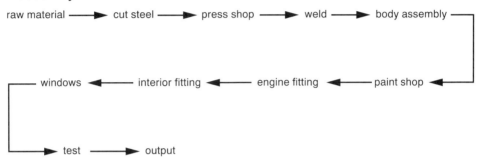

Fig 5.14 Layout by product

This layout is used where large volumes of a small range of items follow the same sequence and progress of operations. The car assembly line is an example of this layout and a fast food chain will organise its layout according to the products it sells, for example, beefburgers and doughnuts. This plant layout benefits

Fig 5.15 Now that is what I call efficiency

from economies of scale as it produces huge volumes of a standardised product.

Cellular layout

This layout is based on group technology principles which combine the advantages of layout by product, fast throughput times, low cost per item made and the layout by process which provides the flexibility of batch production. The 'U' shaped cells provide efficiencies in material and tool handling and inventory movement. This reduces process time and costs. The workers operate in close proximity, which lends itself to teamwork and problem solving. It also encourages job flexibility as workers normally operate more than one machine.

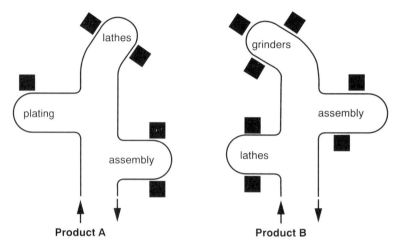

Fig 5.16 Cellular layout

 # Work study

Work study refers to those techniques which attempt to find the most efficient method of utilising resources in an organisation. Two of the techniques used are method study and work measurement. Work study is concerned with finding out whether there is a better way of carrying out and completing an activity. Work measurement relates to how long an activity should take.

Method study

This involves six stages:

◆ identifying the activity to be investigated
◆ recording the present process
◆ asking what is done?
◆ discussing new ideas
◆ implementing new ideas
◆ offering continued support.

Identifying the activity to be investigated

The type of problem to be investigated can be related to any activity for example: goods returned; increasing labour turnover; decreasing productivity; or lost sales.

Recording the present process

One of the problems facing organisations with their existing procedures and processes is they were originally installed to meet the requirements of the organisation at a particular time. As organisations change, develop and grow the procedures and processes may continue to be carried out in a particular way because 'that is the way it has always been done'.

Asking what is done?

The next stage in the work study should be to examine the present tasks, procedures and processes seeking answers to the following questions.

1   What is done, how is it done, when it is done, and who does it?
2   Why is it done that way?
3   Can we think of another way it could be done?
4   Does the task, procedure or process add value to the product?

New ideas

From the investigation new ideas will come forward which need to be discussed with the people concerned. The changes will be successful if the people involved can see how it will benefit them, the organisation and the customer.

Implementing the new ideas

Convincing people of the benefits is the first task since their compliance is important. Planning of the installation of the idea is fundamental to its success. For example, the changes may involve changing the way people work which may require them to learn new skills. Training people will be the key to building their confidence in accepting and implementing the changes.

Continued support

Once changes have been implemented the people involved need to be offered support to maintain their confidence. Until they gain experience in the operations it should be ensured that people do not go back to the previous procedures. During the initial phase any teething problems can be dealt with quickly and efficiently.

 # Re-engineering

Management consultants are making millions of dollars out of re-engineering in America. It is the latest fad in a long line of new cures for business ills. But what is it?

Businesses produce a service or product for their customers. They all manage to do this, otherwise they would not stay in business. Re-engineering examines exactly *how* this is done. Some businesses may have grown in a haphazard way over many years. Other businesses may have planned their growth carefully and are now wondering whether they were going in the right direction. Many businesses are looking for improvements in how they do things, so that costs can be saved and profits increased. Management consultants implementing re-engineering plans (also called 'core process redesign') attempt to identify exactly what processes are taking place in the business to produce the product or service. Questions such as 'What does the company want to achieve?' and 'What is it doing to achieve it?' need to be asked. The answers to those questions provide the starting point to the re-engineering process. It may be that they are not doing the things they need to do to achieve their objectives, or that they could be doing them more effectively.

Traditionally, if businesses wanted to improve their process, they would ask heads of departments to review the performance of their section. The finance director or purchasing manager would write a report on what their department did and how it could be improved. Recommendations would normally be about specific tasks and would often show small improvements. However, re-engineering looks at the *whole* business. It examines:

◆ the strategy the business uses to achieve its objectives

◆ the processes going on in the business to make the product or service

◆ the technology used in the business, especially the information systems

◆ the people who work in the business.

Re-engineering is concerned with major improvements and not with fine details. Traditionally, the production manager of an area which produced small parts for the rest of the factory, who was asked to report on small improvements to be made in their department in the past, would never recommend that the whole department be closed and the work be subcontracted out. Re-engineering takes a look at the entire organisation. Re-engineering can be thought of as being authoritarian with the workers being informed of changes to be made after the decisions have been taken.

In the UK, re-engineering has only been taken up by the financial services sector. The National and Provincial Building Society's 're-design programme' was started in 1990. They plan to reduce eight levels of management to three levels and more than 20 grades of jobs to four grades. The changes are going ahead very slowly because managers may feel threatened by the loss of power. The board of directors is now the 'directions management team' and directors are no longer responsible for functions such as finance and marketing; they are directors of 'customer engagement' and 'customer requirements'. There is a dual system of 'competency assessment' and performance-related pay. The building society hopes to reduce the average time it takes to process a mortgage from 27 days to as little as one day. Re-engineering is not a 'quick fix': it does take years to implement. In America, it is still a growing trend.

Shocking to the core

Re-engineering is all to do with radically reviewing how a business works in order to achieve dramatic improvement. Michael Hammer, the business consultant who coined the term 're-engineering', says those who seriously adopt re-engineering techniques find that they can do the same work with 40–80 per cent fewer employees. One survey respondent admitted the greatest barrier to 'business process re-engineering' (BPR) in his company was 'getting the turkeys to vote for Christmas'.

Rohit Talwar, head of business re-engineering at BMS Bossard:

'Don't underestimate BPR There are obscene levels of hype and false expectations being generated. As a result, some firms are being seduced into expensive and disastrous initiatives. Radical, step-change improvements in service, efficiency and quality can be achieved – but you have to be prepared for a great deal of pain to get them. Why? Because re-engineering means fundamentally changing the "way we do things" and that means changing the culture.'

Re-engineering may not be rocket science but it does require a clear sense of strategic direction and priorities, genuine chief executive and top management commitment and a massive investment in training. Turkeys often drag their feet, but without their vote any BPR effort is doomed. The scale of a purist's re-engineering effort is so vast that many organisations opt for a watered-down version. Re-engineering should not then be blamed if businesses are disappointed with the results, argues Chris Skinner of Highams Systems, who draws a distinction between BPR (changes directed at individual processes in an *ad hoc* fashion) and business re-engineering (BR, a total business rethink):

'Many firms jump in at the pragmatic level of BPR and change some of their simple low level processes without doing anything fundamental to the business. It is like improving the design of your car's hub cap or door. They are components of the car but not the whole car. Business re-engineering means rethinking the entire business. It means starting with a vision of a whole car.'

CASE STUDY 5.4

Sun Life's new policy

Sun Life's Assurance Society started re-engineering three years ago. Now the Bristol based organisation exudes energy, enthusiasm and excitement about its re-engineering experience.

Managing director, John Reeve, is the source of Sun Life's missionary zeal. At the end of the 1980s, recognising that tough times (more competitors, more regulation, more new products, more recession) were ahead, he ordered a radical business review. The findings were only partially encouraging, Michael Baker, project manager of Customer Service Review explains:

'Industry surveys showed quality of service to be increasingly important to brokers. Our reputation was better than most, but our service levels were still only perceived to be fairly average. We were satisfying but certainly not delighting our customers.'

Sun Life plunged into turbulent re-engineering waters in its quest for the delighted customer. In came consultants McKinsey and Hay to plumb the corporate soul: 'Where are we going?' 'Where is the industry going?' Next, they reviewed the core processes. The findings were disturbing. Issuing a new life assurance policy was a typical core process involving administrative steps carried out in different departments. No-one, it seemed, was in charge of a process from beginning to end; each step was hampered by bottlenecks, ambiguity, delays and errors. A process which should have taken 15 days limped along for 46 days. Once a department had done its bit, the paperwork fell into 'black holes' of inactivity.

In June 1991, Sun Life began re-engineering its core process in a two-year, three-wave programme. All processes were put through a five-stage wringer of documentation; analysis; brainstorming ideas; evaluating solutions; detailed redesign; and implementation. The objective was to be a pace-setter – to reshape the organisation into a more efficient and effective one but, vitally, one which has a predominant customer focus. Sun Life's metamorphosis from an organisation based on functional specialists to one based on multi-skilled employees required massive restructuring.

For Sun Life's brave new world redesigned streamlined processes were organised around multi-skilled teams to ensure that responsibility for a complete, end-to-end process was handled in one place. Massive investment in training and communication programmes would broaden and enhance employee roles, responsibilities, skills and competencies. Sun Life's historic hierarchical seven-layer management structure was transformed. A pilot experiment in the 1200 strong customer service department slashed the multiple level hierarchy to customer service managers, team leaders and teams supported by two other roles: a dedicated trainer and a technical expert. Team members, formerly skilled in about 25 per cent of a process, familiarised themselves with the other 75 per cent. New reward structures based on pay for competencies and customer-related performance measures were introduced.

Baker is confident of a two or three year payback period. Already Sun Life boasts 40–90 per cent improvements in process turnaround times; 10 per cent reduction in the unit costs of some processes; and 50–80 per cent quality improvements (work performed right first time). Sun Life confidently predicts a significant increase in job satisfaction among employees and greater customer satisfaction leading to increased business. He reports that the 'black holes' in one process, the Life New Business, have been filled. The process is now completed in 21 days rather than 46. Faults in the company's communication lines are being filled. Employees had a first annual general meeting this year. TV broadcaster Peter Sissons has chaired an 'open house' no holds barred Question Time and while videos, focus groups, attitude surveys and training seminars help keep the momentum Baker says they now have an open style of management which he feels would have been inconceivable three years ago.

Sun Life Assurance's road to re-engineering enlightenment sounds untroubled. It wasn't. Nor is the journey yet complete. 'Anyone who underestimates the size or

CASE
STUDY
cont

difficulty of the task of making the organisation transformation will certainly fail', says Owen. A case of no pain, no gain.

Adapted from *'Shocking to the Core'* by Judith Oliver. *(Source: Management Today, August 1993.)*

DISCUSSION QUESTIONS 5.4

1 Why can re-engineering be considered to be authoritarian?

2 Why do managers feel threatened by changes at the National and Provincial Building Society?

3 What improvements have Sun Life Assurance made to their business?

4 What changes did Sun Life make which would affect their office workers?

5 What effect on workers' attitudes might 're-engineering' changes have in any organisation?

6 How might re-engineering or other major re-organisations of firms, affect the relationship between functions or departments in an organisation?

7 Is organisational culture affected by major reorganisations of the way companies do things?

Work measurement

'Work measurement' is carried out in order to set standards for:

◆ the quantity of work produced by a group or person (output)

◆ the quality of work produced (number of errors in relation to output)

◆ the time spent on work produced.

The setting of standards and recording of actual results for evaluation should not be made in a vacuum. However interesting the resulting information may be, it will not be worth its cost in time, effort and money if it is not *applied* for the benefit of the organisation. Measurement must have specific and useful objectives, such as:

◆ comparing results from a present system with an intended alternative

◆ finding out why costs are rising or productivity falling

◆ identifying errors and their overall effects

◆ identifying bottlenecks and idle time for both man and machine which could be more efficiently organised

◆ evaluating the worth of a particular employee or post for the purpose of wage setting.

It should also be remembered that not all types of work can be easily measured in terms of 'output'. Work which is not easily quantifiable can fall into various categories:

1   Routine or repetitive jobs in production, or in the office, and most jobs involving machine operation and output will be easier to set standards for and measure. For example, how many moulds are filled, or how many orders are processed per hour?

2   Meetings, telephone calls, planning research, non-routine or non-repetitive and 'thinking' tasks will be harder to measure, because the office rarely allows 'pure' and uninterrupted execution of a piece of work (phone calls, unscheduled tasks or visitors arriving, urgent decisions having to be made).

3   It is not easy to determine an accurate time someone spends planning and reviewing work, or managing or 'handling' people. How much of the non-productive time is constructively spent in this way, and how much is simply wasted?

4   Even routine tasks will vary greatly as to time taken and resources used. There may be a particularly difficult shape to cut, or dangerous material to work with, or an illegible draft to word process, or a telephone call from a particularly difficult client or customer. These are not readily quantifiable.

Standard time

In order to be able to express the optimum amount of work that can be produced by a given number of personnel or equipment, some common scale of measurement is needed:

◆ *Standard time* is the total time in which a job should be completed at standard performance by a qualified worker under normal conditions

◆ *Standard performance* is the rate of output which qualified workers will naturally achieve without over-exertion as an average over the working day or shift, provided they adhere to the specified method and provided that they are motivated to apply themselves to their work (British Standards definition).

Standard times are used for a variety of purposes, including the following:

◆ as a basis for pay incentive schemes
◆ for planning machine loading, labour times and overtime/short-time working
◆ as a means of calculating delivery dates and promises
◆ to assist in method study
◆ to determine standard costs
◆ to provide data for budgetary control, estimating and planning
◆ to provide a system of management control through comparisons of work output.

In order to measure the standard of output several techniques might be used with varying degrees of accuracy. The techniques which might be used include direct observation methods and synthetic methods. Direct observation methods is when a trained observer times the tasks on a number of occasions. Using the timings for similar jobs estimates can then be made for work that is yet to be carried out.

Synthetic methods involves estimating the work content of jobs without having to observe them.

Even when actual jobs differ, some tasks making up those jobs will be the same and these can be used as standard data for estimating the amount of time a new job will take to complete. Very small elements of jobs, such as basic hand motions, can be measured and these measurements are known as Predetermined Motion Time Standards (PMTS). PMTS can be used to monitor highly repetitive tasks. It enables very accurate estimates of the exact time to perform a task to be made.

When work is non-routine or unpredictable, guessing the time needed to complete jobs might be the only thing work planners can do. Guesswork should be based on the opinion of a person with a good knowledge of the work involved, such as a section supervisor.

'Work measurement' written by Neil Williams-Slaven, Senior Lecturer in Business and Management Studies, Manchester Metropolitan University. (Copyright reserved)

 ## Changing and amending plans

One of the most famous statements made this century was: 'Houston, we have a problem'. Apollo 13 was due to land on the moon when an onboard explosion fractured the spaceship's oxygen tanks. The immediate response was to change the original plans and implement contingency plans, drawing up new plans to get the astronauts back to earth as quickly and safely as possible.

Some plans have to be changed to meet changing circumstances. However some large scale plans, once implemented, are difficult to cancel. For example, building a steel works which might take seven years becomes difficult to stop mid-construction. In these cases plans are drawn up with projected outcomes and will have built in leeway to accommodate possible changes in variable factors such as changes in interest rates, price changes in raw materials and changes in labour costs. If projects are to take a number of years to complete there might be changes in legislation which could impact on the final outcome of the project.

One of the places where changes occur quickly is the market place. Companies have to be prepared to change their plans if a competitor does something unexpectedly. If a company launches a new product, competitors may have to

Fig 5.17 Some large scale plans are difficult to change!

reconsider their plans on the launch of their own new product. Some industries are in a constant state of rapid change and organisations operating in these markets need to be able to adjust their plans accordingly. The speed of development in information technology makes planning in this industry difficult. The computer industry has seen many companies enter the market and leave very quickly. The performance, versatility and capability of machines is enhanced with the introduction of each new model. Even users of computers who wish to buy and upgrade their existing equipment find it difficult to decide what to do because of the rapid change.

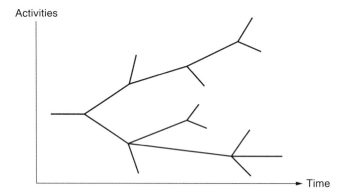

Fig 5.18 Lewis and Clark approach to planning

Planning is also made difficult because there are so many uncertainties and an unpredictable future means many decision points with a number of alternative courses of action: the Lewis and Clark approach to planning. However in a constantly changing environment the few options that are available to the planning function become even more critical because the consequence of any decision taken has a broad and far-reaching impact on the organisation.

Nevertheless, for some organisations the future is clear and it is feasible to plan a move from one point to another without delay or interruption. Organisations are able to utilise the 'Cook's tour' approach to planning because they are operating in a secure and stable environment.

It is important for organisations to plan for expected problems and to have a clear policy and set of procedures for dealing with them. Failure to adopt this approach could force the organisation to deal with each problem as a crisis and adopt a 'fire fighting' approach to management where time, energy, resources and opportunities are wasted because of the lack of planning. The function of planning is to prepare an organisation to cope with the uncertainties of the future. But plans need to have built in flexibility to allow for the possibility of change. Once implemented there should be on-going monitoring, reviewing and analysis of what is happening with the actual performance against the planned activities.

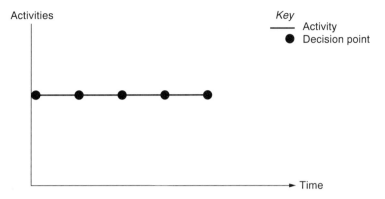

Fig 5.19 Cook's tour approach to planning

Plans can only be amended if there is sufficient accurate and timely feedback of information which can be acted upon.

The planning cycle

This means planning is not a linear activity but is circular. Amending plans as a project is under way is known as adaptive planning, i.e. changes are made which need to be made to allow the planned programme to achieve the goals set.

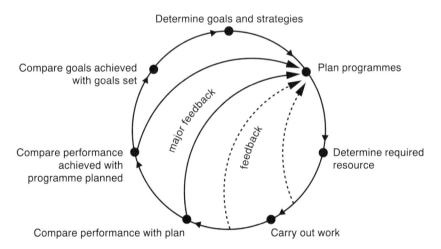

Fig 5.20 The planning cycle

Communications

From reading this chapter you will learn about communications, including:

1   the importance of effective communication;

2   communication channels;

3   communication networks;

4   barriers to communication;

5   orders and instructions;

6   briefing teams;

7   briefing individuals;

8   giving feedback; and

9   information systems.

 ## The importance of effective communication

Without communication an organisation would not survive. Communication involves both the giving out of messages from one person and the receiving and understanding of those messages by another. If a message has been given out by one person but not received or understood by another, than communication has not taken place. Managers spend around 80 per cent of their time in direct communication with others, whether on the phone, in meetings, or in conversation. The other 20 per cent is spent on desk work, much of which is also communication in the form of writing and reading.

Without communications, managers and their subordinates will not be able to function in the organisation. Managers cannot plan, organise and monitor the work without receiving information from internal and external sources. Communication also enables managers to share ideas or pass on information to their managerial colleagues and allows managers to be in touch with their operatives to give instructions. Without instructions the subordinates would be unable to work.

The external environment affects the organisation; events occurring outside such as changes in customer needs or interest rates will impinge upon the work of the organisation sooner or later. Managers need to know as soon as possible about rises and falls in costs or demand for the product or service, as these will affect the survival of the organisation. Communication enables the organisation to be in touch with the external environment. Communication is the means which allows the organisation to send orders to its suppliers, receive orders from customers and be in contact with other essential organisations such as the Inland Revenue, Customs and Excise and local government.

Good communication therefore allows activities within the organisation to take place, for example:

◆ encourages interdepartmental co-operation and co-ordination

◆ keeps the workforce informed about their performance, the performance of others and the performance of the organisation

◆ gives the opportunity to identify and counter dissatisfaction

◆ helps understanding and morale

◆ influences opinions, attitudes and creates better working relationships

◆ facilitates more involvement in decision making and problem solving

◆ keeps employees aware of changes in the organisation.

The manager and effective communications

To operate, the organisation must establish effective channels of communication to enable a free flow of information. This information can be acted upon by institutions, groups of people and individuals. In order to set up effective channels of communication, organisations need to appreciate the complexity of the communication process and recognise it as an important activity in the organisation. Communication allows personnel to operate effectively and efficiently as it gives them knowledge about the current situation. The less effective the communication process, the less effective the manager will be within the organisation.

The communication process

The communication process involves the following stages:

◆ the sender

◆ encoding

◆ transmission

◆ decoding

◆ the receiver

◆ feedback

◆ noise.

The sender

This is the originator of the communication. It may be an individual, group or an organisation. The sender prepares the message, encodes it and enters it into the transmission medium.

Encoding

The message is changed from the idea into the form for transmission. The encoding may include words, letters and graphics. The method of coding should be such that the receiver can decode quickly and understand the message. Language is important because if it is too technical or too difficult to understand the meaning of the message is lost and the communication fails.

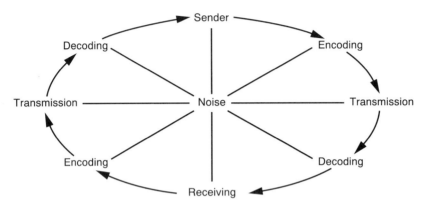

Fig 6.1 The communication process

Transmission

This is the process by which the message is sent to the receiver. The medium is the channel of the transmission. The media used should be selected for the most effective means, for example, a simple instruction may be given over the telephone whereas more complex instructions may require a face-to-face meeting between two individuals supported by briefing notes.

Decoding

This process involves the receiver interpreting the message. This means the receiver has to understand the symbols used in the message conveyed. Usually this is a straightforward process but sometimes the receiver decodes the message incorrectly and this is where misunderstandings occur. People become accustomed to the jargon, technical terms and using initials for processes which to them are everyday occurrences, but an outsider would feel as if they had landed in a foreign country if these were not translated. Some jargon consists of ordinary words such as 'mouse' for computer control which may be misunderstood by those not used to working in the industry.

The receiver

This is the person to whom the message is sent. The receiver is the person who decodes and interprets the message. The ability of the receiver to carry out this process will determine the success of the communication. Successful communication will result in the receiver interpreting the message exactly as it was intended to be perceived by the sender. The reaction of the receiver will act as feedback to the original sender of the communication.

Feedback

For communication to be successful there has to be a response from the receiver. This means there must be some sort of action which acknowledges that the message has been received and understood. If a manager has asked for a file, it is necessary for the right file to reach him or her for the communication to have been effective.

Noise

This refers to anything which can distort, interrupt or disturb the communication process. It may be simply noise on a telephone, people talking in a group or interference during a teleconference. In some cases the rumour grapevine can act as a 'noise' as it distorts a message within the organisation.

◆ ACTIVITY 6.1

Think back over all your communications during the past week, using the following questions as a guide. Write down ways you could have been a more effective communicator.

1   When did you ask someone a question, putting him or her on the spot, rather than stating your own feelings or beliefs?

2   How many times did you say 'Yes, but . . .?' because you

(a)   discounted a suggestion as being too expensive, too difficult, too late, too early, etc.?

(b)   discounted yourself because you're too tired, too old, too young, too dumb?

(c)   said 'Yes, but we tried that before and it didn't work'?

(d)   gave someone a go-ahead on a project you knew wouldn't work, so he could hang himself?

3   Who did you leave out because you don't agree with their views? How did you leave him or her out?

4   How and when did you get defensive, causing communication to be blocked?

5   When did you judge someone because you didn't like his looks, his ideas, or his ethnic background?

6   What happened when you last attended a meeting?

▶

(a) Did you formulate an answer before someone else had finished speaking?

(b) Which of the other participants at the meeting got a deaf ear? Why?

(c) What conversation did you dominate?

(d) What conversation did you not join? Why?

(e) What new ideas did you reject out of hand?

(f) When did you let your mind wander?

(g) What games did you play – that is, when were you not playing it straight?

(h) When were you really certain, in no uncertain terms?

Communication channels

Organisations need to have effective systems and procedures to allow communications to flow freely. By having clear channels of communication instructions can be given, received and acted upon. The internal communication channels are designed to allow information to reach the desired destination quickly and efficiently. Within an organisation there tends to be two main channels: vertical and lateral.

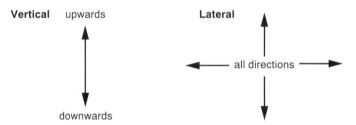

Fig 6.2 Channels of communication

Vertical channels

In this situation information flows down the organisational pyramid. Policies determined at boardroom level are passed down to the next level. Senior managers pass on instructions and decisions to the middle managers who in turn act upon instructions until the relevant communication reaches the lowest level. Feedback relating to production is sent from the lower levels of the organisation, enabling managers to monitor progress and to see how their areas are performing against planned targets.

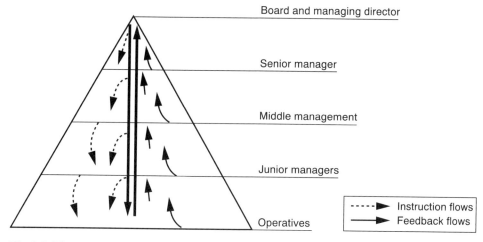

Fig 6.3 The organisational pyramid

Problems with vertical channels of communication

The filtering of information

This can affect information going up or down the organisation. The manager usually decides to pass information down on a 'need to know' basis so that subordinates are only informed of those events which directly affect their work. This means the manager decides what information to leave out when passing on information. However, the manager may decide to pass on information slowly to reinforce or enhance his or her position of power. Information sent upwards will also be filtered if the person responsible for sending the information feels that it is critical of his or her performance. Individuals often distort information so that an account of events shows them to have contributed to a successful project or to have had little to do with an unsuccessful one.

Failure to pass on information

This may arise because managers do not understand the scope of information which is required by subordinates at a lower level. Instructions may be unclear making it difficult for subordinates to operate efficiently.

The length of the chain

The number of layers the information has to pass through can mean a long time lag before people receive information. This is problematic in large bureaucratic organisations because it slows down the decision making process and can reduce the ability of large organisations to react quickly to rapid changes in the market it operates in.

Lateral communications

In any organisation there has to be cross-departmental communication, this allow the work of the marketing department to be passed on, production knows what to produce and the wages section knows how much to pay out. Lateral communication informs, supports and communicates activities across the organisation. It is most effective when each member of the organisation treats others as customers and tries to met their needs for information.

Problems with lateral communications

Filtering information

This will happen where departments do not have a close working relationship and there is perhaps a certain amount of rivalry between departments. The information which is passed on will be that which is required but information may be withheld because it is not asked for or is released only to enhance one of the departments.

Failure to pass on information

Here one department may fail to pass on information, because it deliberately withholds it or because it fails to realise the importance of the information to the other department.

The length of the chain

The longer the chain the longer it takes for information to be processed. In today's competitive markets the quicker an organisation can respond to a situation the more likely it is to succeed. An organisation needs to ensure it can act on information quickly by reducing the time in the communications chain. In many cases this is why organisations have gone through a process of 're-engineering' to speed up their process time.

Which boss

People who work in a particular department know who their line manager is. Problems arise where a person may have cross-departmental roles. They may have problems working for two managers where their manager is in a more junior position to the other manager. Who do they serve first and is the information to be passed on acceptable to the line manager?

Communication networks

Managers managing activities will depend on formal communication networks to ensure their instructions are carried out and they receive the necessary feedback. The effectiveness of their operations will depend to some extent on the structure of the group they manage and the channels of communication they use. The following figures represent structures and channels of communications between group members. The more formal structures are represented on the left and the structures become more informal towards the right.

The *wheel* structure shows a situation where communication is centralised, i.e. where the manager is at the hub of the wheel and all information flows through them. By acting as a gatekeeper the manager allows information to pass on to other people in the structure and as such holds a very powerful position. From this central position he or she will gain job satisfaction because he or she will have a complete picture of what is going on. Those on the rim of the wheel may tend to feel more isolated and frustrated.

The same feeling of isolation and frustration is felt by those who work in a structure called the *chain*. The manager at the centre acts as a sifter, only allowing information to those who need it, and enabling people to concentrate on their own specific tasks. Problems may arise when the manager becomes swamped with work or the manager does not possess the necessary skills or experience to manage their activities. The system becomes inefficient as the work piles up, and the wrong information is given out or kept back.

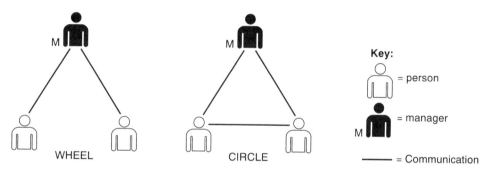

Fig 6.4 Communication in a group with three people

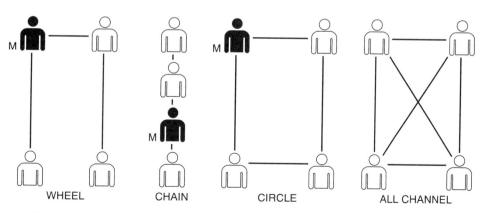

Fig 6.5 Communication in a group with four people

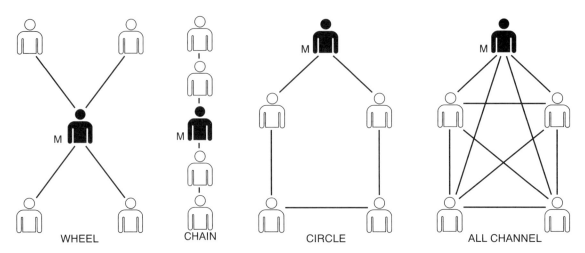

Fig 6.6 Communication in a group with five people

At the other extreme is the structure known as the circle, where information flows freely between each member of the group. This structure will tend to be more informal with the manager having a more open management style than found in the wheel. However, group members may find they are receiving information which they do not always require.

Informal communications

Much of the information a manager receives and uses comes form informal sources, from observing people and practices, face-to-face conversations and informal meetings. The way this information is obtained is called, *Management by walking around.*

The grapevine runs alongside the formal channels and carries formal and informal communication about the organisation and the people in it.

The information is normally passed on orally at face-to-face meetings between individuals and groups. The grapevine becomes most active when something important is about to happen and usually starts off with information which is true. However, the grapevine lacks the full information which gives people the opportunity to jump to conclusions and to fill in the gaps in the information.

The grapevine is not held back by the barriers found in formal communication channels. It can cut across departments, jump over managers and move rapidly in all directions. The flow of information is made easy because people want to know what is happening and to pass the information on to others.

Managers and the grapevine

Managers cannot ignore the grapevine because it can cause harm to the working of the organisation. People can become deflected from their jobs if historically the grapevine has been accurate because they have learnt to believe and act upon information circulating unofficially. For the manager the grapevine can distort information and can undermine confidence in some individuals. Rumours, for example, that a number of workers are about to be laid off will be a cause of concern until the rumours are reported to be false or the layoffs happen. The grapevine will flourish in situations where managers tend to be autocratic and hold on to information.

The grapevine can be a source of information to the manager because it gives him or her a means of finding out how people really feel about the organisation or what is happening at that time. The manager can use the grapevine to his or her own advantage because he or she can feed it information which may reduce anxiety and worry among staff. Also, if the manager is facing a difficult situation, he or she can leak information to the grapevine to see how staff react. From the response of the grapevine the manager can work out alternative strategies.

Barriers to communications

The better the communication system the more effective the manager and his subordinates will be. The extent of their success will depend on overcoming barriers to communications. The barriers can include all the factors involved in the communication process, i.e. the sender, the message, the medium, and the receiver as well as other factors.

The sender

The sender has got to be sure that he or she has chosen the right symbols, the right message, the right medium and identified the right person to be the receiver of the message.

Language can be a major communication barrier. Language is a system of spoken or written symbols which communicate ideas, emotions and experiences. The greater the variety of symbols the more complex the language. There are a number of languages, natural languages such as English or French and artificial languages such as algebra and COBOL.

Natural language is the most complex because of the number of words available for use, and this complexity can create barriers. Words can have more than one meaning, 'run', 'bank' and 'pack' are just three examples. In some cases a word may sound the same but be spelt differently, such as 'through' and 'threw', 'their' and 'there'. In other situations a number of words can be used to describe the same thing, for instance, 'shower', 'drizzle' and 'rain'.

The natural language has so many words that no one person can know them all, and people have differing commands of the same language. Although the wide variety of words makes language a powerful tool for transmitting information, it can cause barriers.

Employees spend a lot of their time talking. This is a particular skill for which the majority of people receive no formal training. Our ability to speak a language usually depends upon our experiences learned from our home and school. People's ability to communicate orally is often dependent on factors outside their control. If a person has received a high level of education and has enjoyed a wide range of experiences then he or she will have a wide vocabulary, an understanding of grammar, and the ability to express him or herself in both written and oral form. The people who will have this higher command of language will probably be the managers.

Managers can create problems by using language which may unintentionally confuse or intimidate the receiver. If managers have difficulty in expressing themselves, their subordinates may form a low opinion of them which will make it more difficult to get their views across.

A further barrier associated with language concerns expressions. Regions of the country have different words or phrases for particular events or situations. 'Ow bin ya' is a friendly welcome in the 'Black Country', in the North 'nesh' means overly sensitive to the cold. Teenagers use everyday words but in different situations, 'cool', 'dead hassling' and 'boring' seem to cover a range of different situations.

Organisations have their own phrases, abbreviations and buzz words. The 1980s saw additions to the business person's language, TQM, TPM, JIT, kaizen, downsizing and negative equity. Other additions came and went as fashion changed such as 'Yuppie' 'Dinkies' and 'NIMBY'.

Noise

There may be barriers which make it difficult for the receiver to understand the message. A manager might be using a mobile phone on the train and having problems with reception, especially when the train goes under bridges and through tunnels. The background noise on the train may make communicating difficult but the manager may need to communicate during the train journey because of the pressure of time. The foreign exchange dealers who work in banks buying and selling currencies seem to operate in what appears to be chaotic scenes. Imagine a situation where a buyer of a company who orders supplies over the telephone, 'Please send 16 000 components tomorrow, I'll confirm in writing' could easily be misheard as, 'Please send 60 000 components tomorrow, I'll confirm in writing ...'

The receiver

It is the receiver who has to interpret the message. When the message is received the mind has to absorb the symbols, see the relationships and then organise the information into a message. The mind has to conceptualise the information. If there are too many symbols, facts or figures, the mind will not be able to cope, and it becomes overloaded.

The behaviour of the listener can create communication problems. The manager may not give their full attention because their mind may be on something else or they may be doing something else at the same time. They may try to interrupt the speaker, criticise or become angry, or may be thinking of a reply to part of the message and not listen to other parts. The lack of concentration means that messages are only partly heard or misheard completely. Nuances, hidden meanings and signals from body language may be lost by the receiver of the communication.

Differing perceptions

People have varying educational backgrounds and experiences. This can mean people perceive or interpret information in a different way. For example if a manager tries to be helpful and supportive, the employees may see this as interference. The manager cannot expect people to understand unless situations are explained. Workers and managerial colleagues can completely misinterpret actions.

Fig 6.7 People can perceive or interpret the same information in a different way

Time

Many managers find themselves under increasing pressure as they have to deal with a rapidly changing business world. They have to master new and important ideas if they are to stay ahead of the field. The greater the demands on their time, the less time managers have to communicate with their colleagues in their own organisation. Managers may find they are always attending meetings which makes it difficult for them to be contacted. This may cause problems if a decision has to be taken quickly. Some decisions may be made without all the relevant information or without spending time to consider all the options.

Time can be a barrier when it places constraints on operations. If people were allowed an infinite period of time to complete a task, either the task would never get done or each task would be completed to a masterpiece standard. Time helps to concentrate the mind and forces people to work to a deadline. Lateness in completing forms may result in incorrect work or poor performance. The logistics manager of a transport firm for example, may not be able to complete scheduling of lorries because he or she is awaiting information. This means he or she cannot distribute the work to drivers and their delivery deadlines are missed.

The globalisation of business

Businesses are becoming more international, trading beyond national boundaries. In Europe there is a move towards a single trading bloc and technical advances have led to some business people talking of 'the global village'. The globalisation of business may create communication barriers because of the variety of languages and culture.

The need for increasingly complex information

Information technology has enabled information to be presented in a variety of ways. This can cause problems in the interpretation of the information for the manager because they need to have their skills continually updated in order to understand and interpret the forms in which the information is presented.

The advances in information technology

Information technology has made the transfer of information in a variety of ways possible. This means technology has enabled information to be saved, retrieved and transmitted at a greater speed. The acceleration of the transfer of information can put the manager under increasing pressure to find the information and convey it to the people who need it increasing the chances of making errors or omitting important information.

The increasing need for information

As the world we live in grows in complexity and is ever-changing, there comes a need for more information. The demand for more information will overload the communication process and cause it to operate less efficiently.

 # Orders and instructions

In order that activities are carried out and the workforce know their roles and responsibilities and are able to perform their duties, managers need to communicate by giving orders and instructions. Orders are directives to carry out a specific task, whereas instructions refer to how to perform a particular task by specifying rules and procedures.

Giving orders

To achieve the objectives of an order the following process can be followed:

◆ be clear what the order relates to

◆ identify the instructions to be given with the order and note them in logical sequence

◆ identify any problems which might arise and decide on the course of action to be followed

◆ if it is necessary and time allows, explain where the order has come from and why the order is being given

◆ give any instructions involved with the order

◆ if the situation permits allow questions to be asked which are seeking clarification.

The methods used to convey an order will depend on the task and the management style of the person giving the order.

The task

If the task is to deliver supplies to the organisation's branches, the logistics manager does not want to engage on a long debate with the drivers about which driver wants to go on which job and by which route. The drivers will receive orders from their manager or the computer system informing them of their work schedule. A doctor will tell nurses the type and quantities of medicine a patient is to receive. The board of directors may decide on a new strategic plan and pass on their decisions to the functional heads to implement. Health and safety requirements lay down rules for the operation of machinery and the safe handling of chemicals. Warning signs will inform people to behave in a particular way, for example, to keep out of an area or to remain silent in a restricted area.

The management style

The management style adopted may depend on the task to be completed, the manager will change his or her management style as the situation changes. For example, as a deadline gets closer, the manager may change from the democratic participant style to the autocratic style, giving orders to meet the approaching time limit. There may be other situations where the manager tells his or her workforce to operate in a set way. This may be because the

Fig 6.8 When the deadline approaches a manager may adopt an autocratic style of management

manager is more comfortable in adopting an autocratic approach to directing the workforce. It could be that the manager is communicating with a new member of the workforce and tells that person what to do, for example, the new apprentice on the building site might be told to clean the plaster off the floorboards of new houses, or to make the tea at 10 o'clock.

How do you rate as a communicator?

Organisational communication is an interpersonal matter. Check your effectiveness by answering 'Yes' or 'No' to these statements.

		Yes	No
1	Most problems between people are caused by failures in communications.	☐	☐
2	A person's cosmology (view of the world) conditions everything he hears.	☐	☐
3	When confronting a subordinate on any issue, it is important to just stick with the facts.	☐	☐
4	Watching body language and sensing what is going on is equally as important as listening to the words.	☐	☐
5	When someone feels he is being judged or controlled, he may become defensive, blocking communication.	☐	☐
6	I always listen attentively and let the other person finish what he is saying before I think of, or begin, my reply.	☐	☐
7	It is important to be very careful of what you say at work. That way, you won't upset anyone.	☐	☐
8	Being personal (being who you are), as opposed to playing a role (acting as a manager) helps the communication process.	☐	☐
9	If you are really clear about what you are saying the other person is bound to understand.	☐	☐
10	Office memos are an ineffective way to communicate.	☐	☐

Answers

If you answered 'Yes' to Question 3, you may be overlooking the real issue – feelings. 'Let's not get emotional around here' blocks out the most important part of the communication.

A 'Yes' to Question 7 may indicate you are engaging in some verbal game – playing. Most people would rather have it straight, even if it upsets them.

Question 9 should have been answered 'No'. Words don't have the same meaning to everyone. Each of our mental filters allows words to come through differently.

Giving instructions

Instructions are usually concerned with laying down rules and procedures. Instructions relate to how to do things; they can refer to learning new skills, re-enforcing old skills or updating and enhancing skills already acquired. Instructions are given to new entrants to an organisation and to existing employees when new procedures are introduced to the organisation. They are made to make the procedure of operations simple, clear and consistent. If a company is considering purchasing a photocopier the salesperson demonstrates how the machine works during their sales pitch. On delivery of the photocopier a representative from the company selling the machine will instruct the photocopier operator on its use by explaining each function. The representative will probably refer to the operations manual as a guide in helping to explain what to do under certain circumstances. The operator will then be able to refer to this manual if they have forgotten a procedure or the

Fig 6.9 Instructions are there to make an operation simpler

machine malfunctions. The operator may have an instruction notice pinned to the wall by the machine giving simple instructions on its use as a quick reminder or as a guide for the people who only use the machine occasionally.

To learn new skills effectively there should be a learning programme. A person who cannot drive will not get into a car and drive off. They need some instructions so they can learn the fundamentals of driving, i.e. steering, changing gear, hill starts and three point turns. The driving instructor passes on his or her skills to the learner driver. The more lessons a learner has, the more experience gained, and the fewer instructions need-

Fig 6.10 To learn new skills effectively there should be a learning programme

ed in the fundamental principles of driving. Once the test is passed the learner is qualified to drive a car without supervision.

Teaching skills to enable a person to perform their work tasks can be done through an organised training session or on an ad hoc arrangement such as observing an experienced worker. The organised training session can be done in-house, by an external agency or a combination of both. These training sessions will have skilled trainers who will have clear ideas on the outcome of the training. They will arrange training sessions which have clear objectives, and the sessions will be broken down into manageable sections of tuition for the learner. Depending on the skill being learnt, there may be theoretical instruction and hands on experience. The instructions which a learner has to follow will be clear and reinforced during the training sessions. The instructions a learner follows when observing an experienced operator will tend to depend on the communication skills of the operative the time the operative has to instruct the student. The bad habits of the experienced operator may be picked up by the learner.

CASE STUDY 6.1

United Norwest

United Norwest is the largest independent society in the Cooperative movement. where John Furlong is General Manager, Warehousing and Distribution:

Fig 6.11 John Furlong, General Manager, warehouse and distribution, United Norwest

'United Norwest's trading area is from Stoke-on-Trent to the Lake District, we are called the motorway society because everything along the M6 is ours. We supply 200 co-op. retailers with groceries and we've got a large pharmacy division, funeral division and travel division. There are 9000 employees up and down the country.

I control the warehousing and distribution of the packaged foods. We also supply fresh food to the retailers within the Norwest area. We've got a depot in Longridge in Preston which supplies our superstores, there is a non-food depot at Haydock which supplies items such as furniture to stores.'

The Stoke-on-Trent distribution centre is located at the bottom of the trading area due to its being on a site which had plenty of land available. The area of the buildings is 350 000 sq ft.

'Stores get about 90 per cent of their orders from us. Store managers send their orders by telephone to the mainframe computer at the distribution centre in Stoke, the orders are produced in the form of a "picking list" (the required items are "picked" from the warehouse to fulfil the order). Small stores send their orders twice a week, whilst large stores send orders on a daily basis. The orders print out throughout the night, the picking lists are collected first thing in the morning and delivery is made later the same day.

At one time all our stores had large warehouse spaces attached to them, but now that we provide same-day delivery, stores have been able to convert that storage space into more shopping space. The warehouse is set out so that groceries can be packed for the stores easily. The heavy items such as tins are at one end of the warehouse, whilst the lighter items are at the other end, the crisps being the last thing to be packed. A lot of thought has gone into it, for example, soap powders and bleaches are picked with tins both before *and after them so that they are sandwiched between products which are not affected by smell.*

It's like going round a superstore as a customer with your trolley, except that the pickers go round and they are picking a whole case of beans at a time. They bring them into the loading bay and they are lined up. Different pickers will pick for the same store and do different sections of the order, the wines, spirits, tobacco and confectionery are in a high-security picking area and have their own pickers. Every roll cage is marked with the name of the store for whom the order has been filled and the loaded cages are then placed into the lorry container designated by the computer for delivering that order. The driver returns with his empty lorry, picks up the full vehicle and away he goes again.

The triplicate copy of the order, which is actually three-part computer paper, then goes to the office for distribution. The top copy goes upstairs to the office for charging the store, the centre page goes in an envelope to the store for checking, the bottom page stays with security in case of shortage claims or discrepancies.

Last year we bought the Longridge depot at Preston as even this depot in Stoke was getting too small. They supply superstores only. We charge stores 4 per cent on cost and at the end of the year, whatever money this depot makes goes back to the stores in proportion to their orders. We're non-profit making, we're just a service, it's all the same organisation.

One hundred and thirty people are employed at the Stoke-on-Trent Distribution Centre. The value of deliveries is £3 million per week, which represents 270 000 cases of groceries. The distribution centre has 20 vehicles, 13 articulated lorries which are 40 foot long, and seven rigid lorries. Deliveries are made to stores furthest away first and the drivers carry out around three journeys each per day. They start at 6 am, so they miss all the hassle on the motorway. If they deliver in Blackpool and Blackburn area, they call in at the Longridge depot and collect goods to deliver to stores on the way back. The Longridge depot stocks a wider range of lines of packaged grocery for superstores. The lorries don't come back down the motorway empty.

Hundreds of suppliers deliver to the distribution centre, a supplier's vehicle is booked in to make a delivery once every fifteen minutes. Once an order has been raised with a supplier by the distribution centre, the supplier telephones for a delivery date and time and they are given a slot. If all the time slots are full, we double book them. Warehouse stock is driven by a radio-controlled computer system called Commander. Deliveries entering the centre are made to a different side of the building to the orders going out from the loading bays. The goods come in and are placed on a pallet and checked against the delivery note, the computer then produces a label which is put on the pallet. The fork lift truck driver types the number into his Commander computer terminal in the truck and the computer screen in the truck then shows which aisle and exact spot along the aisle to take the pallet to. The Commander system controls all the "best before" dates, so that newly delivered pallets are not picked from for deliveries to stores before the existing pallets have been emptied. There are 15 000 pallet spaces in the warehouse which are used in a First In First Out system. Pallets normally stay in the warehouse for no longer than two weeks.

"Paragon" is a computerised journey planner which produces journey schedules for each driver. These tell drivers where to go and how to get there. Each vehicle has an Encripter

CASE
STUDY
cont

machine on it which is a security seal. The manager of each stores takes receipt of each delivery and signs to say that the consignment of goods was sealed at the time he or she received them. This protects the drivers from accusations that they may have taken goods from stores' orders if items appear to be missing. Encripter also monitors the driver's journey, so that Paragon maps out the journey as it should be made and Encripter records exactly where the driver did go and how long the journey took. Drivers can be contacted at any time on the short-wave radios in their cabs. Not only does Paragon map out journeys, but it also takes account of constraints such as the ability of stores to be accessed by a 40 foot vehicle, and that information is fed into Paragon so it won't allocate such a store to a large vehicle to make the delivery. Other parameters such as traffic hold-ups and differences in area taken up by various groceries are taken into account. Examples of differences in volume of groceries: 1 roll case will accommodate 27 cases of grocery, but 192 cases of tobacco, only 23 cases of wines and spirits, and 86 cases of toiletries. The articulated lorries can take 1400 roll cages and the rigid vehicles can house 750 cases. Paragon makes the loads up to suit the vehicle and allocates the stores to each lorry.

At one time we used to have to sit down and say "Well that will go with that and that will go with this", now we just feed it all in and it runs it all off. We've had Paragon for two years and we've been tweaking it throughout that time. You always have to change it because one day you can deliver to a store with an articulated lorry and the next day bollards may be put across the street and access is suddenly limited.

We're shortly going to have an Automatic Branch Replenishment system so that orders are automatically made through the computer system. As stocks in the stores reduce with sales, the computer at the cash register will monitor what is going out of the stores and order more. This saves every manager in over 200 stores having to phone us at least twice a week.'

Communicating with employees

'We have a meeting every week as managers and a monthly meeting with a multi-functional team which I have formed myself. It consists of representatives from drivers, pickers, forklift truck drivers, a health and safety representative and two union shop stewards. We talk about health and safety, I tell them where we're going as a society, and any news such as new systems which we're putting in. I try to communicate with them first, before telling all the staff and then they've got an idea of what I'm going to be talking about when I do tell everyone. My door is always open anyway.

Last year we introduced a Driver of the Month competition. Each month the winner would receive a voucher to the value of £100 of Co-op goods, then from those drivers we chose the Driver of the Year who wins £1000. This was so successful that we decided to give a car to the driver with the most points overall. He arrived at the presentation thinking he was getting £1000 and we surprised him with the car. The competition improved absenteeism levels incredibly. Criteria are daily attendance, personal appearance, customer service, vehicle accidents, vehicle condition and a good tachograph record. It went with a bang, it was really good. After the presentation we decided we were going to go for a warehouse person of the year. Hopefully there will be the same sort of results. Errors at present are only 3 in 1000, and this might improve still further. The prize will be £100 per month for each depot and then an annual award for the best person of around £500. The warehouse people tended to think that they'd been forgotten, we try to keep everyone happy and get the best performance out of them.

There is an in-house magazine to keep all employees informed of events within the society. There is a noticeboard for announcements, I tend to prefer to give everyone a copy of the notice, especially the drivers who work long hours. We often give them notices or memos in with their pay slips.

A bulletin is received by all the stores which acts as a newsletter for instructions. The difficulty is do the managers hand it out to the people who should be getting it? I prefer to talk to the depot managers personally. I drive about 2000 miles a month, I can't just sit here and run all the departments over the phone. Also, if there's trouble with a driver I prefer to talk to him personally.

The staff can come and talk to me, everybody comes. They know that in the past I used to be a picker and my style of management is to treat them as I would like to be treated myself. Management is about getting a good relationship with your staff. I used to be a trouble-shooter so when this new depot opened I saw it as an opportunity to make sure that we had no trouble by asking the best people I'd worked with before to come and work here. Many people here have worked with me for years. I never take YTS trainees if I can't give them a job, three of our supervisors here started with me as YTS trainees and now they're on good salaries.'

DISCUSSION QUESTIONS 6.1

1   Using the casestudy, identify four different communication processes used internally or externally by United Norwest.

2   To what extent is effective communication important to the supply chain at United Norwest?

3   How might the use of IT in communications change the managerial role of the Logistics/General Manager?

4   How has communication improved the motivation of the workforce?

5   Why is layout important for the efficient running of the distribution centre?

6   How does the location of the distribution centre affect its operations?

Briefing teams

The purpose of a team briefing is to pass on information and instructions to a group of people at the same time in an oral presentation format perhaps supported by audio visual material if required. The introduction of teleconferencing has enabled briefing to be more flexible because people do not have to be in the same room or building during the briefing session. A formal briefing session makes for consistency when communicating with groups of people to ensure they all receive the same information.

Usually briefings are used to bring people together who have a common interest in a project, from the launch of a new product to the introduction of a new policy. Departmental managers may call their section heads to a short briefing meeting at the start of each morning. This update enables everyone to know what is happening in the department on a daily basis and helps to remove communication barriers. In many cases people who attend briefings will themselves hold briefings for their colleagues to cascade down the information. In other circumstances people may use different communication mediums to pass on relevant information. Briefings can be part of a programme of communications where after an initial brief, other briefings are called to keep people up to date with developments. Other reasons may be to deliver more formal feedback on a project, for example, the Marketing Director may brief the rest of the board on the success of a new marketing initiative.

As organisations grow briefing methods also need to change. Briefing all the employees in an organisation when it consists of only four or five people is comfortable. However as the organisation increases in size with hundreds of employees, it might be feasible to brief everyone at the same time, but it may be impractical and less effective than other methods of communicating.

Team briefings should be:

◆ held at regular intervals and not just at times of crisis

◆ brief, ideally lasting no longer than 30 minutes

◆ led by the immediate team leader of the work group

◆ face-to-face and not reduced to a series of circulars and memos

◆ structured to cover:

> progress: how are we doing?
>
> people: who is coming and going?
>
> policy: any changes affecting the team?
>
> points: for further action?

◆ monitored to assess their success or failure.

Preparing to present a brief

This process includes a number of stages and incorporates communication skills which the presenter must possess to be effective. The presenter must:

◆ have a clear idea on the purpose of the brief

◆ have a clear understanding of the brief. In planning it may be necessary to consult with others

◆ decide who should attend the briefing

◆ decide on the time allowable set against the information to be given

◆ decide upon the structure of the brief: what to include in the introductory scene setting, the main part of the brief and the information in the recap

◆ decide what if any, audio visual aids are required. The use of the overhead projector is useful for the audience to help them to absorb information as long as there is not too much information on a slide

◆ know when to use information packs and decide: when should they be distributed, before, during or after the presentation.

◆ consider the total physical and human setting for the presentation

◆ decide on when to take questions.

The briefing

The way in which the briefing is conducted will convey to the audience the seriousness and purpose of the briefing. Too many briefings, briefings which go on too long or briefings which are not followed up will test the concentration and attention of the audience. The presenter should be able to communicate to the audience and ensure that they are aware that it is not only what is said but how it is said which is important.

The presenter should:

◆ think of the overtones as well as the basic content of the message. The way in which the message is conveyed, the voice, use of language, the tone of the message will influence the receptiveness of the receiver

Fig 6.12 **Briefings which go on too long will test the concentration of the audience**

◆ think and be aware of how the audience views the speaker. Has the presenter got their back to the audience? Do they walk up and down when speaking? Do they wave their hands, stand with their hands in their pockets? The presenter should keep movement to a minimum

◆ at the start of the presentation introduce themselves and any other speaker, make clear to the audience the likely timetable and the expected outcome from the briefing

◆ when taking questions only deal with questions seeking clarification and deflect questions which are philosophical in nature as they can lead the discussion away from the subject. Also, individuals who question the process and decision making which has led to the briefing should be answered swiftly as this is also leading the briefing in another direction.

Briefing individuals

Briefing individuals can take place on an informal or formal basis. These briefings are usually face-to-face meetings and can be called to pass information between manager and a subordinate or between the subordinate and the manager.

The nature of the briefing which takes place will depend upon the managerial style of the manager and the task to be carried out by the subordinate. If the manager has an autocratic style the briefing will include very clear guidelines on how the project is to be carried out and the manager may request a number of briefing sessions with the subordinate to keep the manager up to date. Whereas the more democratic leader will explain the project and give the individual wider parameters to work within and may have less contact with the subordinate during the project.

The environment in which the briefing takes place will influence the receiver. If it takes place in the manager's office the manager should consider the physical setting, for example the layout of the room. The position of the manager's desk may act as a barrier and reinforce the status of the manager. Where people face each other it is also a possible conflict situation.

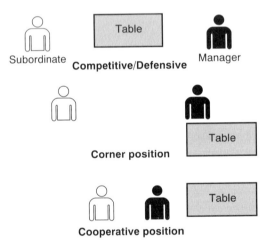

Fig 6.13 The position of the manager's desk may act as a barrier

The briefing

The requirements for briefing an individual are similar to briefing a team. Most of all the manager should know and understand the brief. This instils confidence in the subordinate because it reinforces the manager's position as someone in authority and who knows what he or she is talking about. Therefore it is important the manager knows what it is he or she wants the subordinate to do.

When the manager communicates with the subordinate the manager must think of the way in which the message is conveyed, the tone of voice and the use of language. It would be useful to the manager if they could see things from the subordinate's point of view and if necessary emphasise the benefits which may accrue to the subordinate. This is especially important during periods of change as people need to know the reasons for change and how they might benefit.

Non-verbal communication

Individual briefings tend to mean close proximity between the manager and the subordinate. During the oral communication the participants will be communicating though non-verbal means. People are usually unaware at a conscious level of the non-verbal communications (NVCs), but they form a very powerful part of the message. NVCs may contradict what is being said, for example, if you called on an acquaintance and when they opened the door, their face showed annoyance, no matter how friendly they appeared to be or what they said, the memory of the annoyed look would remain with you as evidence of their true feelings about you calling. Non-verbal communication can be:

- ◆ facial expressions
- ◆ body positions
- ◆ body movements
- ◆ gestures
- ◆ how we talk
- ◆ tone of voice used
- ◆ emphasis on words
- ◆ pauses in speech.

Business people and politicians are trained how to control their body movements and the way they speak so that their NVC is consistent with the message they are conveying.

Non-verbal behaviour

Gestures

Individuals tend to use gestures to reinforce a message or communicate to someone who is difficult to talk to. Gestures are used to support speech, for example, people use their hands to describe what they are talking about. These gestures are called illustrations.

Some gestures give an indication of how a person is feeling. In a briefing a person may be wringing his or her hands – an indication he or she is under pressure. In another situation, the manager may be twiddling their thumbs, which reveals boredom. When a person is nervous he or she may stroke the back of their head or fiddle with a small strand of hair. The manager should be aware of these gestures to know they must try to relax the subordinate.

Posture

The way in which people sit or stand will show how people are feeling. If someone is standing or sitting straight and stiff he or she is probably nervous, whereas someone with their hands in their pockets are relaxed.

The relationship between people can also be illustrated by the way they behave towards each other. If the person is sitting stiff and the other appears more relaxed one may be in a position of authority over the other such as manager and subordinate.

Facial expressions

Facial expressions show how we feel. The way in which we use our eyebrows and our mouth give clues on how we feel. The position of our eyebrows gives messages to the observer – if they are fully raised, this shows surprise, if they are lowered, this will indicate puzzlement or disapproval. The shape of the mouth can illustrate feeling, smiling shows friendliness or happiness, whereas lips turned down at the corners indicates sadness.

What does it mean if someone 'makes eyes at you' or 'you catch someone's eye'? Eye contact shows communication between people, for example, when someone is talking to another person it is important that eye contact is made so the person speaking knows their message is being received. Eye movement gives clues as to when to talk and when to stop, and the extent to which someone is listening.

Speech

Speech is the way words are spoken and may give one message, but the *way* we speak clarifies to the listener what is being said. The way we talk can influence the message through:

◆ the tone of voice
◆ the speed of talking
◆ the level of voice
◆ emphasis on words
◆ pauses in speech
◆ errors made.

For the briefing to be successful from the manager's point of view he or she must take the contribution of NVC as an important part of the briefing process.

Listening

For the subordinate and the manager it is important that they have the skill of listening. Many times people hear what they want to hear and ignore uncomfortable or awkward passages, we can tend to drift off into a daydream if someone talks for a long time and many people try to interrupt with questions or by trying to get their own opinion across. For briefing sessions to be successful the following listening skills will enable the communication process to function with few barriers:

◆ concentrate on what is being said
◆ make a mental note of any important words, phrases and facts which will help the listener to recall information later

◆ observe the person talking and try to keep eye contact. Failure to do so might give the person talking the wrong message, also the listener may miss important other NVC clues from the speaker

◆ give the speaker some positive feedback with positive oral and NVCs response, for example by saying. 'Yes, I understand that . . . Yes I see . . . I'm sure that is fine.' Smiling at the right moment and nods of the head will support the listener's comments

◆ listen to the speech noting the patterns and the tone of the voice, because they will signal the opportunity to ask questions or seek clarification

◆ if the listener is given some briefing notes the speaker will indicate whether it will be in order to go through the notes together. Highlighting important words, phrases and paragraphs. But the listener must not concentrate on the briefing notes too much as important oral and non-verbal combinations will be lost

◆ in some briefings it is better to make notes after the meeting but any notes should be key words only

◆ don't waste time by putting forward your own views unless asked

◆ don't interrupt the speaker.

Giving feedback

This is an important part of managing activities and people because feedback is a source of information for managers. Feedback of information gives the receiver the opportunity to evaluate :

◆ the success of a project; and

◆ the success of the communication process.

Guidelines on giving feedback

1 The feedback should be given as soon as possible after the event.

2 The person giving the feedback should be clear about what they want to say in advance.

3 A check should be made on the understanding of the recipient of the feedback, through occasional questions or requests for them to rephrase what has been said.

4 The person giving the feedback should make it clear that the feedback is their own personal views and that other people might think differently.

5 Feedback should start with positive points.

6 Priority areas should be selected. Too much feedback at one time can be too much for the recipient to take in, particularly if it is negative.

7 Specific actions a person has carried out should be discussed, but general criticisms of the recipient's personality should be avoided.

8 Examples of what could have been done differently should be given, so that the person receiving the feedback can work on changing his or her performance.

9 The recipient should have a choice as to whether or not to act on the feedback.

Customer feedback

Information from customers will give the organisation feedback on the products they have bought and the customer care they received. The organisation will have its own ideas on what it believes the customer wants. However to be sure of this the organisation will carry out market research before the development of a new product and they will seek the customers' views during the testing of the product and after the customer has bought the product.

Customer surveys obtain quantitive and qualitative feedback production data on which the organisation can make modifications to its goods and services. The organisation is seeking customer satisfaction and this will be achieved through high levels of repeat purchases. The organisation will be able to gauge the success of its product through the take up with its warranty and after sales service. From this information the organisation is able to ascertain if there is a common problem with its product. Another source of feedback for the organisation is through comparing actual sales with sales forecasts.

Supplier feedback

Organisations using TQM process will have close links with their suppliers. In order for a close customer/supplier relationship to be established it is important the two organisations communicate with each other. As customer organisations demand higher levels of quality standards from their suppliers it is necessary for the supplier to inform its customer whether it can meet the new standards and if not why. The two organisations can then work together to solve the problem. Without this feedback the level of trust between the organisations and supplier might have been damaged.

Feedback to shareholders

Individuals and organisations who invest money in companies need to know how their investments are faring. This information can be obtained by monitoring the share prices on the stock exchange. This is very limited feedback information but fuller feedback can be obtained from Annual General Meetings, the Annual Report and Accounts.

Feedback within the organisation

Feedback can be given to the managers by their subordinates and also by managers to their workforce and between managers within the same department and between departments.

Management need to know how the organisation is performing and each department will have its own measures of efficiency and effectiveness. Human resources will know how successful their manpower plan is through measuring labour turnover, success in education and training, staff and skill shortages and unmet training needs.

Production can use performance indicators such as percentage defects per measured output, the number of products returned and warranty claims, the percentage of orders completed on time. Sales can use planned sales by region or country, and compare salespersons' actual sales against targets. The organisation's financial performance can be measured against cash flows, and financial ratios measuring profitability and liquidity.

Methods of feedback by the subordinate

This can be of two types: oral (briefings which can be on a one-to-one basis or to a group, or using the telephone) and written (memoranda, e-mail, and reports).

Reports are the usual method of feeding back information to line managers or to a group of people. Formal reports can be requested on a specific topic or are expected on a regular basis. For example, the sales director may be asked to present a report on the success of a new advertising campaign to his colleagues. The sales managers may be expected to report back to the sales director on a monthly basis on the sales of their products.

The report is written and presented in a set format and should include the following:

The title page	This includes the name of the organisation, the name and title of the author and the subject of the report.
Terms of reference	This explains the reason for the report, i.e. the person who asked for the report, the subject to be considered and how the research was to be carried out.
Table of contents	This lists all the main sections in the report and should direct the reader to any appendices as these are used to support the findings and recommendations of the report.
Summary	This should summarise the findings, conclusions and recommendations of the report.
Introduction	This gives the background information of the report.
Main body	This is a clear and concise section of the report which states the information found in a factual manner. Information which supports the findings such as tables and charts will be located in the appendices. Conclusions may be indicated in this section.
Conclusions	Here the conclusions are stated from the findings of the report.
Recommendations	The recommendations are put forward based on the findings and conclusions. They should be clear, unambiguous and concise.

Bibliography	If the report required a literature search, acknowledgments in the form of a list of the texts used are made in this section.
Appendices	This is the information which supports the main body of the report. It includes all relevant data.

Feedback from manager to workforce

The manager will communicate with subordinates on a range of topics, from the implementation of new policies, production and sales figures to wage negotiations. The manager will select the most appropriate medium and which includes:

1 *Written form.* Bulletins and bulletin boards, employee newspapers, house journals, letters inserted in with pay slips, minutes of meetings and reports.

2 *Oral.* Briefing groups, conferences and seminars, departmental meetings, joint consultations and the use of TV and video.

 ## Information systems

An organisation's information is an extremely important resource or asset, in the same way as its capital and human resource assets. Without an information resource, most companies would cease to exist very quickly. The task of managing information is handled by the organisation's information system, defined as the combination of computers and human users that manage data collection, storage, and the transformation of this data into useful information.

The information system must be flexible enough to meet the different needs of users at various levels within the organisation. To meet these needs several different types of information systems are required. One information system may process raw data into information for normal day-to-day operations, and a different one may provide reports to first line managers. Another type of information system may be used to help top-level managers make their decisions.

In the 1960s, the speed and the power of the computer increased, enabling operational data to be processed quickly. Managers were able to use the resulting information more effectively in the decision making process. This led to the development of Management Information Systems (MIS) which solved the manager's problem of searching for information because it produced reports that selected data relevant to decisions and summarised this information in a tabular form. Once MIS became a key source of information for managers, data processing (now often referred to as the Transaction Processing System [TPS]) evolved into the conversion of data to information for MIS and other information systems. *Data Base Management Systems (DBMS)* were also developed at this time to manage the large amounts of data stored in a database.

As well as the Transaction Processing Systems and Management Information Systems there are other information systems which developed as computer power increased.

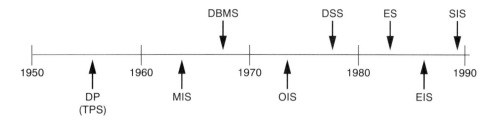

Fig 6.14 Development of information systems since 1950

The most dramatic changes occurred in the early 1980s, when the arrival of the personal computer coincided with the rapid development of telephone and communication technology. The personal computer and its related systems join network software and communication devices like the fax machine to yield an *Office Information System (OIS)* that supports all other information systems.

Although the development of MIS was an important step in providing managers with the information needed to make better decisions, they could not ask questions of an MIS or find solutions to analytical problems. These actions required the reporting function of MIS, graphic displays, and the problem-solving capabilities of management science. The system which combines these factors is called a *Decision Support System (DSS)* due to its emphasis on supporting decision makers rather than just providing reports on past events. Decision Support Systems were found to be excellent for semi-structured decisions, ones where factors influencing the decision are reasonably well known. They are also useful for unstructured decisions where different scenarios may be tried out using the DSS. Middle management usually make decisions of this kind. Top-level executives tend to make highly unstructured decisions where influencing factors are less well defined. To cater for their need *Executive Information Systems (EIS)* was developed. A personal computer-based EIS can link to the company's primary computer and use graphics extensively to display the information needed for executive decisions. Internal and external data may be brought together on-screen and viewed in different ways to give the executive decision maker more feel for the problem.

Two other information systems are becoming important in organisations – *Strategic Information Systems (SIS)* and *Expert Systems (ES)*. An SIS enables an organisation to use strategic information for competitive advantage, and an ES provides workers at all levels with the knowledge and expertise needed to do their jobs better.

The TPS, MIS, DSS, EIS, OIS, and a database interact to form a complete information system that supports managerial decision making. Data from internal and external sources are input through the TPS before being stored in a database. Next, a DBMS is used to find needed data for processing in the MIS, DSS, or EIS. For example, MIS is used to create various periodic reports for the management, or the DSS is used to answer a manager's question.

Management Information Systems

The primary objective of a Management Information System is to create reports which provide useful information to managers. Managers do not have time to sift through reams of operational data when they need to make a decision. A *Management Information System (MIS)* can be defined as 'an integrated user-machine system for providing information to support operations, management, and decision-making functions in an organisation.'[1] An MIS is a primary stage in producing information from data and it underpins the other information systems found in an organisation. The reports that an MIS generates provide support for operational, tactical, and strategic decision making.

Types of reports

Reports can be in as many forms as required by the different management levels in an organisation. Basically, three types of reports are generated by an MIS: scheduled reports, exception reports, and demand reports. Each one serves a different purpose for the organisation, but all are important.

Scheduled reports

These are based on the periodic and historical data produced by an organisation's data processing operations. They reflect the original information with the addition of categorisation and summarisation. Low level managers make use of these reports to make operational decisions to meet objectives set by the higher level managers. For example, a production manager may want to see a daily report on the number of defective items coming off the production line and a weekly report on the number of overtime hours needed for that week.

Exception reports

These are generated when something unusual happens, for example, manufactured items may not be within tolerance levels, or excessive amounts of overtime are being worked. The exception report is useful to the manager in detecting problems. Because a manager is a problem solver, early detection is essential to good management. At the same time, the exception report does not overwhelm the manager with unnecessary information.

Demand reports

These are requested by a manager on a particular subject. Such reports may be predetermined but are not required on a regular basis or they may be the result of an unexpected event in another MIS report or from external information. For example, as a result of an exception report, a manager may request a report on the possible causes of the problem. Availability of data to produce demand reports is a feature of a good MIS.

---

[1] Gordon B. Davies and Margaret H. Olson (1985) *Management Information Systems,* (2nd edn.) McGraw Hill.

Summary

Information systems ensure that the appropriate information is available to managers for better decision making. Computerised information systems consist of

◆ the computer hardware

◆ the software necessary to use the hardware

◆ the data needed by the software to supply information to management and for transaction processing

◆ the personnel needed to operate the system

◆ the procedures necessary to control and operate the information system.

Important types of information systems are TPS, MIS, DSS, EIS, and OIS. The Transaction Processing System converts raw data into either processed information or data for use in other processing operations.

An MIS provides managers with various types of reports, including scheduled reports, exception reports, and demand reports. Decision Support Systems assist decision makers by providing a software environment in which managers can experiment with various alternatives. A spreadsheet can function as a DSS allowing models of a situation to be built and experimented with, for example, cash flow forecasting. An EIS presents information to executives in more graphic terms so they can easily picture the nature of the problem and the alternative courses of action at their disposal.

An OIS expedites all these systems via text preparation, electronic and voice mail, facsimile transmission, EDI, electronic filing, and access to internal and external databases. Many functions are carried out over local area networks.

An Expert System tries to incorporate a human's expertise into an information system using factual knowledge and rules. An SIS helps the organisation remain healthy by providing it with a competitive advantage in the market place. All these systems combined help an organisation to take advantage of information technology to compete more effectively.

(Section on Information Systems written by Sue Coles, Manchester Metropolitan University.)
(Copyright reserved)

Bibliography

McKeown, P.G., and Leitch, R.A. (1993) *Managing with Computers*, Dryden.

Co-ordinating

From reading this chapter you will learn about co-ordinating, including:

1   co-ordinating; and
2   forecasting.

Co-ordinating

Co-ordination involves everyone working together effectively. All the various tasks or parts of an organisation are brought into relation to one another to ensure harmony or effective operation.

A person setting up a printing business for the first time by herself will have to cope with all tasks alone – advertising, answering the telephone, buying paper, getting orders ready, printing their orders off. Orders need to be delivered, customers invoiced and the accounts completed. She cannot spend all day planning a new advertising campaign and leaving the other tasks for another day. Although there seems to be a perfectly logical sequence of tasks – from advertising the service to the completion of the accounts – as organisations grow each task becomes a major activity and within each activity there are sub-tasks which need to be performed. The 'obvious' logic of doing each task can become difficult to see as organisations grow and become more complex. As soon as the sole trader can no longer perform all the tasks, he or she needs to employ another person, and the tasks will need to be divided between herself and the new employee. Co-ordination and communication then start to become very important. Systems will have to be introduced, the owner may have kept information in her head when working alone, but this causes too many problems when other people become involved. If the owner is out visiting customers, she will not be aware of the phone calls and new orders the new employee is receiving in her absence. If the new employee makes a note of orders on odd scraps of paper and gets interrupted by a machine failure or a customer calling round, a new order may be lost or forgotten about. A system for recording phone calls may need to be implemented to aid co-ordination and communication. Complex organisations have hundreds of positions and departments performing incredibly diverse activities. There needs to be lots of liaison within and between departments in order to keep communication and information flowing.

The owner of a small business and senior managers of large businesses have to find a way to tie all departments together. The overall goal of the organisation is to deliver a product or service to their customers, but often employees identify with their immediate department or team and take its interests to heart. They may not want to cooperate or communicate with other departments for the good of the organisation as a whole. Conflict or non-cooperation can sometimes become a more exciting game than working smoothly and effectively with other people. Power and political games provide immediate results. In Lee Iacocca and William Novak's book on Iacocca's time as President of the Chrysler Corporation, they describe the lack of co-ordination between departments:

> *'What I found at Chrysler were 35 vice presidents, each with his own turf . . . I couldn't believe, for example, that the guy running engineering departments wasn't in constant touch with his counterpart in manufacturing. But that's how it was. Everybody worked independently. I took one look at that system and I almost threw up. That's when I knew I was in really deep trouble.'*

Iacocca found a situation where products were being designed which were impossible to manufacture as there was never any communication between engineering and manufacturing. The increased co-ordination which Iacocca implemented enabled the design and production of a new range of cars in only three years, compared with the five years of development previously required.

Co-ordination is important in all types and sizes of business. A small pub or cafe needs to ensure that staff are available to work whenever the business is open. If the manager in charge of drawing up staff rotas allows too many people to have the same evening off, there will be no staff cover for the product to be delivered to the customers and the business will be failing in its most basic aim. Similarly with tasks, even people doing the same job need co-ordin-ation, hospital cleaners

Fig 7.1 Co-ordination between all departments is essential

need to be allocated wards and corridors of their own to work on and their manager or team leader is responsible for ensuring that everywhere is covered and that two people are not cleaning the same area at different times of the day whilst other wards are left untouched.

Co-ordination is especially important in international companies. Managers can design systems and structures to promote communication and facilitate co-ordination. The most important methods for achieving better co-ordination are information systems, task forces and teams and integrating managers.

Information systems

Information systems are the written and computer based internal systems for processing data and information amongst employees. Many businesses which receive customer orders over the telephone, such as the advertising sections of local newspapers, will type the orders straight onto the computer whilst the salesperson is on the telephone. The order is never written down by hand. The computer entry can be printed out to act as confirmation for the customer and as documentation to be acted upon within the company. Information systems include memos, bulletins, and written reports, as well as technological systems such as computers, electronic mail, electronic bulletin boards and teleconferences. Electronic systems have the capacity to process enormous volumes of data across hierarchical levels and departments, thereby enabling greater co-ordination.

Task forces and teams

Teams can be used in various ways to increase co-ordination within an organisation. The simple teamwork principle can be used to get individuals talking to one another about their work instead of acting alone and communicating very little about what they do in the organisation. The quality of work produced is very often improved by getting individuals into a team and encouraging them to discuss improvements to the work. Cross-functional teams can be used for purposes of co-ordination, they can bring together differing experiences and viewpoints from different departments and work together to increase inter-departmental liaison and communication. The Board of Directors is actually a cross-functional team as each Director represents a different function within the organisation.

Task forces are cross-functional teams which have been set up to solve a short-term problem involving several departments. Task force members represent their departments and share information that increases co-ordination.

Integrating managers

An integrating manager is a person in a full-time position created for the purpose of co-ordinating the activities of several departments. Some organisations use product managers to look after one particular line of products and liaise across all departments. Procter and Gamble have several product managers to co-ordinate product lines. Product managers set budget goals, marketing strategies and obtain cooperation from advertising, production, and sales personnel needed for implementing product strategy.

CASE STUDY 7.1

Stretton Leisure

Stretton Leisure supplies 17 000 coin operated machines to sites such as public houses, licensed betting offices and cinemas in the UK. The machines include fruit machines, juke boxes, pin tables, pool tables, background music systems and video games. The depot for the North West area is in Warrington. It serves 2500 customers (or sites) and has 33 workshop/installation engineers who prepare and install the fruit machines. If a machine becomes faulty or damaged, Stretton Leisure will send a field service engineer to the site to repair the machine. Nationally, the company receives 250 000 service calls per annum and prides itself on an average response time of 1 hour 32 minutes. The installation engineers work alongside a sales team who visit customers to sell or replace machines.

The sales team relay information on customer requirements to the workshops, where the workshop teams will prepare the equipment for site. Installation engineers will then visit sites in order to install or replace the machines. The sales team act as Account Managers which entails them monitoring the performance of machines. If the income from a machine falls below a target level, they will make the decision to change the machine.

The other main reason for changing machines is if they have become damaged due to vandalism, burglaries or unavailability of spare parts. Replacing a machine which is unrepairable on site is known as a service change. Service changes are carried out on the same day the customer makes the problem known to Stretton Leisure. The customer pays rent for each machine and therefore Stretton Leisure try to ensure that the customer is supplied with a machine in exchange for the rental payment.

Greg Jackson, Workshop Installations Manager:

'Break-ins are my worst nightmare. There's no control over them and they create unplanned work, it's extra work which we have to do as an emergency. Service engineers can carry out some cabinet repairs on site with the aid of filler and paint, but if it is so badly damaged that it can't be filled and painted, then we'll have to go and change it. We try to get service changes due to break-ins done as quickly as possible because damaged machines on site can

Fig 7.2 Greg Jackson, co-ordinating activities at Stretton Leisure

look bad for our business. Machines are worth between £1295–£1750, so service changes due to break-ins are very costly for our business.'

The installation engineers work in teams of three, one stays in the workshop at the depot and repairs faulty machines, the other two team members install those machines the following day. The teams are rotated so that each engineer spends on average a month in the workshop and then goes out visiting sites to install the machines for two months. The engineers in the workshop carry out a damage assessment exercise on machines which have been vandalised or broken into to ascertain whether it is financially viable to repair them.

Greg Jackson:

'*Even if machines are to be scrapped, they are still worth something for spare parts. A lot of spare parts are interchangeable between machines. The area goes from Anglesey in the west, to Whitchurch in the the south, and up to Carlisle and as far east as Darwin and Blackburn. We do have two small satellite depots in Carlisle and Anglesey and engineers there can change machines. The machines are solid state technology and its very reliable, the manufacturers have improved upon it every year. The company is very image-conscious. When the engineers install a new machine, they will change all the cash from the old machine to the new machine and test the machine. They will then explain the various features of the new machine and how the game actually plays to the licensee. The licensee is also made aware of any special requirements such as token refills for the machine. They leave the site when they are satisfied that the machine is in full working condition. Customers pay the bills, we aim to give excellent customer service, we're very dedicated to the customer.*

My job is to control and maintain the day-to-day running of the department. I shouldn't really get involved with the minor problems installation engineers have because I have got four chargehands to do that for me, but at the moment I'm sharing a small office with the chargehands, so it's very difficult not to. If an installation engineer walks in to see a chargehand, I can't help but get involved. My main function is to improve quality and my performance is judged by the Installation Error Report. This report logs every piece of equipment that we change or install if it breaks down within eight days of installation. When this happens, I have to investigate why it's happened. We're aiming for improved quality all the time. I only get involved with decisions on which teams to send to sites if the chargehands have a problem, but usually that responsibility is delegated to the chargehands.

With 33 installation engineers and four chargehands, there are going to be people who can't get along together. To get the most out of a team, they need to at least speak to each other. It's best to let them try to choose their own teams. However, they may choose someone with whom they are best buddies and bunk off all day, or it may be that they do actually genuinely like working together. If they like working together, they will work more efficiently. At least they'll know each other's quirks and peculiarities when I build new teams. I consult the chargehands because they are closer to the installation engineers than anyone. They visit them on site, train them and check on them on site. I fully intend to carry on building the teams in order to get maximum efficiency out of them. I advertise any vacancies, recruit with the aid of the chargehands whose team has the vacancy.

My day starts at 8 am officially its 8.30 am, but if I get in half an hour early I can finish off things from the night before and be prepared for the day ahead. At 8.30 am, I can guarantee that with 33 installation engineers and four chargehands, the phone is going to ring. When someone phones in sick, I have to find out whether that person was going out as an installation engineer or whether he was working in the workshop. If he was working in the workshop I have 35–40 minutes before I have to do anything about it, but if he was going out I have do something about it straightaway. It may be that the van is due to go and it could be going anywhere in the Northwest. My main priority is to get those off the car park. Once they are off the car park, I can take my coat off and start organising my day.

CASE STUDY *cont*

I liaise with the Sales Managers because they want to know what work was carried out the previous day. If anything was dropped they want to know the reason why. Also, I want to know from them whether they have any special requirements for that day's work in the workshop. We have Hazardous Site Forms and the forms notify me if there is a hazardous flight of stairs or poor lighting or restricted access, so that I have some warning before we go. If it's a hazardous site I will arrange to go and visit it to estimate how many engineers we need to send to get the job done safely.

We occasionally have 10-man team lifts on site as some of the equipment we install can weigh 300–400 kilogrammes and it may have to go upstairs or downstairs. I have given an engineer a friendly warning for putting himself in danger before now; people shouldn't be driven into the ground, they are there to do a good job for us. If someone is injured on site and I have not warned him about possible dangers, I could be liable to prosecution. There's a lot of manual handling and I wouldn't give someone a job I wouldn't be prepared to do myself. I wouldn't hesitate to send the whole installation department onto site if it meant getting the equipment installed safely.

During the day I will liaise with the Sales Managers to produce the Production Lists for the following day and then with the chargehands we can decide who is going where and who is doing what job. Some visits are straightforward, for example, juke box installations require three visits to site. First, to remove any equipment already installed, second, to pre-wire the site with all the necessary cables so that when its decorated all the cables will be hidden. The third visit is for the final fixing and the same installation crew will be involved at all stages, they can follow it through from start to end.

If we're not busy I will speak to the Service Manager to ask if he wants to borrow any staff. It's my philosophy not to stand around doing nothing myself when others are working and not get involved. I don't see why anyone else should stand around and I try to promote that and encourage people to help one another. First thing in the morning, there are nine vans waiting to go out but the most we can fit in on the loading bay is six vehicles, that means there are always three parked outside the loading bay. In the past that has meant that six people have stood around, but now everyone helps each other. It has taken me nearly a year, but they are getting to the stage of thinking "If I help them to load, that will get them out of the way and I can get my vehicle in to load up". The same at night, when they get back early they help one another, and then they can pull off the loading bay to make room for someone else. Instead of working as nine teams, they are now working as one big team, just on these two occasions during the day when they are all together. At least they do when I'm working with them, I don't know whether they do it when I'm not watching.

My chargehands are supposed to supervise the loading operation, but they are usually chasing up last minute requirements for that day's production from Sales Managers or sorting out the workshop teams to get them started for the day. The speed with which the vans get off the car park in the morning is a good indicator of how well the department is running.

The majority of our work is done when the sites we visit are closed. If the site is a pub, the more work the engineer can do before it opens, the better quality his work is. If customers are in the pub, the engineer has to worry about things like the security of the cash he is swapping between the machines. For the furthest distances like Lancaster, Carlisle or Anglesey I give them an incentive of "job and finish". If they start early, they can get the job done, then finish early. They can be on the road for 7 am if they wish. Sometimes the customer requires the work to be finished by 10 am and then it's a mad scramble to get the crew out on time.

I sometimes feel as if I have six plates in the air at once, because once the crews have left I can only get in touch with them by ringing round the sites they are going to go to. If an urgent service change is required I have to make phone calls to every site, then I have to rely on the manager of the site to tell the installation crew to ring me back. The crews can decide for themselves which route they take, the experienced ones go to the furthest site first and work

Fig 7.3 Stretton Leisure prides itself on answering service calls within an hour and a half

their way back. I have to just sit and wait for the engineer to ring me back and the problem can't be cleared up, it annoys me to have lots of ends untied and not be able to finish things off. If a crew has a circular route, we will ask them to call back and pick the machine up, otherwise it involves a crew going out at four or five o'clock in the afternoon. I don't like my engineers having to install machines in pubs at 7 o'clock at night when the public are in, as some of the pubs are in bad areas. I like to protect the engineers because I've done the job myself and it's not nice to walk into a site at night when people are drinking and making merry. We have to get the machines working quickly as they are accumulating "downtime" whenever they are not working and the customer isn't making any money from them.'

('Downtime' is the amount of time taken to get the machine working again. It is recorded from the moment a site rings in the fault.)

DISCUSSION QUESTIONS 7.1

1 Which activities does Greg Jackson have to achieve a balance between each morning?

2 Why does Greg say that 'break-ins are my worst nightmare'?

3 Does the system of job rotation at Stretton Leisure help to build cohesive teams?

4 What factors in the case study indicate that Stretton Leisure does strive to give good customer service?

5 How could communication be improved at Stretton Leisure?

6   What hazards or dangers might the installation engineers face in their jobs?

7   Could Greg delegate or re-organise any of his work in order to be more effective?

 # Forecasting

Mention the subject of forecasting and people either switch off or dismiss it as something that is about unrealistic budgets or unachievable targets set by remote management. Forecasting is not confined to the number crunchers in the accounts department, it is an essential aspect of managing people and activities. Every manager should be concerned about what will happen in the future and how it can be controlled. Managers have to forecast all the time, thus forecasting is an essential part of the everyday life of all businesses, be they in the manufacturing or service industries. The good manager is not so much one who can minimise the effect of past mistakes but rather one who can successfully manage the future.

Look at some of the questions management needs to answer. There are the obvious ones like:

◆   what will next month's/year's sales be ?

◆   what should the sales target be?

◆   how much should be produced this month/year?

◆   how big a stock should be kept ?

◆   what will the cost of raw materials be next month/next year?

◆   what price should be charged ?

◆   what will the profit be ?

However the answers to these questions raise further forecasting needs. If sales are to be increased will this lead to an increase in the

◆   sales force?

◆   marketing staff?

◆   administration staff?

◆   management staff?

◆   telephone staff?

If production is to increase will it lead to an increase in the

◆   production staff?

◆   supervisors?

◆   administrators?

Even if the forecast is that production would remain static or even fall the question of whether this leads to a reduction in staff has to be answered.

It should be clear that these questions and their answers affect all aspects of the business, from strategic planning, market planning, wages structure and so on. To obtain the best practical answers to such questions the ability to produce a viable forecast is essential.

There are three principal methods of forecasting

◆ intuitive

◆ causal

◆ extrapolative.

Intuitive

This is is based entirely on an individual's knowledge and feelings. This is the basis behind many decisions made by entrepreneurs, who thrive on intuitive forecasting, but for every successful entrepreneur there are hundreds of failed ones.

Intuitive forecasting is risky, but it is often the only option open especially when the situation is complex and unquantifiable. One such occasion would be when starting out in a new business. Two disastrous intuitive forecasts were made by experienced managers. One record company manager in 1962 refused to give a contract to the Beatles – his intuition told him they would not sell. The other was by a manager at IBM, who in the 70s stated that mainframe computers were the only option, there was no future in personal computers. That decision put them ten years behind their competitors.

Causal

Causal forecasting is based on identifying events which influence the future. Forecasts are made on the basis of cause and effect and are dependent on correctly identifying the causes. This type of forecasting is principally used in macro economics whereby the effect of, say, major disasters like earthquakes on stock market prices can be predicted or the effect that recovery from a recession will have on unemployment.

Whilst both these methods can be used, in normal management the most popular and frequently used method of forecasting is:

Extrapolative

This is the most popular forecasting method. It is based on identifying past trends and projecting them into the future. This identification is usually of a mathematical or a statistical nature which is used to determine if there is a relationship between two or more variables and then using this relationship to forecast. For example, it could be argued the rate of inflation is related to the level of wages, cost of raw materials and interest rates. To make forecasts correctly using extrapolitive methods the manager needs to be able to identify the appropriate relationship and its stability. The principal models used for extrapolation are regression analysis and time series analysis.

Regression analysis

It is used to determine whether there is a relationship between independent and dependent variables, to study the form or shape of the curve of the relationship and to predict the dependent variable from the independent one(s) using the relationship.

Time series analysis

A time series is a set of values of variables, usually recorded at equal time intervals. In other words, any variable that is measured over time in sequential order is called a time series, e.g. daily, weekly, monthly, quarterly and annually.

(Written by Dr N Shani, Lecturer in Business and Management Studies, Manchester Metropolitan University.)

CASE STUDY 7.2

Assessing engineering companies

Have you ever wondered how small entrepreneurs sell their businesses when they no longer want them? Alan Pinkney buys engineering companies. Alan: *'There isn't an open market for small second-hand companies, people often approach me and ask if I'm interested in buying their business.'* Alan Pinkney is Financial Director of CHK Engineering Limited. The company makes production fabrications in mild steel, stainless steel and aluminium. They also specialise in punching and plasma cutting. Alan Pinkney searches out and assesses other engineering companies to buy which will fit in with CHK's portfolio of products, while his partner, Alan Porter, runs CHK. The partners have recently sold off their minority shareholding interests in several firms and now wholly own three engineering companies. *'We didn't have the degree of control we needed with minority shareholdings and we had sufficiently improved the businesses for the owners to want to buy us out.'*

Alans Pinkney and Porter are married to the two daughters of Eric Churnock, the founder of CHK Engineering. They took over their father-in-law's business in 1976. Alan Porter had been a teacher and Alan Pinkney had played professional football for Crystal Palace for eight years and he had played in South Africa for three years. Alan Pinkney: *'I remember helping my father-in-law with the accounts when he was living in Worthing and still trying to run*

Fig 7.4 Alan Pinkney, Financial Director, CHK Engineering Ltd

the business in Crewe, Cheshire. He used to post the timesheets and envelopes with cash wages in them every week. We used to be scavenging around in the Post Office on the Thursday to see if the wages had arrived. I asked him if he had heard of credit transfer. Once he had let go of the business, everything came up to Crewe and we could run it our way. I looked at the books when I first got back from Cape Town and the turnover for CHK Engineering was £84 000. This year it was £6 500 000.

We did a lot of things on the way to that expansion, we got BS5750 quality approval, a lot of investment in new machinery, changed projects to try to get the staff to cope with what we were planning. We moved out of one league and into another. Up to that point Alan and I were joint Managing Directors and we had taken personal responsibility for most functions in the company. We were advised by our accountants and a consultant that we needed to change our structure. We brought in a second tier of management, a Manufacturing Director, an Accountant, a Sales Manager, and an estimating team below that. It took a lot of courage but it was what we needed to take us forward. We had been creating our own vacuum, where nothing could be done outside mine or Alan's office and it was a constraint. We needed to divest some responsibility downwards, bring in new people, and free ourselves to look after the major decisions.

Alan [Porter] had been in the business longer than I had and was more familiar with its operation, so it was decided that I should develop our other interests. The long term aim was to go out and find related businesses and eventually bring it all back together again, using the eight acre site to provide various forms of engineering sub-contractor services. Our first investment in another business was in 1985. One of our suppliers was a one-man-band toolmaker and he'd done pretty well to get where he was. He didn't have much business experience and he was our main supplier, we did a lot of business with him. I used to call in and help him with funding and various aspects of managing a business. There was a scheme called the Business Expansion Scheme which gave good tax incentives for investing in private companies with no return for at least five years. We pumped our money into this toolmaking business and then began to use the management services of CHK for that and other businesses. We could provide management services such as accurate management accounts to which small businesses normally haven't got access. We used the management skills already available in CHK which meant benefiting from economies of scale. We were approached by a precision engineering company with two owners who were getting on in years and wanted to retire. They had argued and were running the business as two separate entities with their own suppliers and workforces. We then bought a minority shareholding in a moulding company and just kept the Sales Director because he was the one with all the contacts. The basic approach we take is that if someone has a business skill such as selling their company's products, we allow them to get on with that and we provide the other management services from a central point at a very reasonable price.

My skill in assessing which companies to buy came from doing HNC in Business Studies, specialising in accounts, and then through talking to accountants and getting involved in buy-outs, getting behind the numbers, finding out where the weaknesses are. What I'm always looking for is a business with good potential, but with obstacles or constraints. If I can clear the obstacles away and free the entrepreneurial skills that obviously are there then that company could be successful. Obstacles might be lack of vision, lack of investment, no new markets, poor pricing, sometimes it's the individuals who work in the company.

The businesses we bought tended to fit together to offer a product portfolio, this included: production machining, fabrications with machining and toolmaking – this offered customers turnkey solutions to problems. In the past orders for production were given 3–5 months in advance. Today you're lucky if you get orders two months in advance, nobody gives you long lead times any more, everybody wants Just In Time, nobody wants to carry stock. They want you to hold the stock for them and call it up when they want it. If you're strong enough and you've got the systems to control your own material intake and your own production, you can pass that down the line. We're quite happy to offset stock financing on the basis of manufacturing floor times. That means that we can make the product more cheaply in larger quantities. If you can manufacture competitively, but you've got to hold the stock for two or three months, that's to give yourself as much chance to produce effectively and as far forward as the schedule will allow. We do all batch production and its a continual balancing act because costs are lower for producing larger quantities and yet you can't anticipate future demand. Sometimes you think "We could do with doubling up that batch", but you don't have the orders to do it, and if you take a chance you're facing the prospect of producing for stock which may never be sold. There are modifications such as changes in design which might render the stock useless. We are total subcontractors, we make what other people want, so we don't have any control over the design of the product. If we make 1000 extra components in the hope of selling them in the future, we might be making 1000 pieces of scrap. The value of the product is in the engineering and the manufacturing process. If the component isn't needed any more it's worthless. It's not like a pair of shoes or a football where you can trade it in or sell it off as cheap stock. It's only worth the scrap value of the material.

Business people often take business too personally. They can't see that the company is a different entity from them as individuals. Also people try to work together and it's like a forced marriage, it can be counterproductive. Very often in engineering the accounting and finance functions are seen as secondary. The attitude is "You're only counting what I've done after the event", they never use the tools or information. They are still in the mode of writing up the books, giving them to the accountant and then nine months later "He'll tell us whether we've made any money or not". In today's world that's not good enough. If you're borrowing money, you've got to keep the banks and finance partners up to date with what's going on. The bank comes in for a lot of stick, but if you keep them informed of what's going on, generally they will support you. What they don't like is being kept in the dark and hearing the bad news last of all. You need to know where you are with accurate up-to-date information.

The usual routine for buying a business is to have a look at the accounts for the last two or three years, see what the trends are, see how up-to-date the information is. There's always that black hole between the last set of audited accounts and what's happening today. That's the bit you have to find out in the course of negotiations. There's a gap of at least two years since the last set of audited accounts. You've got to do your homework, as soon as you say you're interested you start spending money. It's like buying a house, you get as much information as you can before you involve the professionals, but then you've got to spend some money to find out what's really there.

You can find out quite a lot from looking around and talking to the employees, you get a feel for it. The shopfloor workers will tell you what's going on. Very often they are anti-management and if you say "What do you think of these guys?" they'll tell you straightaway. It gives you a good feel for it. If you ask for up-to-date management accounts and they don't do them, that tells you something straightaway. I look at the age of the machinery, they may not have had the money to invest or they may have been siphoning it off and paying themselves too much. You use the accounts to get the story behind what you're looking at.

You take note of the customer base. It's good if they're a blue chip company. There should be a good spread of customers, you can put all your eggs in one basket by depending too much on one large customer. It might be that before you came in to look at the company, they had lost their major contract. You do a bit of research to find out what's going on.

No one company is the same, they've all got their own peculiarities. The situation in the market matters. It's not so important if the company are in a declining market as long as their products have synergy with ours, if the fit is good you can buy well because the people you're buying from are in a stand-alone position. I always want to know how this business fits into its own market. Is it considered to be the market leader, in the middle, or the bottom and for what reasons? Has it always held this position, or has it dropped? Is it considered by customers as having been a good source of supply in the past, but is no longer? What's the competition? How strong is the competition financially? If we started to compete with them, could we sit out a longer period of competition than they could? It's not the most important aspect. The most important thing is can we buy the place at a price which gives us a very good opportunity of getting us a return in not too long a time. If you want to buy a very well organised company, then you've got to pay for it. If you buy something that hasn't been working, then you're not going to pay very much for it, but you've got to go in there and change what's going on. You can get something quite good by your own efforts and your own approach, your organisation, motivation and your own management skills. It's again very like buying a house. If you buy a run down business, you can rejuvenate it.

Business building is block by block, we get rid of all the excesses and trappings the previous owners have had. You need to dig in for the long haul, keep on investing, keep doing the right things and eventually you'll reach a point where profits start coming. We had 24 years of grafting away to build a solid base. I don't believe that there's easy money to be made.'

DISCUSSION QUESTIONS 7.2

1 What difference did it make to the business when Alan Pinkney and Alan Porter brought in a new tier of management?

2 Why does Alan Pinkney say that they had been creating a vacuum prior to the restructuring and the arrival of the new tier of management?

3 Does Alan Pinkney feel that the JIT system causes problems for the weaker companies?

4 What are the disadvantages of batch production mentioned in the case study?

5 What mistakes does Alan Pinkney consider that small entrepreneurs frequently make?

6 Why does Alan Pinkney sometimes buy businesses which have a declining market for their product?

7 Why is the customer base important in business?

8 Why is buying a business similar to buying a house?

Constraints

8

From reading this chapter you will learn about constraints on activities, including:

1   regulatory control;
2   allocating resources;
3   working in France;
4   external changes; and
5   outer and inner environments.

Regulatory control

Organisational operations are controlled by both external organisations and internal procedures. These controls give order to the way in which organisations behave.

External regulations

There are many ways external forces can constrain an organisation. External bodies which regulate the way an organisation operates include: supranational organisations such as the European Commission; central government, local government, quangos, pressure groups, lobbyists and trade and professional organisations. Also to be considered are legal constraints and legal documentation.

The European Union

The European Union has been having greater influence over the UK affairs in recent years. The Union gets its powers from the Treaties of Rome, Paris and Maastricht. These treaties empowered the Council of Ministers and the European Commission to make three types of legislation and regulation:

1   *regulations,* which are designed to achieve uniformity of law amongst member states;

2   *decisions,* which may be addressed to a company and are binding; and

3   *directives,* which seek to harmonise the law of member states. These are instructions to member states to bring their laws into line by a certain date.

The European Community issues directives which supersede domestic laws and regulations. European regulatory powers, for instance, include consumer protection, health and safety at work, and competitive behaviour between organisations. The beef crisis of 1996 led to the European Union banning all beef products exported from the UK. This caused conflict between the UK government and its European partners, and the resulting ban created hardship to UK farmers.

The UK has opted out of the European Social Charter, although it was agreed by each of the other member states. However, aspects of the different terms of the Charter are being adopted piecemeal in the UK for example, in 1995 European law gave part-time employees the right to the same unfair dismissal procedures as their full-time colleagues. By the year 2000, the UK will probably have to introduce regulations restricting working hours of employees in line with the rest of the European Union.

As part of the harmonisation process, the European Union sets standards for products so there is a common standard throughout the Union. The UK is introducing the metric measuring system to fit in with the rest of Europe which has meant many companies in the UK switching from imperial measure to the European standard.

Other constraints imposed by Europe have included, in transport policy, the tachograph to monitor driving times, the length and duration of rest periods and the speed vehicles travel. Also it became a requirement for coach firms to employ more than one driver on routes to ensure safety standards were met.

All UK courts are bound by the decisions of the European Court of Justice (ECJ) on matters relating to European law. In 1996, the European Court found the UK government had acted illegally in allowing mudflats supporting at least eight species of birds to be covered over to make a car park. The Royal Society for the Protection of Birds had taken the case to the English courts but, eventually, went to the ECJ to get a final verdict.

Central government

The government regulates organisations and competition. The regulation is to ensure the workforce and the consumer are not exploited and competition between organisations is fair. The regulations can be by guideline or by law. Government guidelines usually refer to what the government would like to see happen but for which they would prefer not to legislate. For example, newspapers are subject to the Press Commission and the government has warned the press on a number of occasions about their behaviour regarding privacy of individuals. The government is reluctant to pass laws regulating the press, and therefore it uses its influence through the Press Commission.

Legal constraints

Organisational behaviour is regulated by law administered through the courts. The law determines the way in which an organisation is established, for example a person setting up in business as a sole trader needs to follow few regulations.

When a person decides to trade under his/her own name there is no requirement to register the name. However if the person decides to trade under a name other than the owner's the business name must be registered in order to comply with the Business Names Act 1985. In this case the owner's true name must be disclosed on all business letters, purchase orders, invoices and receipts. The owner can cease trading at any time as long as outstanding debts are paid off. If at any time the owner cannot pay his/her debts then he/she might be forced to dissolve the business through the process of bankruptcy. The sole trader has unlimited liability and is personally liable for all debts incurred during the course of business.

If 2–20 people decide to establish a business they might decide to form a partnership. This business can be regulated by the Partnership Act 1890, or the partners can draw up a Deed of Partnership which is a formal agreement where the partners agree on how much each should put into the business, how the profits and losses are to be shared and the extent of the responsibility and power of each partner. The deed will contain the agreed relationship between partners, how the partnership allows for new partners and how partners may leave the business. It will also state how the partnership can be dissolved. Although the Deed of Partnership regulates the governing of the partnership business it is still regulated by the Partnership Act of 1890, for example if a partner enters into a contract then the other partners are bound by the same agreement.

Company law regulates limited companies whether they are private or public limited companies. The laws which regulate companies are the Companies Act 1985 (as amended by the Companies Act 1989).

The regulations determine the governance of limited companies and lays down clear procedures for the creation of a company and the regulations for some of its operations. The requirements for establishing a limited company depends on set criteria:

◆ a public company sells its shares to the general public

◆ there are more than two members

◆ there is limited liability, limited by share ownership

◆ there is a memorandum stating it is a public company

◆ it is registered as a public company under the Companies Act

◆ has an authorised share capital of more than £50 000.

A private company will have

◆ two or more members

◆ limited liability by share ownership

◆ shares cannot be sold to the general public

◆ an authorised share capital of less than £50 000.

Legal documentation

The documents which regulate the company include:

Memorandum of association

This regulates the company's relationship with its external environment stating for example:

◆ it will publish its name outside every place of business, on all its documents.

◆ where the registered office is located

◆ the purpose of the business

◆ the amount of nominal share capital.

Articles of association

This regulates the internal administration of the company, and for example includes:

◆ the principal matters relating to shares i.e., the allotment, transfer and call on shares

◆ borrowing powers of the company

◆ meetings of the Board of Directors and shareholders

◆ directors' powers and duties

◆ accounts and audit

◆ winding up or terminating the company.

Every public limited company must receive a trading certificate from the Registrar of Companies showing it has complied with raising the minimum cash required to operate. Once all the regulations have been accepted the company is issued with a Certificate of Incorporation which allows the company to trade.

Contract law provides the legal framework and minimum standards for how the company may deal with its customers and suppliers.

In law, for a contract to exist the following conditions need to be met:

◆ *Offer and acceptance:* a clear and unequivocal offer must be made by one party and accepted by the other party. This will lead to an *agreement.*

◆ *Consideration:* each party agrees to exchange goods or services under the agreement, e.g. money for the delivery of office furniture or the performance of employment.

◆ *Intention:* both parties must intend to enter into a legal relationship, and accept the legal consequences of that relationship.

◆ *Capacity:* each party must be capable of entering into an agreement.

◆ *Genuine consent:* each party has entered the agreement freely and understands that consent has been given.

◆ *Legality:* the agreement must not be to perform an illegal act.

◆ *Form:* while many or all contracts are just as enforceable as their physical counterparts, there are some transactions which must be evidenced in writing, e.g. the purchase of property.

A great deal of contract law is not to be found in Acts of Parliament but in common law, as decided by the courts.

Contracts which organisations may enter into with consumers are regulated by laws such as the Sale of Goods Act 1979 and the Supply of Goods and Services Act 1982 and common law such as *Carhill* v *Carbolic Smoke Ball Co* [1892].

These laws exist to protect the consumer from bad practice and the general conditions included in these acts are:

◆ *Title:* the seller of goods has to have the right to sell.

◆ *Description:* the goods will correspond with the description.

◆ *Merchantable quality*: goods must not be damaged or broken and must be fit for the purpose for which they were sold.

If there is a defective product the consumer will be compensated by the person or organisation who sold it. For instance, if a product is bought from a shop, the contract for the purchase of the product is between the customer and the shop owner.

Other consumer legislation which regulates business activity include the:

◆ Trades Description Act 1968, where it is an offence to give false description of products or services

◆ Weights and Measures Act 1963 which makes it an offence to give short measure or quantity

◆ Food and Drugs Act 1955 which makes it illegal to sell food which is unfit for human consumption. It also lays down minimum standards of what may be contained in food

◆ Consumer Credit Act 1974, giving consumers rights such as the right to receive a copy of the credit agreement

◆ Consumer Protection Act 1987, which allows consumers to claim for damages from the manufacturer if the consumer can prove that personal injury or damage to property was caused by defective products

The European Union, through national governments have, over the years sought to protect workers in areas of employment. The areas which have been covered include:

◆ health and safety

◆ employment rights

◆ wage protection

◆ sex discrimination.

The health and safety of the workforce is protected by the Health and Safety at Work Act 1974, as well as the Management of Health and Safety at Work Regulations which are continuously being issued by the Department of Employment. The Regulations expand the obligations of employers to protect the health and safety of their employees since they are able to incorporate aspects of EC law and modern technology which the 1974 Act was unable to envisage. The

1974 Act gave the Health and Safety Executive powers to enforce these standards.

Each employer is required to prepare a written statement of their general policy on health and safety. All managers have responsibility to make sure the policy is carried out to ensure a safe working environment for the workforce. The company, as well as individual managers can be prosecuted if there is negligent practice. Employees are also responsible for their own actions and must take reasonable care for their own safety and the safety of their colleagues.

The Employment Protection (Consolidation) Act 1978 as amended by the Trades Union and Labour Relations (Consolidations) Act 1992, gives workers who have been working for an employer for more than two years protection against unfair dismissal. The payment of wages is covered by the Equal Pay Act 1970 (amended by the Equal Pay (Amendment) Regulations 1983), which ensures that a person is paid the same as another, regardless of gender, who is doing work which is the same, similar, or of equal value.

The Wages Act 1986 defines wages and states what moneys can be deducted from source by the employer.

The Sex Discrimination Act 1975 (amended by the Sex Discrimination Act 1986) made it illegal to discriminate against someone on the grounds of gender or marital status. The Race Relations Act 1976 and the Disability Act 1995 give protection against discrimination on the grounds of colour, race, nationality, ethnic or national origins, and disability, respectively. If anyone feels they have suffered from discrimination they can seek redress through an Industrial Tribunal, or the Commission for Racial Equality.

Regulating competition

The Office of Fair Trading was established by the Fair Trading Act 1973 and its Director-General must keep commercial practices in the UK under review and collect information about them so that he can discover monopoly situations and uncompetitive practices. The Director-General of Fair Trading may refer what he considers to be monopoly situations to the Monopolies and Mergers Commission (MMC) for investigation.

The MMC was set up to make sure that the extent of a company's activities or expected future activities was not against the public interest. The MMC is made up of 30 members with the Chairperson the only person employed full-time. The MMC can be asked to investigate competitive behaviour by the Director-General of Fair Trading, a Government Minister, usually the President of the Board of Trade. It can also ask for an investigation into alleged unfair practices. The companies investigated tend to be those who:

1 substantially dominate a particular industry; or
2 a situation in which there are just a few companies in a market whose combined activities may appear to be operating against the public interest; or where
3 a proposed merger between companies may lead to unfair competition.

For example, if a proposed merger is to take place the following questions might apply. Will the merger:

◆ maintain and promote competition by price, quality and availability of a range of goods?

◆ promote the interests of the consumer?

◆ promote the research and development of new products?

◆ encourage efficient operations by the company?

The MMC can go into some detail in the trading and operating practices of companies referred to it, for example, seeking information about competitors, suppliers, customers, trade associations and government departments. In 1994, the number of mergers referred to the Office of Fair Trading totalled 381, and the main area for merger activity was in chemicals, food, drink and tobacco and distribution. In 1993 the MMC investigated the brewing industry because the government was concerned about the amount of control the breweries had on the outlets of their products. The recommendations included forcing the big breweries to sell off part of their business which was responsible for owning and running 'tied' public houses. The MMC also recommended that some tenants should be allowed to offer a 'guest beer'. The expected result of this was for the price of drinks to fall in the pubs. However, the pressure applied by the breweries on the government watered down the proposals and the recommendations have not had the expected impact.

The Director-General can also refer any agreement or arrangement between suppliers of goods and services which restrict competition to the Restrictive Practices Court. Examples include collusion on prices, dividing up the market and companies trading on the same terms of business. Agreements can be registered at a the Office for Fair Trading if they can be shown that they operate in the public interest. In 1996, the Net Book Agreement collapsed. The original idea of the Net Book Agreement was to prevent books being sold below the publishers' recommended price. This meant small book sellers would not face strong competition from larger booksellers or supermarkets. The popular books sold would also enable less popular, but more specialists books, to be published and sold. In 1996, the pharmaceutical agreement in which some drugs are sold at an agreed price was threatened. Again, this agreement exists to protect the small chemists and allow them to survive and offer a specialist service in the community especially for those who cannot get to the large out of town supermarkets.

Government departments

All organisations have to deal with government departments. Perhaps one of the most commonly used departments is Customs and Excise, due to its operation of the regulation and collection of VAT.

An example where the activities of an organisation has to be restricted by direct government acts is illustrated by the involvement of the government in the TV cable networking. British Telecommunications wanted to deliver a range of services including home shopping and television and film services down its telephone wires. However, in 1991, the government banned British Telecommunications from this market until the year 2001. The ban was imposed to allow the cable industry the chance to develop its own network, but BT objected when the cable companies started to supply telephone services. In 1994, BT applied to the President of the Board of Trade to have the ban on entry into television broadcasting to be lifted. However, BT have been unsuccessful in getting the bid lifted. The government argued that it wanted competition to flourish first before allowing BT into the market to compete.

Regulating the utilities

The privatisation of the nationalised industries was at first the transferring of a state monopoly into the private sector. To ensure that the customers and suppliers got fair treatment from the new companies the government set up regulatory bodies which were to act as watchdogs monitoring, reporting and if necessary, changing the behaviour of the new organisations. One such regulatory body, Ofwat, criticised the Yorkshire Water Company on the way it dealt with the drought in 1995, the charges for water in its region and the profits it made during this time. The company has been forced to find solutions to its water distribution problem. The Ofgas regulatory body monitors the gas distribution and supply industry and regulates the prices and the service offered by British Gas. Ofgas has recommended, for example, that the transportation and storage operations of British Gas should be separated from its production and supply business.

Local government

All organisations have to deal with local government. It might have to deal with the Trading Standards Office, the Local Treasury for the payment of business rates or with the planning office, if the organisation wishes to expand. The local government will enforce national as well as local regulations constraining the activities of organisations.

The Citizens Charter

Citizens Charters were introduced by the government to state the standard of service a customer could expect from public sector organisations for example, the length of time someone could expect to wait in a hospital waiting room. The idea has been adopted by many other organisations and these public statements explain the standards which can be expected. In some cases, if the organisation does not meet its own standards it will compensate the customer.

Pressure groups

Pressure groups consist of people who seek to influence or change the behaviour of organisations. They will try to influence by direct contact with the organisations they are trying to change or else they try to bring pressure on the organisation by influencing public opinion through the media.

Pressure groups can put pressure upon organisations through influencing the sale of its products, for example, during the 1970s and 1980s pressure was put on organisations to stop trading in South Africa. This helped to end the apartheid system in that country.

In 1996, Shell Oil wanted to discard one of its oil producing platforms, the Brent Spa, by sinking it in the sea. However, pressure groups encouraged users of oil based products not to use Shell's oil. Its petrol sales fell dramatically, especially in Germany. Shell was forced to review its plans. The company has the problem of disposing the platform. It has cost £11 million removing it from the sea and has cost the company £35 000 per month to moor it in the deep water of Erfjord, Norway. The environmental lobby would prefer to see Shell decommission the 300 foot platform ashore. But Shell believes this is too costly. There have been many suggestions for alternative uses for the platform from an offshore tax free casino, a wind turbine, the foundation for a high arched bridge spanning the entrance to Poole harbour, Dorset, to a floating hotel with the helicopter deck doubling as an open air dance floor.

The Brent Spa saga indicates another problem facing organisations, the disposal of waste and effluent. Previously, many organisations dumped effluent into streams and rivers to the point where some rivers were devoid of all life. But with the work of pressure groups, the introduction of Clean Rivers Acts, and directives from Europe many organisations have had to find other ways of disposing of their waste.

Pressure groups can exert pressure on companies to modify or stop producing a product which is deemed to be dangerous. For example 'ASH', the anti-smoking group has been successful in reducing tobacco adverts in some parts of the media and banning it from others, e.g. television. The Consumer Association tests products and publishes their findings in their magazine 'Which' magazine.

Pressure groups can operate on a local level such as protesting about the building of a by-pass or the extension to a night club. These tend to be single cause groups compared with Greenpeace which is international and exerts pressure on a range of subjects.

Due to the effect of pressure groups companies must now start to include the social costs of their activities in their overall costings. This will reveal the true cost of production which can then be reflected in the price of the product sold.

Lobbyists

Some industries form a lobby groups to exert pressure on government departments and politicians, for example, during the 1980s the road transport group were successful in persuading the government to increase spending on roads. The brewery industry, with other interested parties, was able to change the hours of opening for public houses and, in the retail trade, pressure was brought on the government to repeal the Sunday trading laws: the pressure group 'Keep Sunday Special' was not sufficiently strong enough to repel this pressure.

Trade associations

Some trades and professions have their own governing groups which lay down rules and guidelines for good practice. They will also make recommendations on improvements to be made in the trade or professions. The British Medical Association sets guidelines for doctors and will publish findings in medical research. For example, in 1996, the BMA recommended that the drink drive level of 80 mg of alcohol per 100 ml of blood should be reduced to 50mg. The BMA argued that co-ordination, reflex skills and mental processes are measurably affected at alcohol levels above 50 mg.

The Association of British Travel Agents (ABTA) regulates the operations of travel agents and has worked to remove the less than-professional operators from the market place. It requires that travel agents deposit a bond with it so that if the agent gets into financial trouble the holiday makers booked through that agent will not be stranded abroad.

Trade associations can also can also operate as a group to defend members' interests for example, they might take action on behalf of its members to curb the power of large powerful suppliers and customer.

Advertising standards authority

One of the most influential business activities is advertising. The Advertising Standards Authority monitors all advertising to ensure that the contract is legal, decent, honest and truthful. Advertising must not cause grave or widespread offence. If the advert is deemed to be offensive, it can be withdrawn.

Internal regulations

The purpose of regulations is to predict and control employee behaviour. The regulatory control in the organisation will be by formal and informal means.

Policies

Policies are general guidelines which state the parameters within which employees are expected to operate. They may cover all the operations of the organisation, for example, each organisation will have policies to cover Health and Safety, recruitment and retirement.

Formal regulations

These usually refer to the procedures adopted to carry out organisational policy and will cover all areas of work. To comply with the Health and Safety policy there will be clear regulations. To make sure the recruitment, selection and appointment of staff complies with company policy there will be procedures laid down as a series of related steps which everyone involved will be able to follow. In many organisations, the procedures are set out in a manual for reference, for example, in the case of purchasing of goods and services the following regulations might apply:

Responsibility	Director of Finance
Operators	Budget holders and their nominees
Purpose	To ensure that goods and services are purchased in line with company financial policies and regulations.
Scope	Allocated budgetary expenditure.

Responsibilities

◆ Designated budget managers are responsible to the Director of Finance for the control of expenditure from the budgets allocated to them. They are responsible for the day to day management of budgets.

◆ Purchase orders may only by placed by persons authorised by the budget holder. These orders will be countersigned by the budget holder.

◆ The list of authorised budget holders together with specimen signatures is held by the Director of Finance.

Purchasing ordering

◆ All orders shall be placed in writing on the serially numbered company order forms only. Stocks of order forms are recorded in a suitable register and are securely stored.

◆ Where as a matter of emergency, goods and services are ordered verbally, an official order number is quoted and written confirmatory order issued within two working days.

◆ Each order will clearly indicate the nature and quantity of the supplies and services required, including prices, costs and whether VAT is inclusive or exclusive.

Informal regulations

The extent of the informal regulations in an organisation will depend on the culture of the organisation. Some organisations, such as the police force or the legal profession, must follow procedures very closely because of the nature of their work. Other organisations will have more informal approaches to their systems of operations and informal regulations may exist where

Fig 8.1

◆ informal groups exert a lot of power

◆ the informal leader has a lot of influence

◆ rules which are implied or have evolved over time and have not been formalised. Tasks are done in a particular way because they have always been done in that way. For example, it may be that the holiday rota always starts with the longest serving member of staff choosing their holiday first and the new entrant has to wait until last, meaning that they have to take their summer holidays in May or October.

◆ bureaucracy is kept to a minimum to enable people to react using their initiative and the need to act quickly in responding to events.

◆ the manager has a strong personality and creates his or her own regulations, for example, no smoking in the office.

CASE STUDY 8.1

Regulatory control and the Kuwait Oil Tanker Company

Peter Morris works for the Kuwait Oil Tanker Company as a captain. The company was created 38 years ago to carry its own crude oil to markets in Europe and around the world. The company has around 32 ships and they charter a further 30 ships. Peter talks about his job:

'My job is to run, efficiently, any of the company vessels to which I'm appointed. My primary concern is the carriage of the cargo and ensuring that cargo gets from A to B in exactly the same condition as it was loaded at the load port. My next task is to maintain the ship and run the crew as efficiently and economically as possible. Depending on the size of the ship the amount of oil carried is between 30 000 tonnes and 500 000 tonnes of oil. The ships range from 30 000 tonne product carriers to 250 000 VLCCs (very large crude carriers) and 500 000 VLCCs.

The average crew these days is about 24. A few years ago it was 50; the ships are run very efficiently now. Most of the crew are Filipinos, most officers are Arabic – from Egypt, Syria, Kuwait; or Pakistan and India. The reason why I am employed on a Kuwaiti ship is because I am British and have a British licence. The insurers all prefer European Ships Masters and make the insurance rates proportionally lower than for other nationalities.

Fig 8.2 Peter Morris, Captain, Kuwait Oil Taker Company, on board ship

The crew members consist of two cooks; one for the crew and one for the officers. There are two stewards who look after internal cleaning and catering, serving and storekeeping. They also do the ship's laundry. We have five able seamen and one bosun who look after the external fabric of the ship, painting, watchkeeping in port and at sea. There are five engineers and a pumpman who assists the Chief Engineer in the maintenance of the deck cargo equipment.

On the deck side, there is myself in command, and the Chief Officer who normally keeps the 4–8 o'clock watch (this involves two watches 4 am–8 am and 4 pm–8 pm). His duties are the running of the crew and being in charge of the general fabric of the ship. His most important job is the loading and discharging of the cargo and preparing to receive the cargo. There are second and third officers who man the other round-the-clock watches, along with various other duties, and a radio officer.

The process of getting business for tankers is that you may have a ship owner who has a ship with no cargo approaching an area of known cargo availability such as the Persian Gulf. He makes it known to all the charterers that this vessel is available for chartering. It's very competitive, very cut-throat; charterers do not make freight rates known publicly. Ninety per cent of the time we carry Kuwaiti oil cargoes, but sometimes a charterer is offering good rates and the Kuwait Oil Tanker Company prefers to earn foreign currency. The charterer will ask the ship's owners certain questions to ensure that it complies with its own legal requirements. Once the deal is struck, the ship is instructed to a designated port to load. The ship has to arrive within a certain time period and the days during which it can arrive are known as 'lay days'. If it misses the lay days and doesn't arrive on time, then it can lose the charter.

As I approach the port of Kuwait, I have to give ETAs (estimated times of arrival) of 78, 60, 36, 24 and 12 hours prior to arrival, one of those has to include the ship's full details. I send these to the ship's agents and he directs them to the different port authorities, depending upon where we're going. As soon as I arrive I give notice of readiness to load. From that moment the payment from the charterer starts. My Chief Officer will have already worked out the capacity and where the cargo is to go. It's important not to overstress the ship when loading. The tanks will already have been prepared on the way to the port. They have to be washed out, you can't put motor spirit with gas oil or aviation fuel in with petrol. Sometimes it's only 12 hours from port to port and there is very hectic activity getting ready for the loading. There's the problem of slops – internationally we're supposed to be able to get rid of our slops anywhere in any port, in practice you can't get rid of it anywhere. We have to maintain it on board in small slop tanks, but we get rid of the water and keep the oil on board. The ship's crew and the loading master do all the loading. Large steel hydraulically operated arms are clamped onto the ship's manifold, the size of pipelines varies from six inches to 24 depending on the size of the vessel. The ship's owner employs an independent surveyor to check on the quality and quantity of the cargo being loaded. It can take between 24 and 48 hours to load the cargo. It's a very busy time, very technically involved. The VLCCs are easily stressed and we have to monitor the stress levels. We shut off tanks, open up other tanks, move the cargo around to minimise the stress on the ship.

On completion of loading we receive the cargo documents. There are three legal receipts to sign Bills of Lading which are the legal transfer; it is my responsibility and my cargo as soon as these are signed. I have to protest about any discrepancies, if the cargo was loaded too slow or there's a quantity difference between what I've taken on board and what they say I've been given, I have to document it. At the end of the loading I'm typing like mad on my computer. I've made special forms for this, to register every single little discrepancy, because if I don't protest it can cost my company millions. If no protests are made my company might be fighting it out in the courts for the next three years about a missing half an hour they have been fined for.

One of the three Bills of Lading is presented to me at the discharge port. Without the presentation of this I cannot discharge the cargo. This Bill of Lading has the terms and conditions of transportation for this particular cargo on it, you need a very good pair of glasses to see the small print, it's very involved. This chartering agreement covers where the ship can go, the speed it is required to go at, costs and how they're apportioned, absolutely everything to do with the cargo and its transportation in fact. I have to arrive at the next port at a certain speed, I can go faster but not slower; if I go slower the ship owner has to pay a fine. They very often set speeds which are unattainable.

The weather has a major hand in the vessel's overall speed. If the weather is anything over Force 5, then the target speed set for that 24 hours is nil and void and the ship owner is not penalised for us going slower than stipulated. I chart the course to take advantage of prevailing currents and weather conditions.

One of the largest running costs of the ship is the fuel it burns. My last ship burnt 85 tonnes per day and this means that for every mile I can save, the company saves quite a bit of money. I had four trips out of Bonny Bay, Nigeria to Galvaston in the USA, and on every occasion the vessel had been unable to maintain the agreed speed. On the fifth trip I chose an alternate route which was 500 miles longer but had more suitable currents. I spent a lot of time persuading my charterers and owners to allow me to do this. I was lucky as I managed to save not only the 500 miles, but an extra 250 miles and over 60 tonnes of fuel. We'd been chartered by BP America who were sending me 'snotty' telexes: normally we have to report twice a week, but they were in touch every day wanting to know why we weren't sticking to the tramline. Eventually, I spoke with them on the phone and got them to understand what was happening.

Before we arrive in a port I have to communicate with the agents at the discharge port. The discharge port can frequently be changed during the voyage, and even more so towards the end of the voyage. It's a nightmare of logistics, arranging for the storing of food, bunkering and crew changes. You have everything set up for Galvaston and you suddenly find yourself down for Loop (Louisiana Offshore Pipeline) hundreds and hundreds of miles away. I send the agents details of arrival 78, 60, 48, 36, 24 and 12 hours before expected because they need to rotate the ships in the port. We send the receiver a discharge plan which might not fit in with their plans and so we communicate backwards and forwards. The pilot meets us and we go in alongside the dock, or a vessel comes alongside us, there aren't many ports in the world where these very large carriers can actually go alongside the dock.

Most ships are discharged in 40 hours. During the first ten hours it's extremely hectic. At Rotterdam recently, there were 26 tonnes of stores and only five crew members to move it. We're short of manpower and at times like that I'm in a boiler suit moving the stores with the crew. All the spare officers get involved too. During the discharge time we're inspected by Port Health to ensure that we haven't got any infectious diseases, Customs and Immigration come to have a chat, and the Port Authorities investigate the ship to ensure it's safe and complies with international requirements. The agent's representative, the charterer's representative, the owner's representative all come to see me. The vessel is inspected on a regular basis and every part of the ship is inspected for safety and construction for its Certificate of Class. The surveyors from the insurance company come every 12 months to inspect the vessel, the equipment and the hull integrity.'

Peter and his officers work four to five months without a day's holiday, the crew work 12 months without holiday. When Peter is leaving for his holiday there is an overlap time of 36 hours during which the new captain and Peter go through a handover procedure which involves information of the ship's characteristics, navigation, current cargo requirements, the accounts. Peter completes all the accounts and pays the staff's wages and overtime.

Peter: *'It's a wonderful job, I never know what's going to happen next. Within a few minutes I can be navigating, then doing a stock check in the fridges, then sewing someone's hand up after he's cut it – I'm also the ship's doctor. I'm on duty all the time. Any problems – poor visibility, close proximity to another ship, personal problems amongst the crew, illness – I'm called at whatever time of the day or night it happens to be and I expect to be called. It's a very hard life, very busy, apart from the officers and crew all working eight hours a day, they do another two or three hours at night on other duties. The biggest part of my job is man management. I like to keep people informed. If any communication comes in, I post it so that everyone knows – that was always a big complaint when I first started as we never knew where the ship was going.*

In my job the buck stops with me. If any of my officers makes a mistake, accidentally causing pollution, for example, it's me who has to go to jail, as I've already found out on two occasions.'

DISCUSSION QUESTIONS 8.1

1　What sort of regulations does Peter have to comply with?

2　To what extent can Peter take decisions concerning the way the ship operates?

3　Why does Peter still enjoy his job, despite the many constraints upon him?

Allocating resources

One of the most difficult decisions which has to be taken in an organisation is distributing scarce resources between their competing uses. This is particularly relevant where an organisation produces a number of products. The organisation has to decide how much raw materials, machines and labour to allocate to each product within a time restriction and be able to maximise its profits. One of the solutions available to the organisation is to use linear programming techniques.

A linear programme is a quantitative tool for planning how to optimise the allocation of scarce resources. It is a linear expression which is an equation linking two variables and can be represented by a straight line. For example, an organisation makes two types of chairs, rockers and straight back. They use the same resources and method of operation and at present the resources used per unit are:

Resources	Total resource available	Rocker	Straight
Timber (ft)	120	30	20
Labour (hours)	9	2	2
Finishing capacity (hours)	24	4	6

1 Plot the constraint equations of the three constraints from the product mix.

Timber constraint: $30r + 20s \leq 120$

Therefore if only rockers were produced and no straights:

$$30r = \leq 120$$
$$r = \frac{120}{30}$$
$$r = 4$$

If only all straights are produced:

$$20s \leq 120$$
$$s = \frac{120}{20}$$
$$s = 6$$

The constraint is then plotted on a graph

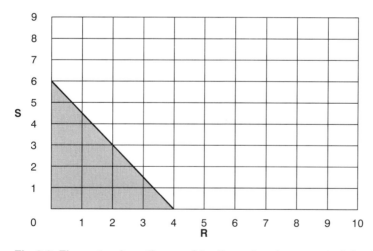

Fig 8.3 Figure to show the combination of rockers or straight chairs made

The area shown inside the constraint is known as the feasibility region. The constraint indicates that either 4 rocker or 6 straights or any combination of the two can be made using the same resources.

The labour constraint: $2r + 2s \leqslant 9$

$$r = 4.5$$
$$s = 4.5$$

This can now be plotted on the graph

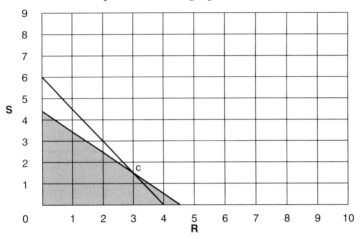

Fig 8.4

The capacity constraint: $4r + 6s \leqslant 24$

If only rockers are produced:

$$4r = 24$$
$$r = 6$$

If only straights are produced:

$$6s = 24$$
$$s = 4$$

This is plotted on the graph

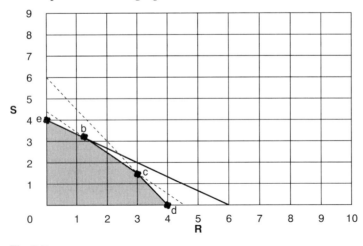

Fig 8.5

2 Once the three constraints are plotted on the graph the feasibility area is shown by 0, e, b, c, d. Any point in this region satisfies the three constraints, i.e. the number of combinations of chairs which can be produced. This can be done by looking at the expected profit from each chair and plotting an isoprofit line.

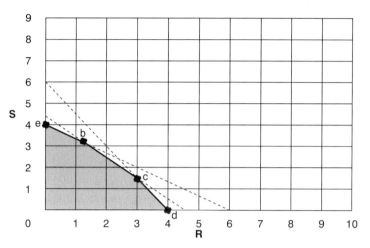

Fig 8.6

This is started at the origin and is moved outwards and parallel to the previous one. It is continued until the last point on the feasibility region is reached, i.e. at c where the optimum number of chairs to produce using the scarce resources it at point c where three rockers can be produced for every 1.5 straight chairs.

Therefore linear programming is useful for determining optimal use of scare resources and maximising profit.

 # Working in France – Regulatory Control

With 57.2 m inhabitants, France has a working population of 24.6 m, of which 5.5 per cent work in agriculture, 28.9 per cent in industry and 65.6 per cent in services. In 1992 the country enjoyed an annual growth rate of 1.9 per cent. Immigrant workers coming from North African countries total around 1.5 m. Algerians are the largest group, with Moroccans and Tunisians making up the balance of North Africans. Workers also come from neighbouring countries (mainly Portuguese, Italians and Spaniards) and have contributed to the growth of the French economy.

In France, 16 years is the minimum legal age to start work. The retirement age is 60 for both males and females, but employees can carry on working up to the age of 65. Temporary work contracts are for a maximum of 24 months. Weekly work is limited to 39 hours and overtime hours cannot exceed nine per week, or 130 per year unless special authorisation has been given. Night shifts are defined as hours taking place between 10 pm–5 am. French workers are given 11 statutory bank holidays per year and if one of those days occurs on a Tuesday or Thursday, companies usually *font le pont*, literally bridge the gap between that day and the weekend, so that employees do not work for four days in a row. Annual leave consists of five weeks and French businesses were reputed to 'fall dead' over the summer months as the French traditionally took their leave during July and August, although this is gradually changing.

French companies divide into four main categories as follows:

1 *Société Anonyme (SA)*. Mostly large companies with a minimum of seven founder shareholders with a minimum legal share capital of FF 250 000. The company can be managed either by a board of between three and 12 Directors (*Counseil d'Administration*) appointed from amongst themselves by the shareholders (*actionnaires*) presided by a chairman (*PDG, Président Directeur Général*), or by a different type of Board named *Directoire*, consisting of a maximum of five members who are appointed along with the Chairman by the shareholders from amongst themselves. Any shareholder can freely trade his or her shares on the French Stock Exchange (*La Bourse*).

2 *Société à Responsabilité Limitée (SARL)*. Limited liability companies. These are the most popular type of company amongst small French businesses (*PME-PMI, Petites et Moyennes Enterprises/Industries*). They have between two and 50 shareholders with a minimum legal shareholding of FF 50 000. The businesses are run by one or several managers (*gérants*) who can own shares. Shareholders can only purchase shares with the agreement of the majority of the other shareholders.

3 *Société en Nom Collectif (SNC)*. This is a general partnership with a minimum of two partners who work in the business (*commercants*). There is no limit concerning the capital invested and all partners have unlimited liability for all debts and obligations of the partnership. One or several managers (*gérants*) appointed by the partners run the business. Partners can only sell their capital shares with the agreement of all the other partners.

4 *Enterprise Unipersonelle à Responsabilité Limitée (EURL)*. Identical to the SARL but with a single shareholder.

Employees play an important role in businesses and are represented at different levels. At shopfloor level, the shop steward (*délégué syndical*) is empowered to negotiate directly with employers whereas the worker's representative (*délégué du personnel*) is elected by all workers in companies of more than ten people and solves individual problems only. At company level and in those employing over fifty people, the works committee (*comité d'entreprise*) is kept informed and consulted regarding planning, results, changes, redundancies, working hours, wages, etc. Both partners, employers and employees adhere to a common agreement (*convention collective*) describing wages, recruitment, redundancy procedures, holiday entitlement and retirement, amongst other issues.

Compared to UK businesses and that of most European countries, French companies are heavily taxed in the form of social insurance contributions. The minimum wage of about FF 5900 per month for adults working full-time contribute, according to many economists, to France's high unemployment rate, which reached 12.1 per cent in 1996. However, the French government also implemented schemes in an attempt to reduce unemployment in which companies could recruit workers on a temporary basis and give them a monthly allowance of £300, providing that they employed them permanently at the end of the time period. These schemes are not always successful due to legal loopholes which allow employers to avoid offering permanent employment at the end of the scheme.

The complexity of French legal procedures, taxation system and powerful trade unions and federations can sometimes discourage foreign investors from expanding into France. There are five nationally recognised trade unions who have the right to establish a branch, even in the smallest company. Striking in France is rarely restricted, although in the public sector some civil servants such as the police, the army or magistrates are forbidden to go on strike, while others are requested to give five days notice. However, surprise strikes and brief and repetitive working breaks are legal as long as they are supported by a group of workers. It is illegal to prevent non-strikers from working, to prevent workers from going on strike to show solidarity towards another company's workers or to undermine the employer's right to his or her property.

('Working in France' written by Nathalie Ormrod-Brunisholz, Lecturer in Business Studies, Manchester Metropolitan University.)

External changes

Organisations operate in an external environment which influences, modifies or changes the organisational activities. Around the organisation environmental influences can be divided into outer and inner layers. The inner layer consists of

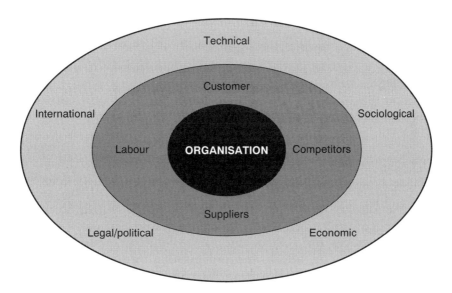

Fig 8.7 External factors which influence an organisation's behaviour

those factors which directly influence the organisation on a day-to-day basis, i.e. its competitors, the labour market and suppliers. The outer layer includes those factors which are more general but can cause far reaching changes in the organisation. Included in this layer are technical developments, legal and political changes, international, economic and sociological factors.

Although it is possible to classify influences under these headings, factors are often multi-influential, for example, changes in the demographic make-up of a country will bring about changes to the sociological and economic factors.

The outer environment

Technological

This includes the technological advances which have been made in the organisation's market as well as society in general. Few industries are untouched by computers and the majority of technical advances being made today are centred on or are aided by computers. The speed of the growth in information technology has led the world to be seen as a global village which would not be possible without computers.

One of the fastest growing industries is the multi-media industry where international players are vying for developing consumer markets. Technical advances in digital television will make it possible for hundreds of channels to be sent down cables or beamed via satellite. Computer games machines and CD-ROM computers will be threatened by these advances.

The health service is a main beneficiary from the technical advances made in medicines and medical machinery and equipment. Consumers are benefiting from products which are made by new techniques and new raw materials. Aircraft are made from materials which are lighter, stronger and more durable than just a few years ago. Technological advances made by one company give it a competitive edge and all the firms in the market must be able to respond to survive.

Alongside the technical advances are changes which have been made in production processes, the use of just in time (JIT) methods and total quality management (TQM) techniques and have revolutionised the way in which organisations produce their goods and services.

International

Many organisations now operate in the international market. If they are not active in a foreign country then they are probably competing in their domestic market against foreign competition. The international market increases the number of potential customers and competitors. At the same time international markets influence the way in which the organisation operates, for example car manufacturers, when giving a name to their models, have to be sure the name is acceptable internationally and does not cause offence or embarrassment.

The changing international economic trading blocs will impact on organisations, for example, the expansion of the EU and the creation of the North American Trade Association has created opportunities and threats to companies.

Organisations within the EU have seen changes take place, for example, the removal of trading barriers such as tariffs, quotas and embargos, the introduction of international standards for products, and common competition laws which restrict monopoly behaviour. The proposed European single currency may yet have the most important influence on trading organisations.

International political changes can alter organisational behaviour. The finishing of the 'Cold War' has meant a fall in demand for military products making this shrinking market extremely competitive. The removal of apartheid and the free elections in South Africa saw the removal of trade sanctions against this country and the opportunity for foreign countries to enter and compete in the South African market. Some organisations may be reluctant to invest in some countries because of political and economic uncertainty.

Economic

This refers to the economic health of the country or region within which the organisation is operating. Economic factors which influence the performance of the organisation will include, for example, the rate of interest, the level of taxation, the unemployment rate and the price level.

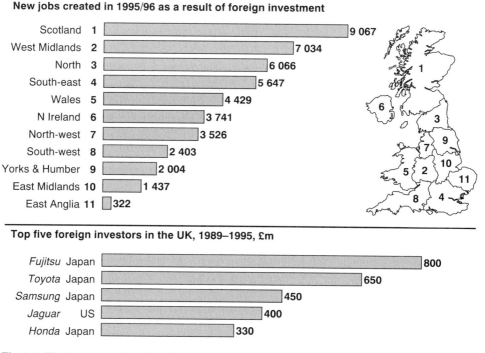

New jobs created in 1995/96 as a result of foreign investment

Scotland 1	9 067
West Midlands 2	7 034
North 3	6 066
South-east 4	5 647
Wales 5	4 429
N Ireland 6	3 741
North-west 7	3 526
South-west 8	2 403
Yorks & Humber 9	2 004
East Midlands 10	1 437
East Anglia 11	322

Top five foreign investors in the UK, 1989–1995, £m

Company	Country	£m
Fujitsu	Japan	800
Toyota	Japan	650
Samsung	Japan	450
Jaguar	US	400
Honda	Japan	330

Fig 8.8 The impact of foreign investment in the UK

Economies have different features depending on their economic well being. If an economy is entering a recession, aggregate demand will be falling and unemployment will be rising. The organisation will have to respond to this change in demand just to maintain its market share. This it can do by perhaps reducing prices, increasing advertising expenditure or it might attempt to reduce costs or export more.

In the UK in recent years one third of total inward investment has come from abroad attracted by government grants, low wage costs and the low cost of land. Some of this investment has been attracted to the UK because of its membership of the EU.

Pay for hours worked, manufacturing industry, £, 1995

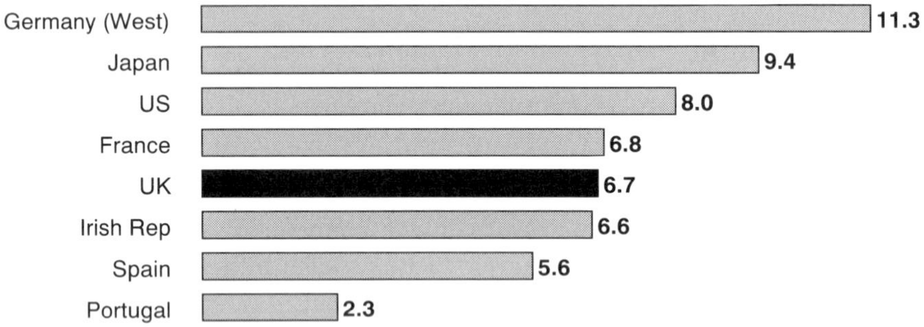

Country	Pay (£)
Germany (West)	11.3
Japan	9.4
US	8.0
France	6.8
UK	6.7
Irish Rep	6.6
Spain	5.6
Portugal	2.3

Fig 8.9 A comparison of labour costs with selected countries

One of the areas which is causing concern is the increasing dominance of large multinational conglomerates who are beginning to dictate conditions in some markets. IBM designed the standard personal computer with millions of their clone machines being produced world-wide. Bill Gates and Microsoft play a dominant role in computer software. In the media Rupert Murdoch's News Corporation plays an important role in supplying newspapers in Australia and the UK. The company also owns or has a major share ownership in television broadcasting companies such as Fox in America, Seven Network in Australia and BSB in the UK. News Corporation is involved in film entertainment in America, owning Twentieth Century Fox.

Legal and political

The Conservative government elected in 1979 was one of the most radical governments since the Labour government of 1945. The Conservative Government moved away from the consensus politics of 30 years to one of implementing clear alternative policies. Controlling inflation and achieving economic growth became the main economic targets and the maintenance of full employment lost its pre-eminence. Making markets work better was a major economic objective and the economic policies introduced to achieve this were predominantly supply side measures. The attempt to regulate the aggregate demand in the economy lost favour. The supply side measures included cutting public sector involvement through privatisation of nationalised industries, reducing public expenditure and direct taxation.

In the legal field, major changes to industrial law were introduced during the 1980s and 1990s some of which saw major changes relating to trade union legislation. Laws concerning consumer protection were widened with the introduction of Supply of Goods and Services Act 1982 and the Consumer Safety (Amendment) Act 1986. The Weights and Measures Act 1985 made it an offence to sell short weight, measure or number, the Food Safety Act 1990 made it an offence to sell food for human consumption which failed to comply with food safety requirements and the Property Misdescription Act 1991 made it a criminal offence to make false or misleading statements about property matters in the course of an estate agency or property development business.

Sociological

Sociological influences on the organisation are brought about by demographic changes as well as the changes in the norms, customs and values of the general public. The UK is faced with an ageing population in which people are retiring earlier and living longer. This will impact the goods and services required, for example there may be a fall in demand for baby clothes and an increase in demand for fashions worn by the elderly. The high spending 'baby boomers' of the 1960s have now moved into another age bracket. There will be an increasing demand on the health and social services. The youth expenditure of the 1960s has given way to the 'grey power' of the 1990s.

Attitudes to family life have changed, the one parent family is a growing institution. The business organisation has had to take this into account when advertising and selling its products. The attitude towards smoking and drinking has changed. There has been a general decline in smoking with many organisations enforcing a total ban on smoking. It is becoming more unacceptable for people to drink and drive, but the drinking of alcohol by teenagers is on the increase. Some organisations have been criticised for producing alcoholic drinks specifically for the teenage market.

The inner environment

The factors within the inner environment are those which have a direct working relationship with the organisation.

Customers

These are the individuals or other organisations which acquire the goods and services from the organisation. Meeting the needs of their customers will allow the organisation to survive. The type of good produced will help to determine the buying habits of the customer, for example, fast moving consumer goods or consumer durable goods obviously have different purchase patterns. The organisation will need to spend time and money to keep the loyalty of their customers. This will be spent on surveys to find out what the customer expects, developing new products and keeping the customer informed of the services provided by the organisation.

Competitors

The nature of the market structure is partly determined by the number of competitors, for example, the petrol market is dominated by a few companies and is said to be an oligopolistic market. The way in which each firm competes tends to be by promotional means rather than on prices. If there is competition by prices then the competition is fierce and can result in a price war. In 1996, supermarkets fighting to gain market share clashed with promotional campaigns and started to compete on prices. Part of the campaign used by supermarkets was to offer loyalty cards to customers and to slash the price of products such as baked beans.

Labour

Labour is the mental and physical effort sold by individuals to organisations in the labour market. Rapid changes have been taking place during the 1980s and 1990s in the labour market, for example, patterns in employment have been changing with more women entering the labour market, more part-time work being done and there has been a decline in full-time work especially in the old heavy industries such as ship building and steel manufacturing. In the future there will be an increase in demand for managers, administrators, and people working in the personal and protective services. However, there will be a fall in demand for people to work in clerical and secretarial jobs, as well as a fall in demand for craft and skilled manual workers and plant and machine operatives.

There has been an increase in the staying on rates at school for youngsters. In 1987/88 47 per cent of 16 year olds stayed on at school, by 1992/1993 this had risen to 69 per cent. More pupils are obtaining GCSEs with girls being, generally, more successful than boys. More students are getting two or more 'A' levels, or their equivalent, and more students are going on to higher education. This means the labour force is becoming better qualified.

Suppliers

Suppliers sell raw materials to organisations. In recent years there has been a change in the relationship between the supplier of materials and the buyer. With increases in quality standards, organisations have been forming closer relationships with their suppliers to ensure a consistent flow of high quality materials. Using just in time order quantities the supplier and buyer have reinforced the need for these closer links.

Meeting the changes in the environment

For an organisation to be successful it must be able to respond and adapt to those changes by which it is influenced. Meeting these changes the organisation needs to forecast and plan, review and modify its organisational structure, and make any necessary investment.

Forecasting and planning

Forecasting is attempting to spot trends and predict future events and failure to do this can mean organisations become uncompetitive. For example, if a company which made adding machines operated by mechanical levers failed to spot that the electronic calculator would be its major competitor then the company would eventually have gone out of business. Lack of planning and forethought can lead to organisations missing out on opportunities or causing avoidable costs to the organisation.

Organisational structures

Those organisations which are in a dynamic environment need to be able to respond rapidly. One of the ways this is made possible is by having an organisational structure which is flexible to adapt to such changes or its management is able to make changes to the structure when dictated by external circumstances. One of the failings of IBM in the 1980s was its organisational structure, which had become too mechanistic and had slowed down decision making in the company thus restricting its ability to respond to the fast changing computer market.

Investment

To be able to compete, organisations need to be able invest and update their capital machinery as regularly as possible. Continued investment in people, through training and staff development will enable the workforce to acquire the necessary skills to adapt to the ever increasing demands placed upon them.

Social responsibility

Social responsibility is concerned with how the organisation's activity impacts on its stakeholders, i.e. employees, customers, owners, suppliers and investors and individuals and society as a whole. Social responsibility can be categorised under economic, legal, and ethical.

Economic

The organisation should employ its resources efficiently and effectively to produce the goods and services which society needs and maximise profits for its owners. These profits are made by fair competition without exploitation of its labour and its customers. Organisations in the past have had a low regard for the environment the result of which is clearly visible today with derelict buildings, spoilt countryside and polluted rivers. Although organisations should not produce goods which harm the environment, in many ways it is probably too late as it has already been predicted that by the year 2050 Kent will the same climate as the South of France due to global warming.

Legal

Organisations should produce products by means which do not break the law or infringe on workers' rights or intentionally produce defective goods for consumption. Organisations must perform within the framework of the law.

Ethics

Ethics are the set of moral principles and rules of conduct which govern individual and group behaviour. Therefore ethics help us to understand what is good or bad behaviour. Business ethics should regulate organisational behaviour so that it does not gain at the expense of individuals or society. The Italian fashion company Benetton, was criticised for its advertising campaigns which deliberately set out to shock viewers, for example, by using a person dying of Aids in an advertising poster. Questions were raised as to the ethics of such a campaign. Obviously the problem facing organisations is the conflict between ethical behaviour and the desire to make profits. Some companies make their position on different issues public, for example, the Co-operative Bank will not accept business from companies which operate in countries which have a poor human rights record. The Body Shop will not use products whose raw materials have been tested on animals.

There are some companies which are established to make quick profits and are not concerned with the long term customer satisfaction. These are usually business activities which are set up with low capital investment, minimum cash injection and a quick completion time. Double glazing companies and property developers were particularly renowned for sharp practice. On a larger scale some companies buy other companies and rather than run them they sell off the more valuable parts (asset strip) to make a quick return on their investment.

Some companies produce harmful products and continue to sell them, for example for many years the tobacco companies denied links between smoking and cancer. Several previous employees of the asbestos industry are suffering from asbestosis and the manufacturers of the product are being sued by the employees.

DISCUSSION QUESTIONS 8.2

1 How have the technical advances which have taken place in the last five years impacted on your:

(a) work;

(b) homelife;

(c) leisure.

2 Which international companies do you deal with in your work? What benefits do they offer which could not be met by a UK competitor.

3 If Spain, Portugal and Greece all have lower wage costs than the UK why do firms such as Fujitsu and Toyota invest in the UK?

4 To what extent should directors of companies be liable for acts of social irresponsibility by their organisations?

5 At what point does business activity become unethical?

Leighton Hospital

The hospital

Leighton Hospital in Crewe, Cheshire, became a first wave Trust in 1991–92, which meant that rather than being managed directly by a Health Authority, it became an independent provider of healthcare services. The hospital now sells its services to health authorities and GP fundholders.

Leighton Hospital employs 1899 full-time equivalent staff and has 45 785 in-patients and 163 000 out-patients per year. The annual income is £60 million of which 66 per cent is spent on staff, four per cent on drugs, seven per cent on medical and surgical equipment, three per cent on administration and just over three per cent on expenses such as heating and lighting. There are three statutory targets the hospital has to meet:

◆ keeping within an external finance limit

◆ breaking even

◆ achieving a six per cent return on capital.

Margalit Stott, Financial Controller: *'So far, we have always achieved our targets, the six per cent return on capital is the hardest to achieve. We meet our contracted numbers and exceed our target numbers in terms of patients, and our waiting times have come down. The meeting of targets is achieved by very tight financial control, and we've had some windfall gains which have helped us.*

Fig 8.10 Margalit Stott, Financial Controller, Leighton Hospital

We have to market ourselves to GPs and other health authorities who may purchase some of our services. We have to try and persuade them to do more work with us. Giving GP fundholders the choice of hospital potentially reduces our funding, as previously we would have received the entire sum for the healthcare we provided from the health authority, but now the GPs get a share of that funding based on historic activity. Thus the funding is no longer guaranteed to be returned to us, but we still have all the costs.'

Healthcare provision contracts

There are three types of contract for healthcare provision:

1 *Block contract.* This how the system started back in 1991. This type of contract says 'Here's £50 million, go away and do all the activity you can, it must be at least three per cent more than you have done previously for the same money. We will not pay for any excess activity.'

2   *Cost and volume contract.* This type of contract says 'Do £45 million worth of activity and don't ask us for permission, but once you've spent that there is another £5 million to spend, but we want you to talk to us about it first.'

3   *Cost per case contract.* A bill is sent out for every patient treated. The hospital doesn't have to seek permission prior to doing the work. The bill will go to the health authority or a GP fundholder.

'If you haven't got a contract and you are going to treat a patient who is not resident in your area, it's called an "extra-contractual referral". You have to get permission beforehand from the health authority in order to treat that patient, otherwise they will not pay the bill. There are two varieties: emergencies and non-emergencies, emergencies do not need permission in advance. If someone from another town collapsed in the street and was brought to Leighton Hospital here in Crewe, the health authority is obliged to pay for the treatment, provided we informed them within a defined time limit of the treatment. If we fail to inform them in time, they don't have to pay us. Where a GP has referred the patient to a particular consultant in the hospital, and it's not an emergency, then we have to get permission beforehand.

All three types of contract are operating together. With all our GPs we're on a cost per case contract, with all smaller health authorities we're on a cost and volume, and with our main purchaser, South and East Cheshire Health Authority, we're on a block contract. To deal with the contracting side, we've had to have more administrators. There are more people who go out and negotiate the contracts as well as people who invoice and monitor. Resources are becoming tighter which means that health authorities and GPs seem to look for any excuse not to pay our bill. We now have an extra six staff who deal with finance, contracts and support. Part of my job is now supporting others who go out and negotiate contracts, but I'm not counted as part of extra staff needed to service the new arrangements.

We try and manage our contracts and work to contract so we're not doing work we won't be paid for. We will still see anybody who is regarded as urgent. Communications throughout the whole of the organisation have improved tremendously because of the need to meet these objectives. The clinicians are far more involved in the management of the hospital. We often have meetings at eight o'clock in the morning before the consultants go to their clinics, or we're sitting waiting in the evenings for them to finish theatre so that we can have a meeting. They are not cutting their medical commitment, but they are taking on more of the administration. They understand what's going on much better now and within medical ethics they try and keep us on an even keel. They always see medically urgent people, but where someone can wait, we ascertain that we will be paid for payment for our services prior to seeing the patient. There's no additional money, so if we see more patients than our contract says, we are paying for it from funds we've allocated to other priority areas.

Leighton Hospital is a general hospital and works in partnership with a private hospital on the same site. Before the private hospital opened we had private patients, but now we have an agreement with them that will we not take any private patients. In return we get a guaranteed income from them every year and we supply them with any goods and services they require at a slight profit. We are not rivals and we will occasionally take their patients and they will take ours when we haven't got a bed. It isn't we haven't literally got a bed, it's the staff to staff the bed that we haven't got. A fair number of our consultants do work for the private hospital. Consultants do not work full-time for the NHS. After they have worked for the NHS for three years they can work maximum part-time and they can then go and work some private sessions.

The Budgeting Process

The hospital is organised into a directorate structure similar to large departments. There are 13 clinical directorates and two non-clinical directorates. Each directorate is headed by a clinical director who is a consultant, or an executive director. Each of those directorates is given a budget which is divided down to ward level, giving a series of budget holders within each directorate. In budgetary terms every member of staff is costed individually. In addition to staff costs there are non-staff costs. Budgets are formally re-costed once a year, and pressures such as increased costs of new drugs and equipment are identified. Informally we have monthly meetings to monitor what's going on. From the formal process, all the clinical directors meet together and they agree what is a reasonable cost pressure and what is an unreasonable cost pressure and how they should fund new expenditure.

The first point of call for new funding is to the purchasers such as the health authority, saying: "These are the developments, will you pay for them?" The answer is generally "No". We either have to do without the developments or find a way of behaving more efficiently in order to fund the development. In theory we should be able to say: "That's what we want to provide, and we'll go out and sell our services in order to pay for it", but it's a closed market and that doesn't happen. In practice you're at last year's budget level, but the directors can't agree between themselves to swap funding between departments. We have now introduced the system of recharging between the directorates for work which one directorate does for another under the heading of service-level agreements. For example, radiology and pathology are demand led and the clinicians who are demanding more and more have got to make decisions as to whether they do want more and if they decide that they do want more, they know their department is going to pay for it. They must decide what they are going to give up to get all the radiology and pathology services they want, whereas the radiology department are saying, "We're getting all this money from the extra work other departments are now paying for, we could afford a new consultant". This has never been recognised before, it all just happened in an uncontrolled fashion. The understanding of budgetary control by the clinicians has increased as a result of having to get more involved in management. We still have tantrums and table banging, but at the end of the day most of them actually accept what is going on. Two or three years back we had a major financial crisis, we had to cut £3 million worth of costs back. It resulted in redundancies among administrative staff. We had business managers at that stage, and they represented most of the job losses, and many of the clinical directors actually would like those business managers back again now that they understand more about administration.

Efficiency savings

As a finance department, we co-ordinate the budgeting process by writing to the Directorate to ask them to identify their needs. The Directorate produce a business plan for the year which identifies cost pressures, equipment needs, development bids, and their training needs. I will extract different elements from those business plans and produce a lists of "bids" from the directorate. Those lists then form the basis of the discussion of their requirements. We just pull things together and support the directors in making their decisions.

In order to keep making three per cent efficiency savings every year, we've cut back on everything we can. We just don't know how we can do it again next year. There aren't many administrative staff to cut now and if further cuts are made, we would be cutting clinical staff. We can't economise on staff salaries by employing less experienced staff. Anyone coming into the NHS starts at the bottom of the scale and moves up the scale annually. We need specialist, experienced staff and those coming from another NHS employer will have to be paid the same by us. A staff nurse coming to us from a different NHS hospital will move sideways on the incremental scale. We haven't got much ability to economise on staffing costs, we need trained staff.

There are a number of a national agendas which we are supposed to be meeting without any resources being put in, like the junior doctors' hours. We should be reducing their hours and doing structured teaching. It sounds fine in theory, but the financial effect of that is £350 000. Now nobody will give us £350 000 to undertake this national agenda. We spend less than £100 000 per year on training which is very low compared to the ideal situation for a hospital. It's the easiest thing to cut. It's short-sighted, but when money is tight, the benefits of training are not immediately tangible. We do a lot of in-house training and that is not costed as training.

All our services such as laundry and catering are provided by in-house staff. We put them out to tender, but the in-house staff have always been successful in winning the contracts. We buy our supplies from a supplies division, although we can go for outside deals if we want to. If someone has specialist knowledge or contacts who can get good deals, then we'll make use of that, but generally we get most of our supplies from the NHS supplies division.

We're not a charity so we can't raise money for our day-to-day running, but we do have charitable funds to run appeals to raise money for specific pieces of equipment. We've got a fund at the moment for an MRI (Magnetic Resonance Imaging) scanner which will last for two years. We can market our services to a small extent in order to generate extra income, but the effect of that is short-lived because we have to knock off that income from our prices in the following year. Each year we have to work out our prices and reduce it by any income we receive. This is one way of achieving the three per cent efficiency savings.

There's beginning to be a recognition that acute hospitals are under-funded. All the new money available to the NHS has gone into community provision. There's nothing wrong with that but acute services have been neglected. There's only so much one can do. Most staff in the hospital work far more than their contracted hours and don't get paid for overtime. They're a dedicated bunch and they are interested in treating the patients and doing their best for them.'

9 Reviewing and monitoring

From reading this chapter you will learn about reviewing and monitoring activities, including:

1   value analysis;
2   systems analysis;
3   just-in-time;
4   total quality management;
5   performance standards and indicators;
6   benchmarking; and
7   the impact of technology

 ## Value analysis

In a competitive world organisations will only survive by updating their existing products and bringing out new ones to satisfy consumer demand. In the computer industry a number of manufacturers have been unable to compete and have disappeared from the market place. The price and the versatility of desk top computers put IBM, the world's leading manufacturer of mainframe computers, under pressure and made it revalue its products range. When price is the main form of competition, organisations need to look at the relationship between the cost of manufacture, profit levels and the function of the product.

Value analysis enables an organisation to ensure that products are made in the most effective way and at the lowest cost while still meeting the needs of the customer. Costs refers to price of the inputs in the production of the product; raw materials, labour and overheads. Each unit produced can be costed in terms of pounds and pence. Value is how much something is worth to the customer in terms of the performance of the product for its intended job, its quality, and reliability. Value is a means to make comparisons with similar products enabling customers to make their choice. Therefore, value analysis is about looking at ways to reduce cost of the product to the organisation while either maintaining or improving the value of the product for the customer.

Value analysis uses procedures for the identification of unnecessary costs in the manufacture of components and unnecessary components in the product. The procedures are based on the function of the product. All products have a primary function while many also have a secondary function. Once the primary and secondary functions have been identified creative alternatives are developed which can reduce the cost and or increase the value of the product. For example the primary function of a CD holder which can accommodate 50 CDs, is to house and facilitate the easy retrieval of the CDs . However, the secondary function may to beas a piece of furniture and to support an ornament.

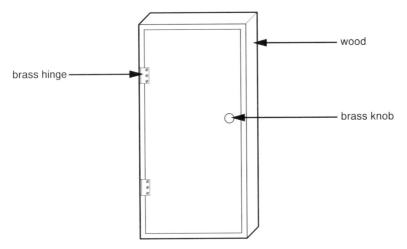

Fig 9.1 A CD holder

Questioning the detail of each component focuses the organisation on the function and cost of the product.

Therefore the value analysis procedures to reduce the cost and improve the value of the CD holder are:

◆ What is its purpose?
◆ What do the customers expect?
◆ What are the dimensions?
◆ What are the raw material, (the type of wood, the number of screws, glue)?
◆ What are the number of components?
◆ What is the cost of each component?
◆ Is each component needed?
◆ Is there a cheaper raw material which can be used?
◆ Is the way in which it is manufactured the most efficient and cost effective?
◆ Can similar parts be bought in?

It could be that the wood used can be substituted by contiboard, and nails in place of screws. There is no need for glue and the door can be removed. The CD holder is cheaper to produce but maintains its primary function of holding 50 CDs.

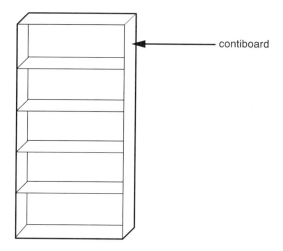

Fig 9.2 A modified CD holder

 # Systems analysis

A system is a set of interrelated activities which together have a specific outcome. The Post Office has a queuing system where customers stand in line guided by a roped off area. When one of the counter clerks is available the customer at the head of the queue goes to that window. This system was introduced to replace the one where people selected their own queue at a window. Some queues moved faster than others which led to queue hopping. The present system reduces frustration. A filing system is a way of storing documents in a regulated sequence in a designated location. A small business owner may file their invoices in a folder according to invoice number. Some systems are sub systems of much larger systems. Keeping invoices for future retrieval and reference is perhaps only a small part of a whole accounting system which records payments received and payments made.

In order for any system to operate effectively and efficiently there has to be order, monitoring and control as well as ease of access and usage. New people who join an organisation need to be able to use the system quickly with few errors and understand how their contribution fits into the whole.

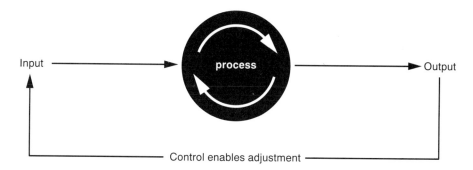

Fig 9.3 A simple information system

Each department in an organisation will have their own system to suit their needs but where there is overlap then a system should be common to both. For example, Human Resources will have their own system for the selection and recruitment of staff, and purchasing will have a set way requisitioning materials. In order to support these systems, and for future reference, the information is normally recorded on paper or computer and filed.

Systems tend to evolve and grow over time, especially in small organisations they develop to meet the needs of the owner. In large organisations the system needs to develop in a way which meet the growing demands made on it but remain consistent to allow different people over time to operate it. People who work in one job for a long period of time tend to personalise the system to meet their own needs and may ignore certain procedures. The more important the person, the greater the tendency to personalise a system. In some organisations systems have tasks or routines because they have always been done in a particular way, and even though time has moved on the routine stays the same. In some situations organisational procedures have developed to meet new demands and tend to grow in an *ad hoc* way. Systems and bureaucracy may eventually slow operations down which, in an economic climate where the competitive edge is making decisions quickly, a slow lumbering bureaucratic organisation may become uncompetitive.

From time to time, especially when organisations wish to computerise their systems, there is an opportunity to review and analyse the system to look for improvements. This function was usually the domain of the work study engineers whereas today it is usually the systems analyst who will carry out the review and recommend changes.

Analysing a system

The following are the stages of an investigation an analyst will follow when they are analysing an organisation's system:

◆ investigate how a present system operates

◆ analyse the system's present performance against its original requirements

◆ decide if a new system is required

◆ identify, develop and evaluate ideas about how the present system could be improved

◆ design a new system to meet the requirements identified

◆ implement a new system to meet the requirements identified

◆ modify and make necessary adjustments.

During the first stages of the analysis the systems analyst will carry out a feasibility study to assess whether there is good reason on technical, social and economic grounds to justify a change in the present system. During the feasibility study the systems analyst will become aware of problems likely to be faced with improving the old system or when introducing a new system. Examples of problems facing the analysts include:

◆ investigating the present system and trying to predict the future requirements on the system

◆ deciding who should be involved with the investigation and the ability of those people to communicate with the analysts

◆ investigating whether the manager's view of the systems requirements are the same as other users of the system

◆ identifying the black holes into which the information may disappear

◆ what are the present level of computer skills within the departments?

◆ will the organisation be able to cope with the change?

◆ costs versus benefits of a new system.

A major factor when investigating the feasibility of a new system is to weigh the costs and running of a new system against the benefits which accrue from it. The costs are clearly identifiable: the cost of the consultancy; the cost of equipment and software; training costs; costs of conversion; and running costs. The benefits are less quantifiable but may include: better planning; better information for decision making; greater flexibility; and an improved customer service. As a result of the feasibility study the analyst will be able to make recommendations including a description of the present system, a description of alternatives and an evaluation of alternatives.

Investigation

However, a more detailed investigation of the organisation's operations and a study of procedures to identify who does what, when, where, how and why will be necessary. By observing procedures it will enable the analyst to identify which procedures are routine, controlled and exceptional. The investigation will show up activities which are duplicated, how and where errors are made and the amount of errors in the system. From the investigation the analyst will need to identify which records are kept on file and why, and the number of times they are accessed and by whom. The analyst will want to know where the information goes and whether there are any communication barriers.

By analysing the findings it is possible to identify how the systems perform against the requirements of the organisation and from this the analyst will be able to see which parts can be reduced, which can be improved or expanded and where new system sub-sets need to be introduced.

The analyst will have gathered information by employing the following methods:

Interviewing

This will be face-to-face interviews where the analyst can find out what each person does and how it contributes to the system. Staff will have to justify objectively the procedures which are performed especially those of an historical nature and in some cases the original reason for carrying out the task may have disappeared.

Questionnaire

This can be used where only a small amount of information is required from a large number of people.

Examination of records and procedure manuals

This can show the analyst what the organisation's procedures should be compared to what happens in practice.

Observation

This enables the analyst to see the system in operation. Tracking a document through its procedural path will show the actual route against what should be the real route. It will show what happens to it at each stage and where and why there might be bottlenecks and delays. It will also alert the analyst to those processes which don't add value to the process. Analysing procedure will identify what decisions are made by whom and how the decisions are made.

Designing a new system

When designing a new system the analyst has to work within constraints of which the main two are: the objectives of the system and the resources available to the organisation. The design must be accurate and reliable. Frustrations occur when information is incomplete, inaccurate or simply disappears. Frustration turns to anger when the system crashes.

All subsystems in the overall system must be compatible and no subsystem should stand alone. Although it is difficult to predict the future the system should be of a standard which will be able to be expanded to meet forecasted future demand. Security needs to be an integral part of the system so information stored can only be accessed by those people who have authority to use it. This protects confidentiality, the loss of information and helps to build confidence in the system.

The implementation of the new system

Once a system has been designed and is ready to be implemented there needs to be plans made on how to introduce the system. People need to be informed beforehand about the system, what they can and cannot expect from it and they may need to be trained so they are competent to use it. It is important the system is tested beforehand to allow people to understand how it works and also to iron out last minute problems.

Replacing the old system can be done in three ways each having their own advantages and disadvantages but the selection will depend on the requirements of the organisation:

1 *The immediate changeover.* This is where the old system is stopped and the new one introduced. This is the simplest and least costliest method but it is also the most risky. There must be absolute confidence in the new system.

2 *Running parallel.* This method is used where it is possible to run the old system alongside the new one. This helps boost confidence in the new system and gives people time to solve problems in the new system. It allows staff the opportunity to train on the new system. However, it is more costly as two systems are running at the same time and there is obvious duplication in some areas.

3 *Stepped approach.* This is where there is gradual change from the old system to the new. This enables the organisation to cope with the changes gradually and problems can be more easily identified because they can only be in a part of the system rather than having to investigate the whole system. The problem with this approach is the time scale. There might be a reluctance to move on to the next stage until everything is sorted out and this can be a costly exercise.

After the introduction of the system there will be a time for checking the system to make sure it is meeting the requirements of the organisation. Questions such as:

◆ what is the standard of service?

◆ are there any bottlenecks?

◆ are there any errors? How many are there? Where are they?

Minor adjustments can then be made. Modifications over time can be done as an updating process rather than sudden adjustments to the system.

Just-in-time

In the past, most companies using the continuous flow method of production built up high stocks of raw materials and components, relying on buffer stocks to protect the flow of production 'just-in-case'. For example, have firms ordered large amounts of stocks because their supplier had a history of being unreliable in delivery or in the quality of the components supplied. Sometimes firms would use more than one supplier to guarantee supplies. Other factories which used batch production and had long machine set-up times would run their machines for as long as possible. This meant the factory built up large stocks of finished goods which then had to be stored in a warehouse until required.

The Japanese, in contrast, used a 'just-in-time' approach to stockholding and production. This method reduces stocks, reduces work in progress and streamlines operations. One view of just-in-time (JIT) is to see production as a stream. The water level is the inventory and at the bottom of the stream are rocks which represent problems relating to quality, suppliers, delivery and machine breakdowns. The water level is kept high enough so that the rocks will pose no danger and the stream of production keeps flowing. The JIT approach is to lower the water level gradually to expose the rocks which can then be dealt with, that is, the problems relating to production can be tackled. The water level can be lowered again and more rocks are exposed and eliminated until all the rocks are broken down leaving small pebbles on the stream bed and the stream flows smoothly at a low level.

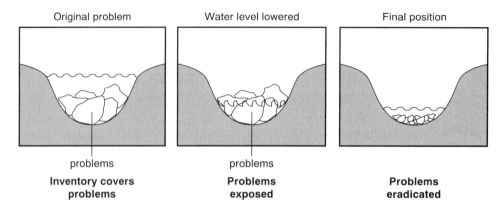

Fig 9.4 'Just-in-time' procedure

The ultimate aim of the JIT is to get to a point where stock is arriving JIT to go straight into the production process. For production to work at this level the production process must operate its inventory on a 'demand pull' basis i.e. demanding stock when it is needed from the supplier and not pulling it out of stores.

The JIT method of production uses the 'Kanban' system. 'Kanban', meaning 'card' in Japanese, was originally based on a system of cards which the workers used to signal to the previous workers in the production process that new parts were required. The signal indicates the next part of the process is ready for more parts. An organisation can use any signal to meet its own needs but the important point is that the signal pulls the components into the next stage. Under the old 'batch inventory system' different sections of operations used to push out components as they were completed irrespective of the demand for them (supply push). This meant they had to be stored in a warehouse or stores area. Stocks were also stored next to the production line. Just-in-time means that the organisation operates a lean production system.

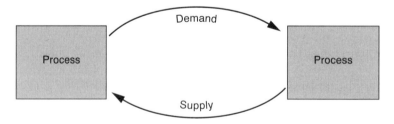

Fig 9.5 'Just-in-time' inventory system: demand pull

Just-in-time: The advantages of this system are:

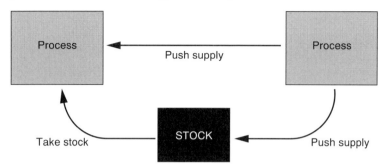

Fig 9.6 Batch inventory system: supply push

Advantages internal to the organisation

◆ stock levels of raw materials and finished products can be reduced, releasing capital for other uses

◆ there are no stocks of work in progress because those products in the production process will be completed from start to finish

◆ cost of storage is reduced as there is a reduced requirement for storage space and savings are made on lighting and heating the stores warehouse

◆ flow routes around the factory can be reduced and layout simplified

◆ the production chain is reduced and lends itself to closer working in teams and cells

◆ the system cannot afford stoppages therefore any problems in the production process have to be solved quickly. Maintenance needs to be preventive rather than corrective

◆ the quality of the final product is improved

◆ managers can look at each operation involved in the production process to identify those stages which do not add to added value to the product. For example moving the product from one workstation to another does not add value, therefore reducing the time the movement takes may lend itself to modifying the production layout

◆ the production process can operate on smaller batches and meet customer demand and changes in product design

◆ the organisation has better delivery and response times.

Advantages external to the organisation

◆ can meet consumer demand and changes in demand more easily

◆ there has to be a closer relationship with suppliers because the purchasing of materials has to be JIT. Carrying low stocks does not allow for wastage through poor quality components or poor delivery times

◆ there will be fewer suppliers because duplication of suppliers will no longer be necessary

◆ there will be a long term relationship between the buyer and suppliers of materials which means stability and mutual dependency for both.

Disadvantages of just-in-time

◆ the system is a more controlled process which means there is tighter control over the workforce which they might find stressful as they concentrate on their job continuously

◆ the opportunity to make social contacts is greatly reduced as workers no longer spend time on such activities as walking to the stores for spares which is also built in relaxation time for workers

◆ just-in-time creates a greater reliance on suppliers and the system is time consuming to set up, involving such close co-operation between customer and supplier that it often seems as though they have become part of the same organisation

◆ if an organisation has the ability to demand stocks from its suppliers whenever it needs them, this often means the supplier has to keep the stock in readiness. Just-in-time therefore often represents a solution for a large firm and a problem for their smaller suppliers.

It is questionable just how far it is possible to use JIT. Japan is beginning to experience problems. The JIT system in Japan relied on the availability of labour, proximity and ease of access to the customer. Each day frequent small deliveries would be made using small delivery vans. However, suppliers are having to locate further away from their customer because of labour recruitment problems. This means longer distances to travel and the small Japanese roads are getting congested which delays deliveries. Suppliers therefore are reluctant to make a number of deliveries in a day preferring just to deliver larger quantities just once a day. The result has been some production problems and has forced some firms to hold stock 'just in case.'

Total quality management

A quality product is one which meets customer needs. Organisations today are more aware of the need to produce products of high quality in order to compete. However, quality products are not the sole quality targets of an organisations but total quality within the organisation: total quality management (TQM). Total quality management is an approach to getting everything right first time, for example, making products with zero defects, operating procedures with a minimum of mistakes and the realisation that everyone employed in the organisation is responsible for quality.

The success of TQM is based on removing the sole responsibility for quality away from managers, the quality control department and control systems and incorporating quality into the whole organisational process. Quality is not the responsibility of one department, TQM represents an acceptance that quality should pervade the whole organisation and everyone is responsible for the quality of their own work. This requires a change in organisational culture from having acceptable quality levels with built-in defect allowance to having incremental improvements in quality. The ultimate aim is to achieve zero defects where emphasis is on the prevention of defects, rather than correcting defects at a later stage, thus saving time and money. This requires more time to be spent on planning and problem prevention and less time is spent on inspection and control. As the management of quality is the responsibility of every employee the workforce has to be trained and trusted to take more care in their work and produce quality products.

To ensure that the process is continuous it is important the organisation has close links with its external suppliers to meet the organisational quality standards. Within the organisation each worker is seen as both a customer and a supplier. At every stage and process the product goes through, the person who completes a part of the process is seen as the supplier and the next person in the process is seen as the customer. This means everyone can identify with 'customer' needs. The eventual beneficiary is the final customer who purchases the product.

The idea of TQM and continuous improvement was advocated by the American, W.E. Deming, whose 14 management principles state:

1 Create constancy of purpose toward improvement of products and services with the aim of being competitive and staying in business for the long run rather than making short run profits.

2 Adopt the new philosophy by refusing to allow commonly accepted levels of mistakes, defects, delays and errors. Accept the need for change.

3 Cease dependence on mass inspection. Rely instead on building quality into the production in the first place and on statistical means for controlling and improving quality.

4 End the practice of awarding business on the basis of price tag alone. Instead minimise total cost. Reduce the number of suppliers by eliminating those who cannot provide evidence of statistical control of processes.

5 Improve constantly, and forever, systems of production to improve quality and productivity and thus constantly reduce costs.

6 Institute training on the job for all employees.

7 Focus management and supervisors on leadership of their employees to help them do a better job.

8 Drive out fear. Don't blame employees for 'systems problems'. Encourage effective two-way communications. Eliminate management by control.

9 Break down barriers between departments. Encourage teamwork among different areas such as research, design, manufacturing and sales.

10 Eliminate programmes, exhortations and slogans that ask for new levels of productivity without providing better methods.

11 Eliminate arbitrary quotas, work standards, and objectives that interfere with quality. Instead, substitute leadership and continuous improvement of work processes.

12 Remove barriers such as poor systems and poor management that rob people of their pride in their work.

13 Encourage life-long education and improvement of all employees.

14 Put everyone to work on implementing these fourteen points.

The three main components of TQM are:

1 *A well documented quality management system.* Many organisation have achieved recognition of their quality guidelines and procedures by obtaining BS5750 and ISO 9000.

2 *The use of statistical tools and techniques to measure quality.*

3 *The use of teamwork including the autonomous working group.* A group of workers, normally working together, are responsible for a particular task or area of work. The group will meet regularly perhaps before the start of a shift to discuss the previous day's work and any problems which arose. They may have extra meetings as the need arises. They will often have a team leader who can make decisions, for example, calling in suppliers to discuss quality of supplies. The group is responsible for achieving production and quality targets, for training one another, solving problems on a daily basis and for improving the work process.

The cost of quality

If the organisation cannot get quality right first time it incurs costs such as rectifying faults or having to throw away defective products which costs money and ultimately customer loyalty. The cost of quality can be divided into; control costs and failure costs.

Control costs are concerned with prevention and appraisal costs which remove defects from the production flow before they reach the customer.

Appraisal costs relate to incoming materials inspection, the process inspection, and the inspection process.

Prevention costs include:

◆ *quality planning.* The cost of preparing quality manuals and procedures

◆ *new product review.* Preparing the specifications for new products and determining customers' quality requirements

◆ *training.* Preparing training programmes

◆ *process planning, quality data* and *improvement projects.*

Failure costs relate to internal and external failure costs. Internal failure costs are those incurred during the production process and external failure costs are those incurred after the products leave the organisation. Internal failures include:

◆ *scrap* i.e., the cost of the lost labour input and raw materials when errors occur

◆ *rework* is the cost of rectifying errors on products which do not conform to standards

◆ *retest* once the product has been reworked, checking to see if it reaches the required standard

◆ *time* wasted because people and machines are standing idle because of failures.

External failure relates to the cost of warranties, the cost of refunds or repairing faulty products, and also the cost of dealing with complaints.

TQM reduces overall costs and strengthens the organisation's ability to compete on price. The final result will be higher profits, maintaining or increasing market share and long term survival of the organisation.

The disadvantage to organisations implementing TQM include managers who expect unrealistically high results, both in changes to the production process and the quality of products. Middle managers may feel they have lost authority and status because responsibility for production has been delegated to the workers and workers may feel that the new system is

Fig 9.7 TQM requires more planning and less inspection

unfair as their jobs have grown without any recognition through the pay packet.

CASE STUDY 9.1

Quality circles at Wedgwood

Transporting a truck (or dolly, as they are called in the pottery industry) full of fine china across a factory can be hazardous. The tall coffee pots on the top of the dolly often wobbled over and crashed to the ground at the Wedgwood factory in Barlaston, Stoke-on-Trent. A team of workers in the lithographing department (the department where patterns are put on the china) decided to do something about the constant breakages. Their idea was to design dividers to support and separate the coffee pots. Now all dollies are equipped with the new plastic dividers and coffee pots ride steadily through the factory. The implementation of workers' ideas at Wedgwood is common practice and is achieved through their Quality Circle programme.

A Quality Circle is a group of people who work in the same area, who meet together regularly to analyse and provide solutions to problems which affect them. When the group first meet they identify the problems they are experiencing. They discuss all the problems and choose one which they all agree they would most like to find a solution to. They analyse the causes of the problem, get facts to back up their ideas, look for a solution, try out the solution and then make a recommendation to management for their idea to be implemented. All Quality Circle members receive training before they join a circle.

Wedgwood are a strong driving force in the Quality Circle world. Their Chief Quality Circle Facilitator, Graham Finney, chairs the annual conference of the National Society for Quality through Teamwork held annually at Warwick University; he is also Midlands Regional Co-ordinator for the National Society. Wedgwood were a founder member of the National Society when it started

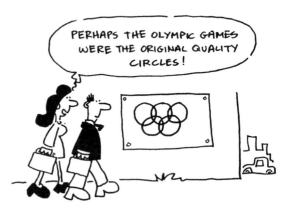

Fig 9.8 Quality Circle Awareness Day

in 1985. Since Wedgwood started their Quality Circles in 1980 they have been helping other companies to set up their own programmes. Graham Finney:

'I have lots of companies wanting to come and talk to me, I could spend all my time telling people about our programme.' Wedgwood are in such demand for their advice on setting up Quality Circles that they hold an annual open day for companies. Graham: *'Within two weeks of advertising the open day this year, it was filled and we had to turn companies away, which was a shame.'* The open day is held in March every year and can accommodate 105 company representatives. This year the programme included Quality Circle team presentations, speakers and a tour of the factory.

Wedgwood have 150 Quality Circles and five full-time Quality Circle Facilitators. Twenty two per cent of the 4000 strong workforce are Quality Circle members and meet for an hour each week to discuss a problem. There are seven different factory sites in the Potteries area, which include Coalport, Masons Ironstone and Johnson Brothers brand names and each site has a Quality Centre which provides accommodation for Quality Circles to hold meetings. Graham:

'We'd like 30 per cent of the workforce to be Quality Circle members by 1995. We really have pushed up the numbers involved, it used to be less than 10 per cent.'

Graham encourages more people to join Quality Circles through Awareness Days. These involve a meeting of those workers not already in Circles and the format normally consists of a talk from the Production Director, a description of the work of Quality Circles from Graham and a presentation from a Quality Circle team on how they operate. Then five or six Team Leaders from different sites show their projects to the interested parties on an individual basis. The participants of the Awareness Day then fill in a questionnaire to say whether they would like to become involved. Graham: *'There will always be a proportion of people who don't want to be involved. We've trained 60 per cent of the workforce in problem solving training.'*

CASE STUDY cont

The Decorating Dollies

One of the first tasks any Quality Circle set themselves is to choose a name. The Decorating Dollies are five women who work in the lithographing department. At present if a worker does not know how to lithograph a particular piece of ware, she has to ask her supervisor to demonstrate how to do it for her or find a method sheet, which are in short supply. The Decorating Dollies decided to set about producing a manual which will provide instructions for lithographing each item and every pattern available. This will save both the supervisor's time and the workers' time as they will not have to wait until the supervisor is available before they can start work on a new piece. The supervisor's role will then be to check the finished piece of ware. This Quality Circle started on their project in April 1994 and completed it in November 1994. They attended a conference in November 1994 at East Midlands Airport and made a presentation of their work as a Quality Circle. Graham:

'There's no pressure brought to bear on Quality Circle members to complete a project in any set time. It's voluntary and there's no benefit to them as far as money goes. Their satisfaction is working on something and seeing their idea implemented.' Wedgwood reward Quality Circle members who give presentations of their ideas to management or outside bodies, and anyone who has served for more than two years on Quality Circles with Wedgwood receives a stick pin. In June of each year there is a buffet lunch and presentation ceremony for those being awarded pins. Graham:

'The best way of rewarding people is to take them out to conferences. At the annual national conference at Warwick University there were over 20 Quality Circle members from Wedgwood. It was a reward and a thank you to them. They meet other people involved with Quality Circles, attend workshops and are developing their skills. Other conferences include an annual Team Leader's conference in a local hotel and a Members' conference at Christmas, both involve presentations and lunch for participants.'

Graham Finney considers that the success of the Wedgwood Quality Circle programme is due to a number of factors:

◆ voluntary participation by members

◆ top management support

◆ operational management support

◆ facilitator guidance for every group

◆ training

◆ the similar work background of all group members.

'The main reason we started in the 1980s was to improve communication and to get people involved. We were losing touch with the people on the shopfloor, there was too much "us and them".'

In the early days of Quality Circles, some middle managers were suspicious of what Quality Circles were going to do. Graham:

'There was fear, some managers prevented their people from coming. Even now some of them don't like us asking the workers for their ideas.'

Now, no-one is prevented from attending Quality Circles. Those who are uncomfortable about making a presentation to management are given the choice of presenting informally which Graham hopes will encourage more people to sign up: *'Now they know they haven't got to stand up and present, it will draw more people to us.'*

Quality Circles are encouraged to look at small projects when they first start. Graham:

'They are pleased to look at those little niggles that annoy them in their daily work. The problems are always more involved than they first thought. We've got to make it interesting for them.'

There is no restriction on sources of help for any Quality Circle. Graham:

'They can ask other factories, suppliers, anybody in the company. They can get Directors to talk to them if they wish. There are no limits on the amount of help they can ask for with their projects.'

One group who did go outside for help worked in the lining department (they paint gold and platinum lines on the china). The group decided to look at the problem they were having with paint brushes. The brushes being supplied to them were not the right shape and the workers were cutting them to the desired shape with scissors. The Quality Circle visited the brush manufacturers and explained the problem to them. The manufacturers were able to rectify the problem without delay. This saved time for the painters in the lining department, the quality of work improved which benefited the company and the manufacturer had the benefit of knowing customer requirements.

Every six weeks a newsletter 'The Circle Report' is distributed to all managers, directors, factory sites and facilitators so that everyone is kept informed of what projects are being worked on by all Quality Circles. Senior management are very supportive of the Quality Circle programme. The Production Director chairs the Steering Committee meetings on Quality Circles which are held every six weeks. Graham: *'The Steering Committee is made up of senior people. They are the people who can make decisions, they don't have to go away and ask somebody else.'*

The Steering Committee, which is made up of senior people who can make decisions, looks at projects currently being worked on by Quality Circles, discusses any problems and any outstanding actions which have been promised and not fulfilled. Graham:

'If a Circle has worked on a project for a long time and now they're waiting for some action by management, they want to know what is going on.'

Team Leaders meet one week prior to the Steering Committee meeting in order to discuss any issues they would like putting forward to the Steering Committee. There are between 700 and 800 people involved in Quality Circles at Wedgwood. Each person is released from their work for an hour every week. Graham:

'We're not in it for the money, we lose those man hours each week. I budget for their time and I've never been asked to justify my budget. We do keep a record and submit estimates of savings that are made as a result of the ideas generated by Quality Circles.'

Wedgwood regularly involve local schools in solving problems. Teams of schoolchildren work with Team Leaders on a problem for 12 weeks. One school has designed an electronic digital instrument to measure the hardness of clay as the previous instrument became damaged very easily. Graham:

'I don't think we'll run out of problems to solve, there are still plenty of projects to be carried out at the beginning of the production process.'

The Quality Circle programme is very flexible. Graham:

'People may drop out for a year and then come back again. Some people have been in Quality Circles since they started with the company. That's what makes it successful, it's an open shop for them. When I think of where we first started, it's tremendous where we've advanced to and the support and commitment that's been given to it.'

DISCUSSION QUESTIONS

1 What are Quality Circles?
2 How might Quality Circles increase workers' motivation?
3 What benefit are Quality Circles to companies?
4 How do Wedgwood encourage cooperation between companies?

Performance standards and indicators

Setting performance standards and indicators allows managers to compare actual performance against desired outcomes. Standard setting allows managers to take corrective measures if the organisation varies from the planned process and to avoid or reduce problems in the future. Performance standards and indicators can be set at organisational, operational and individual levels. Early identification of deviation from standards set can avoid major problems in the future. Organisations need to have systems to enable them to react to information gained from assessing performance indicators. These systems must be able to ensure smooth operations of activities, feedback of information through effective communication channels and be flexible enough to allow remedial action to be taken.

Setting standards and indicators helps managers to cope with external and internal influences such as:

◆ uncertainty
◆ opportunities
◆ production
◆ marketing.

Uncertainty

Strategic planning sets goals for a three to five year time period. The goals which are set are those to be achieved in the future which is unseen and therefore uncertain. The goals can only be 'best guess', based on the performance of the organisation, customer behaviour, competition and the state of the economy. In the UK during the 1980s it was a period of economic uncertainty, for example, during 1981/82 the economy entered a deep recession hitting the manufacturing sector worst. The country lost about 25 per cent of its manufacturing base. By 1987 the country was enjoying an economic boom with ever increasing demand. It was the period of the 'Yuppie' and the 'Dinkies'. By 1991 the economy was in deep recession. This cyclical nature of the economy makes it difficult for organisations to plan for investment, production and labour. If a company decides to invest in 1996 when interest rates are low, can the interest rates of 1998 be forecasted?

An organisation might trade with France and experience uncertainty with the exchange rates. In 1985 the exchange rate was FF10 = £1, by 1996 this had changed to FF7.50 = £1. An exporter might see this as an opportunity because the price of their goods have fallen in France, however for the importer the price of imported goods from France will have increased. Two uncertainties arise:

1   how this change in the value of currency will influence demand;

2   how certain the rate of exchange is.

Exchange rates are notorious for having sudden swings, the UK is more vulnerable because of the floating pound, i.e. the value of the pound to other currencies can change day-by-day.

A time period of three to five years can see changes in governments. With the election of a new party there is always uncertainty as to the economic and industrial policies of a new government. The governments since 1979 have been radical in reducing government intervention in the market place and has shifted power away from labour to organisations. For example for many industries pay was negotiated nationally, but now there is more emphasis on local pay agreements.

The greater the uncertainty facing organisations the more unlikely it is to take risks, and yet less risks taken may indicate more opportunities lost.

Opportunities

Companies need to be able to exploit opportunities as they arise, this may increase sales, market share or the survival of the organisation. For example, retailers can cater for seasonal variations, however, it is the unexpected changes in demand which cause problems. A period of hot weather can boost sales in particular products such as garden furniture and barbecue sets. But problems arise when there is a sustained demand for the product and the retailer and the producer have underestimated demand. During Euro 96 the upsurge in support for the England football team increased the demand for flags. The flag manufacturers had underestimated demand and had to change their production schedules. The manufacturers knew that demand would only remain high as long as England remained in the tournament. From this experience the flag manufacturers can identify an opportunity to make more flags every time England plays at home. But what should the target numbers be?

Production

Some organisations do produce to order whereas others try to identify future demand and produce accordingly. Each August sees the introduction of the new car registration. Car manufacturers know they need to gear their production to meet this sudden increase in demand. Huge amounts of raw materials and finance of the car manufacturer is tied up waiting for this particular buying time. It is important production targets are set appropriately to accommodate changes in demand. However, failure to hit production targets may indicate that something is wrong with the production process; a mismatch of labour skills to production needs; or poor operational layout.

Marketing

Marketing is the key to all other activities because this is the link between the market place and the organisation. The marketing department needs to be able to communicate to the organisation as a whole so that departmental and organisational targets can be set.

From their own target setting marketing can be alerted to changes taking place, for example, the customer care service will become aware from the amount of complaints and returned goods of the level of customer dissatisfaction with a product. This will require action by the organisation. Customer service will be able to monitor what happens to customer complaints over time to see the effectiveness of the action.

Benchmarking

Benchmarking is the examination of a firm's products, services, processes and performance measured against those organisations identified as 'the best'. It is undertaken to share information, learn from others' experience and improve performance.

Benchmarking can be one of three types:

◆ *internal.* Comparing departments within the same organisation

◆ *competitive.* Comparing your organisation with the leader in your industry

◆ *general.* Looking at a company with similar practices to yours but operating in another industry.

Benchmarking is about comparing your organisation with the best performers and initiating procedures and practices which bring your organisation more into line with them. The purpose of benchmarking is to achieve superior performance that results in a competitive advantage in the market place.

Steps in the benchmarking process

This involves five phases:

◆ planning
◆ analysis
◆ integration
◆ action
◆ maturity.

Planning phase

1   Select benchmarking candidates.
2   Identify organisations to compare with.
3   Select data-collection methods and collect needed information.

Analysis phase

1   Identify gaps between company practices and the industry best practices.
2   Forecast future performance levels if the chosen benchmarks are implemented.

Integration phase

1   Communicate benchmarking findings and gain acceptance by the workforce.
2   Establish functional goals.
3   Develop action plans.

Action phase

1   Implement plans and monitor progress.
2   Review benchmarks and replace as needed.

Maturity phase

◆ Achievement of leadership position.
◆ Benchmarking fully integrated throughout the organisation.

Applying benchmarking

The five-phase sequence of applying benchmarking begins with planning. Participants select the companies they want to benchmark and determine how they will collect information. The benchmarking product should focus on critical success factors, these are activities and functions considered most important in gaining a competitive advantage and achieving long-term success.

The analysis phase involves team members studying their own company practices and comparing them with those firms considered best in their industries.

The third step, integration, begins with communicating the results of this comparison to the members of the organisation. Benchmarking results should be communicated to employees so they understand the reasons for change, the opportunities for improvement, how they can help implement these changes, and how these changes impact on the organisation's overall business strategy. Goals and action plans are then are developed to incorporate these superior practices.

The fourth phase, action, involves putting the plans in place and monitoring their progress. The new processes are measured against the benchmarks, which are replaced as needed.

In the final stage, maturity, the organisation achieves a leadership position in its industry by integrating the best industry practices into all organisational functions. Many firms strive for a zero-defects standard as a performance goal. H.J. Heinz use an error-free standard of 99.9997 per cent, which is 3.4 defects per million units. Xerox uses a standard of one mistake per 1000 transactions recorded by its accounting department, and is working towards a goal of one mistake per million. Benchmarking is a component of most firms' quality programmes and it is used as a standard tool for measuring quality.

Performance indicators

The organisation might be set overall performance indicators as stated in the strategic plan. These may include: maintaining its market share; increasing market share; or achieving ISO 9000 award or the Investors in People Award. Some organisations may be seeking to achieve a Queen's Award for Industry. Each of these is quantifiable, however performance indicators such as having a highly motivated workforce is more subjective and difficult to test. The following are performance indicators many of which are specifically directed to a department or individuals and will contribute to the performance of the organisation as a whole

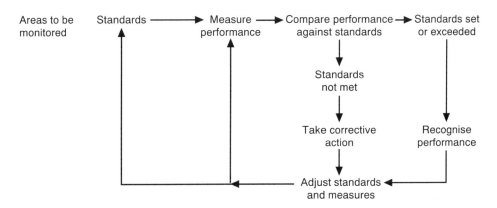

Fig 9.9 Review, monitoring and evaluation of performance indicators

◆ finance

◆ human resource management

◆ marketing

◆ stock turnover

◆ operations management.

The stakeholders in the organisation will be interested in the performance of the company. The shareholders will be interested in their investment which can be assessed as follows:

Fig 9.10 Performance indicator at work

Interested group	Measurement	Indicator
Shareholder	Earnings per share	$\dfrac{\textit{Net profit after tax-preference dividend} \times 100}{\text{Number of ordinary shares issued at end of accounting year}}$ High company shares are normally a good investment.
	Dividend yield	$\dfrac{\textit{Gross dividend per ordinary share (in pence)}}{\text{Market price per ordinary share (in pence)}}$ High good return for ordinary shareholders.
	Price earning ratio	$\dfrac{\textit{Market price per ordinary share (in pence)}}{\text{Earnings per share (in pence)}}$ High investors have confidence in the company.

The stakeholders including owners, workers and creditors will be interested in the profitability of the company. Competitors will want to see how other organisations are performing and the profitability can be measured by the following

Interested groups	Measurement	Performance indicator
Owners, employees, suppliers	Gross profit margin	$\dfrac{\textit{Gross profit}}{\text{Turnover}} \times 100$ Higher profit margins are the rule but those with the quicker turnover tend to have lower ratios.
	Net profit margin	$\dfrac{\textit{Net profit}}{\text{Turnover}} \times 100$ This indicates how well the management can control indirect costs.

Finance

One of the performance targets which is crucial for any organisation is their liquidity ratios. A liquidity ratio shows how quickly the organisation can turn their current assets into cash. There are two liquidity ratios: the current or liquidity ratios and the acid test ratio.

The current or liquidity ratio

This shows the relationship of current assets to current liabilities

$$\text{Current Ratio} = \frac{\text{Current asset}}{\text{Current liabilities}}$$

Ideally the ratio should be between 1.5 and 2. If it is any less than this the organisation may have a problem paying its debts. If the ratio is any greater then too much cash may be tied up in the current assets.

Acid test ratio

Stock is the least liquid of the current assets and therefore it is deducted from the other current assets to show how much of the remaining current assets can be converted into cash.

$$\text{Asset test ratio} = \frac{\text{Current assets} - \text{stock}}{\text{Current liabilities}}$$

The ratio should be at least 1. That is for every £1 of debt there is £1 of current assets to cover it. But for some organisations it may fall below 1 as in the case of supermarkets.

Human resource management

The performance indicators refer to employees of the organisation which in turn relates to skills and education attainment, the amount of training costs to payroll and the rate of absenteeism. One of the areas of concern for an organisation is labour turnover which is calculated by:

$$\text{Net labour turnover} = \frac{\text{Total separations in period}}{\text{Average working force}} \times 100$$

Some labour turnover is acceptable, i.e. Natural Wastage Rate and some organisations have an historical high turnover rate such as in the hotel and catering industry. But in those organisations where there is a high labour turnover it is costly in terms of recruitment and where it is unusual for the industry this would indicate there is something wrong with the organisation.

Marketing

The performance indicators for this department can also relate to the performance of the organisation as a whole, i.e. trend in sales, market share and market penetration. Sales representatives can have targets such as number of sales per month. This enables comparison to be made with their previous sales record and colleagues in the region and nationally.

Stock turnover

The stock turnover ratio is measured by:

$$\text{Rate of stock} = \frac{\text{Cost of goods sold}}{\text{Average stock}}$$

This ratio shows how long on average an item is in stock. An organisation will want to have as high a rate as possible within limits of stock turnover. Each product will have an optimum time in stock; perishable fruit will have a high stock turnover whereas a product such as beds will have a longer time in stock.

The stock turnover ratio taken with the gross profit rate will give an indication of the performance of the organisation. If there is a low gross profit rate, there is expected to be a comparatively high stock turnover, 'stack it high sell it low'.

Operations management

The usual measure here is productivity, i.e. output per person. However, performance indicators are more far reaching than this for example:

◆ purchased components: defect ratio

◆ equipment failure: unscheduled down time/real time

◆ waste: percentage rework or scrap

◆ quantity of output: actual v target

◆ reliability: warranty claims and cost

◆ quality: percentage conforming to standards

◆ lead time: completion time to fulfil orders.

The more quantifiable the indicator the better an organisation can monitor its performance, take early remedial action so as to be more effective.

The impact of technology

Technology is a set of processes, tools, methods, procedures and equipment used to produce goods and services. The use of technology improves productivity and control mechanisms of an organisation and when used effectively releases managers from 'fire fighting' situations to being able to focus on their tasks.

Computers

Computer technology has influenced all sectors of industry and has changed working practices in the extraction industry, manufacturing and banking. The computer has had a great impact because it can be used in the design, the manufacture and the support operations of producing a good or service. Computer applications are often incorporated as an integral part of consumer products operating for example in diverse consumer products such as washing machines and cars.

Computers have enhanced the just-in-time production process, for example, by ordering stock as it is required. In retailing, the electronic point of sale can inform the computer which products are being sold, monitor and calculate stock levels and can automatically order more supplies when stocks reach the re-order level. As illustrated in the United Norwest case study, the computer in Distribution receives orders from the retailers, and works out the goods required and the loading order. Another computer calculates the routes to be taken by the lorries to restock the stores.

A further advantage to the retailer is if the customer pays by credit card or uses a loyalty card, the retailer can monitor the buying patterns of customers and can, using this information build up customer profile database. From the knowledge they have gained the retailer can send out direct mail such as personalised letters to their customers from the knowledge they have gained, rather than sending out direct mail on a 'scatter gun' approach.

Computers have aided management information systems because they are able to sort, edit and process large volumes of data quickly and accurately. It can repeat the processes just as quickly and accurately and make any adjustments as it is instructed. This speed and flexibility allows management information to be produced and disseminated quickly and effectively. Reports can be generated which are up to date, detailed and specific to the people or departments to which they are addressed. Therefore computer driven information systems enable more efficient support for planning and more effective control and operations of an organisation. The speed of the computer aids operations management and decision making by quickly providing past, present and future orientated information about operations and external influences. Computers therefore improve the 'What if?' scenarios.

A major impact of computer technology which has taken place in the manager's office is the computer which is placed on his/her desk. This enables them to call up information quickly without having to call upon a subordinate. This means that information is available to the manager without some of it being filtered and they are able to make decisions more quickly.

Computers aid communications internally within the organisation and with the outside world. Utilising the fax,

Fig 9.11 People can now communicate via computers

e-mail and the Internet the use of computers and their accessories will reduce the demand for people to sit in offices and enable people to work from home. It is feasible for people to communicate and hold meetings by tele-conferencing thus reducing the time and expense to bring people together for face-to-face meetings.

The computer technology is having a tremendous impact in the banking industry where they are able to centralise their operations and locate away from city centres. They now operate direct banking 24 hours a day offering many of the services normally offered by the local branch. In direct banking where workers are dealing with telephone enquiries the employee does not need to know all the services available. They can usually deal with enquiries by asking questions displayed on the computer monitor. The customer gets a standard service and the employee's supervisor can monitor the employee's performance by timing each response.

It will be the organisations which can make computer-aided decisions more quickly than their competitors who will survive.

Computers have been able change the leisure industry. Football matches have electronic screens which can show playbacks of the game, 'White knuckle' rides at leisure parks are not only designed by computer but are also run by them. This has enabled the leisure parks to become a major force in the leisure industry. Computers have also played an important part in computer games machines.

In the educational field the use of computers is beginning to change the facilities and resources available for learning. Students use the computers to glean information from a number of sources including the Internet. The simple calculator has long since replaced the abacus.

Fig 9.12 **A place for everyone and everyone in their place**

In industry computers have also been able to improve the quality of the products made. *Computer Aided Design (CAD)* uses a computer to help in the production of design drawings and produce data for computer aided manufacture. Data for the CAD can be input by keyboard or by light pen straight onto the screen and the computers provide a visual display for the engineer and designer. This enables new product design to be developed more quickly, giving greater design flexibility and control. Using CAD, designers have been able to utilise resources more efficiently, thus reducing manufacturing costs. The fashion industry has to meet rapid changes in tastes and preferences as well as the seasonal variations in fabrics and fashion. Using CAD the fashion industry is able to adapt to changes very quickly.

Computers can improve the manufacturing process using *Computer Aided Manufacture (CAM)*. The computer controls the manufacturing system, for example, in the clothing industry the information from CAD can be fed into a computer controlling the cutting machines which will cut out the required pattern parts. The process is as accurate as the information which is fed into the machine and the machine can cut out unnecessary waste of materials and time. All the products will be standardised to the same quality level.

Some manufacturing processes are completely automated and controlled by computers. The computers in the *flexible manufacturing system* can instruct each machine in the integrated process to change parts as the product changes or as a part becomes worn out. The computer can also control delivery vehicles within the factory to carry stock or finished goods to their destination.

The fully automated production line is coming to fruition. In Japan, Honda has introduced automated guided vehicles where the vehicle can

◆ be raised or lowered to the most suitable assembly position

◆ stop to allow the robots to instal components

◆ vary their speed to catch up gaps.

In these systems body shells pass through the final assembly process on self-propelled motor driven carriers which have replace the traditional assembly line. Each movement can be individually controlled at a set pace and each can be stopped at a specific location depending on the model being carried and the component to be fitted.

Robotics

This a machine with artificial intelligence which is programmed to perform various tasks. The part of the robot which makes it distinctive from other computerised machines is the 'hand' or gripper and the arm which can make human-like movements. Robots tend to be limited in the production process to performing repetitive production jobs such as welding, painting and fixed assembly work such as those found in car manufacture. The benefits to the organisation include the reduction in direct labour costs, 24 hour operation, and the reduction in the number of repetitive and dangerous tasks. The disadvantage of using robots is their limited scope, they tend only to be able to perform simple tasks and as technology advances they quickly become obsolete.

Technological advanced materials widens the scope for existing products and creates the development of new products for example, fibre optics which has improved the speed and opportunities for communications.

However, the impact of technology on organisations will set many challenges. Some organisations will not be able to compete because they will not be able to afford the new technology. Some may choose the wrong technology and cause costly replacements. In many cases technology will demand that there is continual updating of skills. The challenge for the future is for technology to release workers from basic operations and allow them to contribute to the process of adding extra value to the products made.

British Rail

NRS Service Centre is a wholly owned subsidiary of British Railways Board. NRS specialises in the manufacture, service and repair of electronic, electrical, electro-mechanical equipment used throughout the railway infrastructure.

Fig 9.13 Mervyn Evans, Cell Supervisor, British Rail (centre) with his two assistants

There are approximately 150 people working in the Service Centre at Crewe. The majority are engaged on repair work and some are involved with procurement and materials management. There are three Service Centres in Britain – Crewe, Brighton and York and they are contracted by Railtrack to repair 'strategic material' no longer available from original equipment manufacturers. The four departments within the Centre: the Electronics Section, the Relay Section, the Auto-Warning Systems (AWS) and the Electro-mechanical Section. The Electronics Section repairs VDUs, modems, printers, power supplies, printed circuit boards and amongst other things, manufactures level crossing barriers.

The Electronics Section has 30 staff which include the Cell Supervisor, Mervyn Evans, and his technical assistant, and his administration assistant. The repair staff are split into teams: radio team, modems and printers team, VDU team and miscellaneous. Mervyn:

'We don't get large quantities of things, we get a lot of orders for one-off repairs.'

There are also two people in the stores area who take receipt of new jobs and dispatch completed jobs. Mervyn:

'There are three team leaders who help me distribute the work to the lads in the shop. They're not lads, they're all ages from 20 to late 50s. They are all qualified and have done apprenticeships. A number of them have an ONC or HNC in Electronics or Electrical Engineering.'

It is difficult to judge repair times for the faulty items entering the workshop. All items for repair have to be stripped down, cleaned, have their faulty components repaired and reassembled. Mervyn:

'We have called our pricing system "emerging cost" because we don't know how long it will take to repair and therefore how much to charge the customer until the job is completed. We can then charge the customer for the amount of hours the job has taken plus the cost of the parts.'

However, the company is actively forcing a move towards fixed price repairs, as we feel the customer wants to know the cost before sending equipment in for repair.

'The men don't need much supervision. We've got a good mix in the workshop, the older men exert authority over the younger ones. They all get on well. Occasionally you might have to say something to somebody, but the majority of the time there isn't any problem. It's satisfying work because each job is different to repair and they enjoy it. The position of the office may affect the workrate as I look out across the whole workshop, so they might feel watched from the office. There are windows all around the office. There might be some messing about when I'm not there, they wouldn't be human if there wasn't an element of that. The system of emerging costs is measured by each man clocking on to the computer terminal through a barcode system to record that he has started a new job. The time he takes is then monitored, so we know how long they've taken to do every job throughout the week. So they are being watched from the point of view of the computer system as well.

I'm sure they think it's a good place to work. The workshop is very clean, and has windows all around and there are big double doors which we can open in the summer time. That sort of thing helps. I've worked at another firm where there were no windows, no skylight, you didn't know what was happening outside.

We can't do time and motion studies of how long a job takes because there are so many individual jobs which we have no average times for. Because of the nature of the job, the lads might struggle with a particular fault which they haven't come across before and someone will give them a hand with it. They build on one another's experience and they are helpful to one another and they are very helpful to us in the office.

When quarter to five comes round, they all want to go home, but if there's a rush job which has to be completed, they will stay. They are conscious that the job is not just for their own ends, it's a job of work that's got to be done. We've got customers to satisfy.

We've got a good relationship in the workshop. I've been with the company for four years and doing the supervisor's job for two years. For the first two years I was on the bench myself and basically I think that because I've got experience of other companies I was able to help other people as well as them helping me. They know I'm capable of doing the job. You've got to treat people properly. I know the lads and try to treat them the right way. I don't do as much walking about as I should, I spend a lot of my time with my head buried in the computer terminal. I have to do a report on each employee's work: the time sheet analysis, which lists the work completed during the week. I can make sure they haven't gone over the top with the amount of time they have spent on any particular repair. They shouldn't spend too long on one job, because if they're having a problem they can come to us and ask. The customer is charged on how long we've spent doing a job, so it's best to check these things, mistakes do happen sometimes. We might make a wrong booking when clocking on and off the system, the terminal can misread the barcode on the repair card. I have to do reports as to how long a job has been in the department, this includes other information such as how long the material has been on order for the job. Customers ring up wanting to know how long their job will be. The system can tell you where the job is, who is working on it and what stage it has reached in the workshop. We use the computer to monitor the work.

In the past every job would have its own paperwork and the team leader would spend a day each week gathering all the pieces of paper together and recording how long had been spent on each job. It's so much quicker now, they don't have to go out into the workshop to look

CASE
STUDY

cont

for jobs to find out what's happening. The team leaders have got more time to spend on repair work. Initially, there was a certain amount of suspicion of the computers from the men, they felt that they were being watched by management and that we wanted to know their every move. That died down a long time ago and they accept the computer system now. Instead of them filling in a piece of paper at the end of each day to say what they have done, it's recorded through the barcodes as they go along.

We go out in the evening together occasionally. We go out for a Chinese or Indian meal and then the older blokes go home and the younger ones go off out to the pub. At least we've all got together. I go to football matches with some of them now and again. Most people go to the social functions, at Christmas time if you don't turn up people want to know why.'

DISCUSSION QUESTIONS 9.1

1   Why is the repair work at NRS Service Centre expensive to undertake?

2   How is the workrate monitored?

3   Do the men in the workshop train one another?

4   Has the computer system helped to increase productivity?

References for further reading

Adair, J. (1979), *Action Centred Leadership*, Gower.

Adair, J. (1984), *The Skills of Leadership*, Gower.

Cole, G.A. (1988), *Personnel Management*, DP Publications.

Curson, C. (1986), *Flexible Patterns of Work*, Institute of Personnel Management.

Curtis, S. and Curtis, B. (1996), *Behaviour at Work*, Pitman Publishing.

Daft, R.L. (1994), *Management*, The Dryden Press.

Daft, R.L. (1995), *Organization Theory and Design*, (5th edn.), West Publishing Company.

Evenden, R. and Anderson, G. (1992), *Making the Most of People*, Addison-Wesley.

Gaither, N. *Production and Operations Management*, Dryden Press.

Garratt, B. (1990), *Creating the Learning Organisation*, Director Books.

Handy, C. (1990), *The Opportunist Learner*, Honey and Mumford.

Honey, P. (1990), *The Opportunist Learner*, Honey and Mumford.

Iacocca, L. and Novak, W. (1984), *Iacocca: An Autobiography*, Phantom Books.

'Labour Force Survey', *Department of Employment*.

Likert, R. (1961), *New Patterns of Management*, McGraw-Hill.

Lockyer, K., Muhlemann, A. and Oakland, J. (1993), *Production and Operations Management*, (6th edn.), Pitman Publishing.

Makin, P., Cooper, C. and Cox, C. (1989), *Managing People at Work*, British Psychological Society and Routledge Ltd.

Moorhead, G. and Griffin, R. (1995), *Organisational Behaviour*, Houghton Mifflin Co.

Mullins, L.J. (1996), *Management and Organisational Behaviour*, Pitman Publishing.

Schroeder, R. *Operations Management*, McGraw-Hill International.

Senge, P. (1990), *The Fifth Discipline: The Art and Practice of the Learning Organisation*, Doubleday.

Vroom, V. and Deci, L. (Eds) (1992), *Management and Motivation*, Penguin Books.

Vroom, V. and Yetton, P.W. (1973), *Leadership and Decision-Making*, University of Pittsburg Press.

Index

Index of case studies